RosaMaria LaValva

The Eternal Child

The Poetry & Poetics of Giovanni Pascoli

Annali d'italianistica, Inc.
Chapel Hill, NC 27599-3170

AdI, Studi & Testi 2
A collection of monographs sponsored by
Annali d'italianistica, Inc.
and directed by Luigi Monga & Dino S. Cervigni.
The University of North Carolina at Chapel Hill
Chapel Hill, NC 27599-3170

Library of Congress Catalog Card Number: 99-072079

ROSAMARIA LAVALVA
    THE ETERNAL CHILD: THE POETRY & POETICS OF GIOVANNI PASCOLI
    1.   Giovanni Pascoli (1855-1912)
    2.   Criticism, theory, interpretation.
    3.   Italian literature: 19th & 20th Centuries

    ISBN 0-9657956-1-6

Studi & Testi 2

directed by

LUIGI MONGA & DINO S. CERVIGNI

A COLLECTION OF MONOGRAPHS OF
ANNALI D'ITALIANISTICA
THE UNIVERSITY OF NORTH CAROLINA AT CHAPEL HILL
CHAPEL HILL, NC 27599-3170

To my children
and to all my students

CONTENTS

PREFACE

Giovanni Pascoli (1855-1912) is a major figure in modern Italian letters and his work is considered of signal importance in the development of contemporary poetry. "Crepuscular," "hermetic," and impressionist poets are indebted to the wealth of Pascoli's poetic devices: use of analogies and synesthesias, chromatic imagery, creation of unusual onomatopoeias and rhyme structures, decisive rejection of conventional syntax. In particular, his *Myricae* and *I Canti di Castelvecchio*, two collections of poems published in 1891 and 1903 respectively, are viewed among the poetic masterpieces of this century.

It is well to recall these facts, long known to Italian scholars, because, quite surprisingly, an author of such stature has been poorly represented in the Anglo-Saxon literary world and not adequately considered even by strictly academic critics. While Pascoli's contemporaries, Gabriele D'Annunzio and Luigi Pirandello, have been the object of numerous conferences and symposia and of many noteworthy critical studies in English, the scholarly treatment of Pascoli is almost non-existent. Even translations of his poems are rare and insufficient, a situation due, at least partly, to sheer linguistic difficulties. For Pascoli is a poet who, for example, invents verbs from adjectives and nouns, expands vocabulary by assimilating Greek and Latin roots into Italian, chooses special, often scientific, terms for objects and actions, and privileges unusual word sounds for their suggestive musicality. Furthermore, he is a poet who firmly believes that words have the capacity to condense the very experience conveyed in the poem, and that the author must constantly experiment with language, never reaching final answers.

Whatever the reasons, we are presented with the curious case of a major Italian author who is virtually absent from the Anglo-American awareness of Italian literary history. It is as if, in dealing with the fourteenth century, the name and works of Petrarch were passed over in silence. The primary reason for my present study on Pascoli stems from a desire to bridge this serious lacuna, and part of my work focuses on the modernity of Pascoli's poetry, which is so keenly intent upon discovering a new dimension of consciousness.

The central focus of my research, however, is one of Pascoli's prose works, *Il Fanciullino* (literally, *The Little Child*): a brief theoretical

RosaMaria LaValva, *The Poetry & Poetics of G. Pascoli*

treatise on the nature of poetry, first published in a literary journal (*Il Marzocco*, 1897) and appearing ever since in a collection edited by the poet himself under the title *Miei pensieri di varia umanità* (Messina, 1903) and in his *Pensieri e discorsi* (Bologna, 1907), the latter published while the poet was still living.

Il fanciullino is a discourse on modern poetics of considerable significance. But, with the exception of a few important articles, the essay has not received the full critical attention it deserves. In fact, most of the critics who have studied Pascoli's prose works have not considered this essay as an autonomous work on aesthetics of broad philosophical value, but rather as a simple illustration of his poetry. The latter approach cannot be easily discounted, of course, because Pascoli's poetry entails a constant appeal to the reader to regain certain invaluable affects and an unspoiled perception of beauty in all things, as is typical of childhood. I will seek to show that *Il fanciullino* may well serve this interpretive function.

It is my conviction that this short essay by Pascoli should command a more general scholarly interest and that the lack of critical attention is due primarily to the unfavorable, almost hostile, remarks of Pascoli's first readers: Benedetto Croce, Renato Serra, and Emilio Cecchi: in a word, the sharpest and most influential Italian critics of the early twentieth century. These readers were constantly baffled and irritated by the elusiveness of a poet who not only defied classification in any specific school, however innovative, but also challenged and frustrated their very ability to reach a firm critical judgment.

More recent studies have reopened the question of interpretation and invited inquiry into the cultural sources of certain concepts articulated by Pascoli in his essay. These ideas center on a fundamental notion, which can be very simply summarized: a child lives within each of us and does not grow into an adult state; he remains buried within us, preserving the sensations and the images we all experienced in our tender years. When we listen to him, we revert to the child we once were; and if, after listening only to him, we decide to express what he has inspired us *to see* and *to hear* as before, then we become poets.

The Child who does not die, *The Eternal Child*, as I prefer to call him in my essay, is then the source of poetic representation, residing within but remaining separate from the adult poet himself. Thus, we are presented with an original dichotomy that divides the self, the traditional subject/object of lyric poetry. And we face a continuous dialogue between the 'I' that knows history and myth, time and space, feelings and actions, and a very special interlocutor and actor who, instead, never knows more than what he sees, dreams to see, or imagines to see. The world fills the

Child with wonder and awakens his reverence and piety, although not his aggressive feelings. Here is certainly the major difference from the Child of D'Annunzio's poetry: a divine adolescent eager to possess, manipulate, and appropriate his natural surroundings in virtue of his own youth and talent. Here, certainly, is a reason for the diminutive form of the noun deliberately chosen by Pascoli. *Fanciullino* is not so much a term of endearment as a specific connotation of age. This child is small, far from beginning that process of individuation that may in time make him an *Übermensch* and decree his eventual fall: self-love, ambition, assertiveness, will to power. And this Child, like all real children, is not attracted by what is generally known and recognized of importance in adult eyes; rather, he is fond of small things.

Giorgio Agamben, in an essay entitled *"Pascoli and the Thought of the Voice,"* which prefaces the most recent edition of *Il fanciullino*, finds the sources of Pascoli's poetics in the religious writings of early Christianity. His observations are important for what they say about the peculiar quality of Pascoli's language. For in *The Eternal Child* language is also a repository of objects that were alive and now are frozen, at the edge of life, waiting to be re-animated. Before anything else, the poet strives to revitalize the dead things held captive in language, cutting through and cooperating with language, in order to exorcise death. Agamben's conclusions, however, are not equally convincing about the origins of Pascoli's themes and ideas.

In this study, I would like to establish these sources, which at times were clear to the poet himself and at other times reached him indirectly through an unconscious web of cultural memories and theoretical suggestions and were re-elaborated by him to form a decidedly original system. I am convinced that the roots of Pascoli's poetics are not to be found in mediaeval theology, but much closer to his own time. These roots are to be found, first of all, in the great precursor of Romanticism, Giambattista Vico, who, in *La scienza nuova*, represents the beginning of creativity as the child-like expressions of the immediate feelings man experiences in contact with nature and the objects it presents to him. Secondly, the roots of Pascoli's poetics are also to be found in some of the major Romantic texts: Schiller's essay *Über naïve und sentimentalische Dichtung*, the poems and reflections on childhood by Wordsworth and Coleridge, and Leopardi's observations regarding the influential power of infancy and youth on the adult man.

I propose to examine the different manifestations of this central idea of the myth of childhood, a theme the Romantics handed down to the rest of the nineteenth century. For there is an intimate connection between the activity of fantasy and the repressed and subconscious material of

infancy. In creative fantasy and dreams, the poet finds the traces of his oldest and now forgotten desires. In this light, however, returning to childhood does not mean regression and entrapment; rather, it stands for the possibility of discovering a new life system and is the indispensable condition for every creative act as suggested by the modern phenomenology of mythical figures. Carl Gustav Jung, Eric Neumann, James Hillman, and Henri Corbin, among many others, have written important studies regarding the symbolic language of the psyche and the importance of the archetypal world of the individual for his own creativity. Even the specific polarity of the *Puer-Senex* archetype, of which Pascoli is obviously unaware, provides a significant tool for the understanding of his poetry, which is literally obsessed with imagery of infancy and old age, cradles and tombstones.

Nor should it be overlooked that in Pascoli's own time a strong creative current was producing a new literature for children. I am thinking of works from Peter Schlemil to Peter Pan. Such works may have contributed, although in an indirect way, to Pascoli's understanding of childhood in its relation to the creative process.

While didactic stories and moral tales continue to prevail in works written for children, many important authors choose to present the first few years of life as the special province of fantasy and nascent intelligence, and they highlight the dangers inherent in the process of growing up. In fact, it is not difficult to recognize the enduring presence of their ideas in the major literary figures of our century, from T. S. Eliot and Nabokov to Kafka and Beckett, for example. For all of them, the passage from the vague and unruly impulses of the *instincts* to the rigid incarnation of an apparently benevolent and rational *Superego* does not occur without some loss. What follows is a new dimension of childhood, represented in a gallery of poor, lonely children, troubled and in pain, who find escape in dreams and construct their destiny through the power of cleverness and imagination. These are the wonderful heroes of the new fairy-tales: *Thumbelina, Puss 'n Boots, Cinderella, Little Red Riding Hood.* All these works mark a radical switch taking place in children's literature, mostly under the influence of Romantic ideas, articulating a new approach to children and elaborating a new concept of childhood itself. Andersen allows his magical children to know evil within themselves as well as without, while remaining impermeable to it and holding on to their inner serenity. Theirs is the mission of the poets: it is up to them to keep alive the ideals that guarantee human salvation. More tragically, Collodi's *Pinocchio* surrenders, almost without regret, his fun-loving nature to become a good little conformist, respectful of law and order. The wooden puppets and the masks of the

circus are replaced by the masks of authority; and the subversive energy of the rebellious child is outgrown like the colic or the measles, so that the social order may exercise its power of formation, and de-formation, of the soul. Lewis Carroll aligns his work with that other fundamental quality of childhood: the imagination that makes children react to the "real world" in a unique and absurd way revealed, principally, by the playful and transgressive use of language.

Thus, Pascoli's Child is born in a climate of precise reflections articulated around the child and childhood and is in tune with the images outlined in the new fairy-tales. He is autonomous and dependent at the same time, full of life and fascinated by death, not at all one-dimensional, but, rather, troubled by conflicting desires, pleasure, and sadness. Most importantly, this Child wants to examine and explore; he needs independence and solitude and, at the same time, he craves sympathy and immediate communication. Consistently underscored throughout Pascoli's poetry and theoretical reflections is his special awareness, full of wonder and pain. Every human being experiences in childhood the curse of the Platonic prison from which there is no exit. The child learns that he must become what he does not want to be, and he suffers a growing awareness of conflicts. A ludic and also a tragic dimension is needed, acting in opposition and yet complementary, to mark the first stage of man's journey. Childhood is, indeed, the time of the first and most sorrowful catastrophe: the tension between reality and imagination must be resolved with the necessary acceptance of concrete facts and the induction into adulthood. But, Pascoli claims, what is defeated cannot disappear. It may become smaller and smaller, it may stay marginal and neglected, but it remains inside as the exciting double of the man. It is the perennial invitation *to be other*, simpler, and more authentic and to remember what each one was before the conformities that entrap us at the end of the first initiation.

This *fanciullino*, then, is part of Pascoli's conscience and consciousness, indeed of his entire world view. To follow the Child does not mean to be exclusively open to wonder and to react spontaneously and freely to people, things, and events, while being protected by one's innocence. It also means to recognize one's loneliness and fragility and be aware of the mysterious power of all that is yet unknown. In fact, in Pascoli's view, childhood is not the privileged space for pure little beings. It is the wellhead and symbol of all beginnings. Furthermore, meditating on the mystery of origins brings the poet to a certain lyrical mystique of the physiological aspects of love and fecundation and to a renewed appreciation of the matter in a perspective different from that of positivistic thought, since the substance does not oppose nor become subject to the spirit, but

rather contains it. Therefore, far from enclosing his Child only within the mother's loving arms, or projecting it as the harbinger of a superior order, Pascoli makes it an object of study and an answer to questions of life-style and poetics.

***

In the present study, I make constant reference to Pascoli's text, and so I have decided to premise my work with a complete translation of *Il fanciullino*, up to now unavailable in English. I am confident that making his work accessible will help stimulate the interest of American critics concerned with the poetics of late Romanticism and Symbolism.

The translation itself presented some major problems. Pascoli's prose is uneven in style, ranging from formal, rhetorical, and literary flourishes to loosely connected series of elliptical phrases. I have tried to reproduce this variety of registers, in the conviction that Pascoli's style is an important indicator of both the content of his arguments and the relative importance he attached to them. I also opted to furnish some necessary background information in the course of my own study rather than to overburden the text with too many explanatory notes. For my intention was not to interrupt the attention of the reader and thereby run counter to the anti-academic intention of the author. The choice of the personal pronoun was of particular difficulty in both the translation and my essay. After some hesitation, I preferred not to betray the original language in the name of current political correctness, and I used the masculine singular personal pronoun every time I made reference to the child.

I should like to thank Professor Joseph Tusiani for his striking translation of some of Pascoli's poems (*From Marino to Marinetti. An Anthology of Forty Italian Poets*. New York: Baroque Press, 1974). With prompt generosity he gave me permission to use them in my commentary. For the most part, however, I had to resort to my own prose translation, and hope that the literal, if less eloquent, rendering helps clarify my interpretation.

To my good friend and colleague, Professor Anthony L. Pellegrini, I owe a debt of sincere gratitude. His innumerable suggestions for revisions, especially in the translation of Pascoli's difficult essay, his extraordinary linguistic sensitivity for both Italian and English, along with his well-known editorial acuity, have been instrumental in bringing this work to completion.

IL FANCIULLINO

I

È dentro noi un fanciullino[1] che non solo ha brividi, come credeva Cebes Tebano che primo in sé lo scoperse, ma lagrime ancora e tripudi suoi. Quando la nostra età è tuttavia tenera, egli confonde la sua voce con la nostra, e dei due fanciulli che ruzzano e contendono tra loro, e, insieme sempre, temono sperano godono piangono, si sente un palpito solo, uno strillare e un guaire solo. Ma quindi noi cresciamo, ed egli resta piccolo; noi accendiamo negli occhi un nuovo desiderare, ed egli vi tiene fissa la sua antica serena maraviglia; noi ingrossiamo e arrugginiamo la voce, ed egli fa sentire tuttavia e sempre il suo tinnulo squillo come di campanello. Il quale tintinnio segreto noi non udiamo distinto nell'età giovanile forse così come nella più matura, perché, in quella occupati a litigare e perorare la causa della nostra vita, meno badiamo a quell'angolo d'anima d'onde esso risuona. E anche, egli, l'invisibile fanciullo, si perita vicino al giovane più che accanto all'uomo fatto e al vecchio, ché, più dissimile a sé, vede quello che questi. Il giovane in vero di rado e fuggevolmente si trattiene col fanciullo; ché ne sdegna la conversazione, come chi si vergogni d'un passato ancor troppo recente. Ma l'uomo riposato ama parlare con lui e udirne il chiacchiericcio e rispondergli a tono e grave; e l'armonia di quelle voci è assai dolce ad ascoltare, come d'un usignuolo che gorgheggi presso un ruscello che mormora.

O presso il vecchio grigio mare. Il mare è affaticato dall'ansia della vita, e si copre di bianche spume, e rantola sulla spiaggia. Ma tra un'ondata e l'altra suonano le note dell'usignuolo ora singultite come un lamento, ora spicciolate come un giubilo, ora punteggiate come una domanda. L'usignuolo è piccolo, e il mare è grande; e l'uno è giovane, e l'altro è vecchio. Vecchio è l'aedo, e giovane la sua ode. Vainamoinen è antico,

---

[1] PLATONE, Phaed. 77 E: E Cebes con un sorriso, "Come fossimo spauriti," disse: "o Socrate, prova di persuaderci; o meglio non come spauriti noi, ma forse c'è dentro anche in noi un fanciullino che ha timore di siffatte cose: costui dunque proviamoci di persuadere a non aver paura della morte come di visacci d'orchi".

THE LITTLE CHILD

I

A little Child[1] lives within us, who not only trembles with fear, as Cebes the Theban believed who first discovered him in himself, but also has his own tears and his own joy. When we are still of a very tender age, he melds his voice together with ours, and of the two children, playing and fighting, always together, experiencing fear and hope and pleasure and pain, one would note only one quiver, only one shout, only one whine. But then we grow bigger, while he remains small; our eyes light up with new desires, while he holds firm in his eyes the old serene wonder; we grow up and let our voices roughen, while, in spite of everything, he always makes us hear his chimes, tinkling like a little bell. And in our youthful time we do not listen to this secret tinkling as distinctly as we do in our more mature years, because, then, too busy struggling and pleading for our existence, we do not attend as much to that corner of our soul from which the little Child often calls. And also, the invisible Child himself is more hesitant with the young man than with the mature and the old, because he sees the former more different from him than the latter. In truth, the young man rarely and only fleetingly stops to be with the Child, scorning his conversation, as if ashamed of a past still too recent. But the older and peaceful man loves to talk with him, to listen to his noisy chattering and to answer back in tune with him and gravely; and the harmony of those voices is very sweet to the ear, like the voice of a nightingale trilling near a murmuring brook.

Or by the old gray sea. The sea is weary with the anxiety of life, and with white foam it shrouds itself and gasps along the shore. Yet, between one wave and another, ring the notes of the nightingale, now in sobs as if wailing, now brief and quick as if in jubilation, now intermittent as if questioning. The nightingale is small and the sea is large; and the one is young while the other is old. Old is the poet and young is his ode.

---

[1] Plato, *Phaedo*, 77E. And Cebes with a smile, "Then, Socrates, you must argue us out of our fears — he said — or better, not as if we were afraid; rather, think that there is perhaps within us, a little child who is afraid of such things: him too we must persuade not to be afraid of death as of the grimaces of ogres."

RosaMaria LaValva, *The Poetry & Poetics of G. Pascoli*

nuovo il suo canto.[2] Chi può imaginare, se non vecchio l'aedo e il bardo? Vyàsa è invecchiato nella penitenza e sa tutte le cose sacre e profane. Vecchio è Ossian, vecchi molti degli skaldi. L'aedo è l'uomo che ha veduto (*oidè*) e perciò sa, e anzi talvolta non vede più; è il veggente (*aoidos*) che fa apparire il suo canto.[3]

Non l'età grave impedisce di udire la vocina del bimbo interiore, anzi invita forse e aiuta, mancando l'altro chiasso intorno, ad ascoltarla nella

------

[2] Che Femio sia vecchio, non si dichiara da Omero con parola espressa, ma indirettamente con l'epiteto *periclytos* (*Od.* I, 325) comune all'altro aedo Demodoco (ib. 8, 521 e al.), e specialmente con ciò che Femio stesso afferma di sé (ib. 22, 347):

> *Sono maestro a me io, ché, un dio piantommi nel cuore*
> *Ogni ragione di canti...*

Il che consuona con ciò che di lui dice Penelope (ib. 1, 337 seg.):

> *Femio, poi che sai molt'altre malie de le genti*
> *Opere d'uomini e dèi...*

E il vecchio Femio con la canzone più nuova o più giovane (ib. 351 sg.):

> *Poi che gli uomini pregiano ed amano più quel canto*
> *che il più nuovo all'intorno de li ascoltanti risuoni.*

Quanto a Vainamoinen, ricordo da quel meraviglioso frammento di versione dovuto al mio P.E. Pavolini (Sul limitare, pag. 75 seg.):

> *L'antico e verace Vainamoinen*
> ....
> *Quindi l'antico Vainamoinen*
> ....
> *Quando udirono il nuovo canto,*
> *Sentirono il dolce suono.*

[3] OMERO, *Odissea* 8, 499, *phaíne d 'aoidén.* Badiamo che io non intendo affermare l'etimo di *aeidèin* da *a* privativo e *vid-*vedere. No: intendo asseverare che codesto etimo era presente agli antichi cantori. Si confrontino i due versi di *Odissea*, 1, 337 seg. che terminano il primo con *oidas* e il secondo con *aoidoi.* Si mediti il 64 di 8: Degli occhi, sì, lo privò, ma gli dava la soave *aoidén.* Si ripensi l'espressione su riferita: "mostrava l'*aoidén.*" Persino, oso dire, giova osservare, riguardo l'accecamento di Polifemo, mangiator d'uomini e bevitor di vino, che *polyphemos*, oltre a essere il nome del terribile Ciclope, è epiteto dell' *aoidos* Femio (22, 376), *Phémios* il cui nome somiglia del resto a quello di *Polyphemos.* E il Ciclope che mostra nella Odissea la sua musicalità solo quando (9, 315): "egli con sufolo molto parava le pecore al monte," musicalità che del resto è nel suo nome, se esso vale, come in 2, 150, "pieno di sussurri o di voci", il Ciclope è presso Teocrito un dolce cantor d'amore, e nessuno dei Ciclopi sa sonar la piva come lui (THEOCR., Id., I l).

Vainamoinen is ancient, and his song is new.[2] Who can imagine the *aedus* and the bard to be other than old? Vyàsa became old in penance and he knows all things sacred and profane. Old is Ossian, old many of the skalds. The *aedus* is the man who has seen (*oide*) and therefore knows; moreover, at times he is blind; he then becomes the seer (*aoidos*) who causes his song to come forth.[3]

Thus, old age does not keep one from hearing the tiny voice of the little Child within, rather, it is inviting, perhaps, and it is helpful, in the absence of other surrounding noise, to listen to that voice in the half-light

---

[2] That Phemius be old is not expressly stated by Homer but indirectly, with the epithet periclytos (*Odyssey* 1, 325) which is also given to the other aedus Demodocus (*ibidem* 8, 521 and elsewhere), and especially with what Phemius states about himself (*ibidem* 22, 347):

> Teacher I am to myself, since a God planted in my heart
> every means for singing...

This accords with Penelope's words (*ibidem* 1, 337 ff.):

> Phemius, since you know many other sorceries of people,
> Works of men and of gods ...

And the old Phemius with the youngest or the newest song (*ibidem* 351 ff.):

> Since men prize and love more that song
> Which sounds newest, around about the listeners.

As for Vainamoinen, I remember a marvelous fragment of a translation owed to my P. E. Pavolini (*Sul limitare*, pp. 75 ff.): "The old and truthful Vainamoinen / [...] /Hence the old Vainamoinen /[...] / when they listened to the new song / they heard the sweet sound.

[3] Homer, *Odyssey*, 8, 499; *phaine d'aoidén*. Let us note here that I do not intend to establish the etymon of aeidein from a alpha privative and vid vedere (to see). No; I mean to assert that this very etymon was present to the old poets. Let us compare the two lines of *Odyssey* 1, 337 ff. which end the first with oidas, and the second with aoidoi. Let us consider line 64 of 8: "Of his eyes, yes, he deprived him, but he gave him sweet aoidén." Let us recall the above mentioned expression: it showed aoidén. I even dare say it is helpful to observe in regard to the blinding of Polyphemos, eater of men and drinker of wine, that polyphemosis is not only the name of the terrible Cyclops, but the epithet of the aoidos Phemius (22, 376), Phémios, whose name clearly resembles that of Poliphemos. And the Cyclops who in the Odyssey shows his musicality only when (9, 315): "he, with his pipes drove the sheep to the mountain," a musicality which is moreover right in his name, if it means as in 2, 150 "full of whispers or voices." According to Theocritus the Cyclops is a sweet singer of love, and not one of the Cyclops can play the pipes as he does (Theocritus, Id., II).

penombra dell'anima.[4] E se gli occhi con cui si mira fuor di noi, non vedono più, ebbene il vecchio vede allora soltanto con quelli occhioni che son dentro lui, e non ha avanti sé, altro che la visione che ebbe da fanciullo e che hanno per solito tutti i fanciulli. E se uno avesse a dipingere Omero, lo dovrebbe figurare vecchio e cieco, condotto per mano da un fanciullino, che parlasse sempre guardando torno torno. Da un fanciullino o da una fanciulla: dal dio o dall'iddia: dal dio che sementò nei precordi di Femio quelle tante canzoni, o dell'iddia cui si rivolge il cieco aedo di Achille e di Odisseo.[5]

II

Ma il garrulo monello o la vergine vocale erano dentro lui, invisibilmente. Erano la sua medesima fanciullezza, conservata in cuore attraverso la vita, e risorta a ricordare e a cantare dopo il gran rumorio dei sensi. E la sua fanciullezza parlava per ciò più di Achille che d'Elena, e s'intratteneva col Ciclope meglio che con Calipso. Non sono gli amori, non sono le donne, per belle e dee che siano, che premono ai fanciulli; sì le aste bronzee e i carri da guerra e i lunghi viaggi e le grandi traversie. Così codeste cose narrava al vecchio Omero il suo fanciullino, piuttosto che le bellezze della Tindaride e le voluttà della dea della notte e della figlia del sole.[6] E le narrava col suo proprio linguaggio infantile.

Tornava da paesi non forse più lontani che il villaggio che è più vicino ai pastori della montagna; ma esso ne parlava ad altri fanciulli che

---

[4] Ricordo che tutto porta a credere che la *Comedia* sia stara cominciata dal poeta nell'anno quadragesimo ottavo della sua età, o dopo. E quello è il poema della contemplazione, opposta alla vita attiva.

[5] Così in vero lo rappresentò il Manzoni con le Muse (bastava una) che l'accompagnano: "la mal fida Con le destre vocali orma reggendo".

[6] Non solo i poeti moderni, così assolutamente fissati sull'amore e sulla donna ma anche gli antichi poeti tragici e persino i poeti corali immediatamente successi alla poesia epica, si diedero a colorire l'elemento femminile ed erotico dei poemi omerici. E le donne designate e mentovate in essi poemi, non bastarono, e se ne crearono di nuove. Ciò accrebbe l'interesse drammatico del ciclo, ma segna in esso la diminuzione di essenza poetica. Così Orlando innamorato e furioso per amore è più drammatico ma meno poetico di Rolando nella Canzone.

of the soul.[4] And if the eyes through which he looks outside, cannot see any longer, well, then, the old man sees only with those larger eyes that are within him, and has before him only the vision which he had as a child and which all children usually share. If one had to represent Homer, one would have to portray him old and blind, led by the hand of a little child incessantly speaking while looking all around. By a little boy or by a young girl: by the god or the goddess: by the god who planted many songs deep in the heart of Phemius, or by the goddess to whom the blind aedus of Achilles and Odysseus turns.[5]

II

But the garrulous urchin, or the talkative virgin, were within him, invisibly. They were his very childhood, kept in his heart throughout his life, and now resurfaced to remember and to sing after the great turmoil of the senses. That is why his childhood spoke more of Achilles than of Helen, and preferred to linger with the Cyclops rather than with Calypso. It is not love not women, however beautiful and goddess-like they might be, that matter to children; but bronze lances and war chariots and long journeys and great adventures. Such were the things, not the beauties of Tyndareus' daughter and the pleasures of the night goddess, and of the daughter of the sun,[6] his *fanciullino* narrated to Homer. These were the stories he told him in his childlike language.

Homer would come back from lands perhaps no more distant than the closest village to the mountain shepherds; but he spoke of them to other children who had never been there. He spoke of them at length, with

---

[4] I recall that all evidence leads us to believe that the Comedy was begun by the poet in his forty-eighth year, or later. And that it is the poem of contemplation, in contrast to the active life

[5] And this is the way in which Manzoni represented him with the Muses (one would have been enough) who accompany him: "With their clever voices the unsteady steps sustaining."

[6] Not only the modern poets, so absolutely set on love and on women, but also the ancient tragic poets and even the choral poets who immediately followed epic poetry, started to emphasize the feminine and erotic element of Homer's poems. And the women designated and mentioned in those poems were not enough, and new ones were made up. This added to the dramatic interest of the cycle but marks its decreased poetic essence. Thus, Orlando, in love and maddened by love, is more dramatic but less poetic than Roland in the *Chanson.*

non c'erano stati mai. Ne parlava a lungo, con foga, dicendo i particolari l'un dopo l'altro e non tralasciandone uno, nemmeno, per esempio, che le schiappe da bruciare erano senza foglie. Ché, tutto a lui pareva nuovo e bello, ciò che vi aveva visto, e nuovo e bello credeva avesse a parere agli uditori. La parola "bello" e "grande" ricorreva a ogni momento nel suo novellare, e sempre egli incastrava nel discorso una nota a cui riconoscere la cosa. Diceva che le navi erano nere, che avevano dipinta la prora, che galleggiavano perché ben bilanciate, che avevano belli attrezzi, bei banchi; che il mare era di tanti colori, che si moveva sempre, che era salato, che era spumeggiante. I guerrieri? Portavano i capelli lunghi. I loro caschi? Avevano creste che si movevano al passo. Le loro aste? Facevano una lunga ombra. Per non essere frainteso ripeteva il medesimo pensiero con altra forma: diceva "un pochino, mica tanto!", "vivere, mica morire!", e anche "parlò e disse", "si adunarono e furono tutti in un luogo". Non mancava di quelle spiegazioni che chiudono la bocca: "ubbidite, perché ubbidire... è meglio", "solo devo rimanermene senza dono? Non sta bene". La chiarezza non è mai troppa: "I pulcini erano otto, e nove con la madre, che aveva fatti i pulcini", "Aias, quello più piccolo, non grande come l'altro, ma molto più piccolo: era piccino...." Qualche volta riusciva sublime, ma senza farlo apposta: saltava qualche circostanza, per giungere a ciò che importava più e che era più sensibile. Un divino arciere tirava l'arco "e per tutto si vedevano cataste accese per bruciare i morti". Il dio supremo mosse il sopracciglio e scosse i capelli, "e scrollò l'Olimpo che è così grande". Sopra tutto, per far capire tutto il suo pensiero, in qualche fatto o spettacolo più nuovo e strano, s'ingegnava con paragoni tolti da ciò che esso e i suoi uditori avevano più sott'occhio o nell'orecchio. E in ciò teneva due modi contrari: ora ricordava un fatto piccolo per farne intendere uno grande, ora uno maggiore per farne vedere uno minore. Così rappresentava un mare agitato che con le grosse ondate spumeggianti si getta contro la spiaggia, e strepita e tuona, per dar l'idea d'una moltitudine d'uomini che accorre in un luogo; e descriveva uno sciame di mosche intorno ai secchielli pieni colmi di latte, per esprimere il confuso e vasto agglomerarsi d'un esercito di guerrieri.

Questo era il suo solo artifizio, se pure si può chiamare artifizio ciò ch'egli faceva così ingenuamente che spesso la cosa, mediante il suo paragone, riusciva più piccola sebbene sempre paresse più chiara; come quando confrontava il fluido parlare di alcuni vecchi savi all'incessante

passion, telling every detail, one after the other, and not omitting one, not even, for instance, that the stubble for burning was without leaves. For everything that he had seen there seemed new and beautiful to him, and new and beautiful he thought it would appear to his listeners. The words "beautiful" and "big" kept recurring in his telling, and he always embedded in his talk a note by which things could be recognized. He would say the ships were black, with a painted prow, that they could float because they were well balanced, that they had beautiful equipment, beautiful benches; that the sea was of many colors, that it was always moving, that it was salty, that it was foaming. The warriors? They had long hair. Their helmets? They had crests that moved at every step. Their spears? They cast a long shadow. In order not to be misunderstood, he would repeat the same thought in a different form: he would say: "a little bit, not a lot!" "to live, certainly not to die!" and even "He spoke and said," "they got together and they were all in one place." Nor did he lack peremptory explanations: "obey, because to obey... is better," "must I remain by myself, without [my] gift? It is not right." Clarity is never too much: "The little chicks were eight and nine with the mother that made the chicks." "Ajax, the smaller one, not as big as the other one, but much smaller: he was quite small..." Sometimes he attained the sublime, but without trying: he skipped some circumstance, to get to what was more important and more noteworthy. A divine archer bent his bow and "everywhere lighted pyres could be seen to burn the dead." The supreme god moved his eyebrow and shook his hair "and he shook the whole Olympus which is so great." Most of all, in order to have his thoughts fully understood, when dealing with a fact or an event that was newer and different, he tried to work with similes that were very familiar to him and to his listeners. And, in so doing, he followed two opposite ways: at times he remembered a small fact to make a big one understood; at others he used the greater one to set off the lesser. And so, he represented a rough sea casting itself against the shore with big foamy waves, roaring and thundering, in order to indicate a multitude of men arriving in one place; and he described a swarm of flies around a pail filled to the brim with milk, in order to express the vast and confused massing of an army of warriors.

This was his only artifice, if one can call artifice what he did with such simplicity that often, through his similes, the objects of his song became smaller, though they always appeared clearer; as when he compared the flowing speech of some old wise men to the incessant chirping of the cicadas, or the stamina of a great hero to the indifference of an ass grazing in a meadow from which young children wanted to chase it with their

frinire delle cicale, o la resistenza d'un grande eroe all'indifferenza d'un asino che seguita a empirsi d'erba nel prato donde i bimbi vogliono cacciarlo a suon di bastonate. No no: il fanciullino del cieco non tanto voleva farsi onore, quanto farsi capire: non esagerava; perché i fatti che raccontava, gli parevano già assai mirabili così come erano. Ed egli sapeva, né per altro argomento se non perché parevano anche a lui, che mirabili dovevano parere anche agli altri bambini come lui, che erano nell'anima di tutti i suoi uditori. I quali ora come allora lo ascoltano con maraviglia. E non sarebbe ragionevole, di cose che dopo trenta secoli non si credono più verosimili. Ma dopo pur trenta secoli gli uomini non nascono di trent'anni, e anche dopo i trent'anni restano per qualche parte fanciulli.

III

Ma è veramente in tutti il fanciullo musico? Che in qualcuno non sia, non vorrei credere né ad altri né a lui stesso: tanta a me parrebbe di lui la miseria e la solitudine. Egli non avrebbe dentro sé quel seno concavo da cui risonare le voci degli altri uomini; e nulla dell'anima sua giungerebbe all'anima dei suoi vicini. Egli non sarebbe unito all'umanità se non per le catene della legge, le quali o squassasse gravi o portasse leggiere, come uno schiavo o ribelle per la novità o indifferente per la consuetudine. Perché non gli uomini si sentono fratelli tra loro, essi che crescono diversi e diversamente si armano, ma tutti si armano, per la battaglia della vita; sì i fanciulli che sono in loro, i quali, per ogni poco d'agio e di tregua che sia data, si corrono incontro, e si abbracciano e giocano.

Eppure è chi dice che veramente di generi umani ve ne ha due, e non si scorge che siano due, e che l'uno attraversa l'altro, sempre diviso ma sempre indistinto, come una corrente dolce il mare amaro. Vivono persino nella stessa famiglia, sotto gli occhi della stessa madre, e vivono in apparenza la stessa vita germinata da uguale seme in unico solco; e questi sono stranieri a quelli, non d'un solo tratto di cielo e di terra, ma di tutta l'umanità e di tutta la natura. Essi si chiamano per nome e non si conoscono né si conosceranno mai. Ora se questo è vero, non può avvenire se non per una causa: che gli uni hanno dentro sé l'eterno fanciullo, e gli altri no, infelici!

sticks. No, no: the *fanciullino* of the blind man did not want so much to be admired as to be understood: he did not exaggerate; because the facts he narrated seemed to him to be wonderful enough just as they were. And he knew, not for any special reason other than because they appeared to be so, that they had to seem wonderful to the other children like him, who were in the souls of all his listeners. The ones who listen to him, now as they did then, in wonder. And this would not be reasonable to expect of things that after thirty centuries are not considered likely any longer. But even after thirty centuries men are not born at age thirty, and even after they are thirty, they remain, in part, childlike.

III

But is the child of the Muses [literally the music-like child] truly in each one of us? That he may not be in some one, I would not like to believe if others told me so or even if he did himself: so great would his misery and his solitude appear to me. He would not have within him that resonant breast from which the voices of other men could echo; and no part of his soul would reach the soul of his fellow human beings. He would be linked to humanity only by the chains of the law, to be borne, whether lightly or heavily, like a slave: rebellious out of love for something new, or indifferent out of habit. For it is not the men who feel like brothers among themselves, men who grow up different and arm themselves in different ways, yet all take up arms for the battle of life; but the children within them, who, as soon as there is the chance for a little respite, hasten to meet together and hug each other and play.

And yet there are those who talk of two kinds of humanity, not discernible from one another, with the one running through the other, always separate and always indistinct, like a sweet water current through the bitter sea. They even live in the same family, under the eyes of the same mother, and, to all appearances, they live the same life generated from the same seed in one furrow; but the one is alien to the other as if they were separated not by a mere stretch of sky or land, but by all of humanity and all of nature. They call each other by name but do not know each other, nor will they ever know each other. Now, if this is true, it can happen for one reason only: that some have within them the Eternal Child and the others, poor wretches!, do not.

But I do not want to accept so much unhappiness. It may seem that the Child is not in some people; some people may believe he is not in

Ma io non amo credere a tanta infelicità. In alcuni non pare che egli sia; alcuni non credono che sia in loro; e forse è apparenza e credenza falsa. Forse gli uomini aspettano da lui chi sa quali mirabili dimostrazioni e operazioni; e perché non le vedono, o in altri o in sé giudicano che egli non ci sia. Ma i segni della sua presenza e gli atti della sua vita sono semplici e umili. Egli è quello, dunque, che ha paura al buio, perché al buio vede o crede di vedere; quello che alla luce sogna o sembra sognare, ricordando cose non vedute mai; quello che parla alle bestie, agli alberi, ai sassi, alle nuvole, alle stelle: che popola l'ombra di fantasmi e il cielo di dei.[7] Egli è quello che piange e ride senza perché, di cose che sfuggono ai nostri sensi e alla nostra ragione. Egli è quello che nella morte degli esseri amati esce a dire quel particolare puerile che ci fa sciogliere in lacrime, e ci salva.[8] Egli è quello che nella gioia pazza pronunzia, senza pensarci, la parola grave che ci frena. Egli rende tollerabile la felicità e la sventura, temperandole d'amaro e di dolce, e facendone due cose ugualmente soavi al ricordo. Egli fa umano l'amore, perché accarezza esso come sorella (oh! il bisbiglio dei due fanciulli tra un bramire di belve), accarezza e consola la bambina che è nella donna. Egli nell'interno dell'uomo serio sta ad ascoltare, ammirando, le fiabe e le leggende, e in quello dell'uomo pacifico fa echeggiare stridule fanfare di trombette e di pive, e in un cantuccio dell'anima di chi più non crede, vapora d'incenso l'altarino che il bimbo ha ancora conservato da allora. Egli ci fa perdere il tempo, quando noi andiamo per i fatti nostri, ché ora vuol vedere la cinciallegra che canta, ora vuol cogliere il fiore che odora, ora vuol toccare la selce che riluce. E ciarla intanto, senza chetarsi mai; e, senza lui, non solo non vedremmo tante cose a cui non badiamo per solito, ma non potremmo nemmeno pensarle e ridirle, perché egli è l'Adamo che mette il nome a tutto ciò che vede e sente. Egli scopre nelle cose le somiglianze e

---

[7] Augusto Conti narra di una sua bambina: "Quando mirava la luna o le stelle, metteva voci di gioia, e me le additava, e chiamavale come cose viventi; offrendo loro quel che avesse in mano. anche le vesti." Rivado col pensiero a tutte le poesie che ho lette: non ne trovo una più poesia di questa!

[8] Tale, p. es., è quello di Andromaca che piange su Ettore (*Il.* 22, 510):

nudo, e si che di vesti ce n'hai ne la casa riposte
morbide e graziose, lavoro di mani di donne!

them; and maybe it is a false appearance and a false belief. Perhaps men expect from their Child who knows what wonderful deeds and demonstrations, and since they do not see such deeds, either in others or in themselves, they judge that the Child is not there. But the signs of his presence and the acts of his life are simple and humble. The Child is the one who is afraid in the dark, because in the dark he sees or believes he sees; he is the one who in the daylight dreams or appears to dream, remembering things he has never seen; the one who talks to the animals, the trees, the stones, the clouds, the stars: the one who fills the shadows with ghosts and the sky with gods.[7] He is the one who cries and laughs without cause, at things that escape our senses and our reason. He is the one who, at the death of a loved one, comes out with that little word which makes us burst into tears and saves us.[8] He is the one who in the wildest excitement utters, without thinking, the grave word which restrains us. He makes bearable both happiness and misfortune, tempering them with bitterness and sweetness, and making of them things equally sweet to memory. He makes love human, because he soothes it like a sister (oh! the whispering of the two children in the midst of wild beasts bellowing), he caresses and comforts the little girl who is in the woman. He is in the heart of the serious man, there to listen, in wonder, to fairy tales and legends; in the heart of the quiet man to hear shrill fanfares of trumpets and bagpipes; and he is the one burning incense on the altar he kept in a little corner, inside the soul of the non-believer. He makes us lose time, as we go about our business, because he wants to look, from time to time, at the singing titmouse, or pick the sweet-smelling flower, or touch the glittering stone. And he chatters in the meantime, without ever stopping; and without him, not only would we not see many things to which we ordinarily do not pay attention, but we could not even think them or say them, because the child is the Adam who gives the name to all that he sees and hears. He discovers

---

[7] Augusto Conti tells of one of his little girls: "When she looked at the moon or the stars, she screamed with joy and pointed them out to me, and called to them as living things; offering them whatever she had in her hands, even her clothes." In my mind I go over all the poems I have read: I do not find one that is more poetry than this!

[8] Such is, for example, that of Andromache, crying over Hector (II, 22, 510):
Naked, and yet of clothes you have many stored in the house,
Soft and graceful, the work of women's hands!

relazioni più ingegnose. Egli adatta il nome della cosa più grande alla più piccola, e al contrario. E a ciò lo spinge meglio stupore che ignoranza, e curiosità meglio che loquacità: impicciolisce per poter vedere, ingrandisce per poter ammirare. Né il suo linguaggio è imperfetto come di chi non dica la cosa se non a mezzo, ma prodigo anzi, come di chi due pensieri dia per una parola. E a ogni modo dà un segno, un suono, un colore, a cui riconoscere sempre cio che vide una volta.

C'è dunque chi non ha sentito mai nulla di tutto questo? Forse il fanciullo tace in voi, professore, perché voi avete troppo cipiglio, e voi non lo udite, o banchiere, tra il vostro invisibile e assiduo conteggio. Fa il broncio in te, o contadino, che zappi e vanghi, e non ti puoi fermare a guardare un poco; dorme coi pugni chiusi in te, operaio, che devi stare chiuso tutto il giorno nell'officina piena di fracasso e senza sole.

Ma in tutti è, voglio credere.

Siano gli operai, i contadini, i banchieri, i professori in una chiesa a una funzione di festa; si trovino poveri e ricchi, gli esasperati e gli annoiati, in un teatro a una bella musica: ecco tutti i loro fanciullini alla finestra dell'anima, illuminati da un sorriso o aspersi d'una lagrima che brillano negli occhi de' loro ospiti inconsapevoli; eccoli i fanciullini che si riconoscono, dall'impannata al balcone dei loro tuguri e palazzi, contemplando un ricordo e un sogno comune.

IV

Se è in tutti, è anche in me. E io, perché da quando s'era fanciulli insieme, non ho vissuto una vita cui almeno il dolore, che fu tanto, desse rilievo, non l'ho perduto quasi mai di vista e di udita. Anzi, non avendo io mutato quei primi miei affetti, chiedo talvolta se io abbia vissuto o no. E io dico sì, perché ivi è più vita dove è meno morte, e altri dice no, perché crede il contrario. Comunque, parlo spesso con lui, come esso parla alcuna volta a me, e gli dico:

— Fanciullo, che non sai ragionare se non a modo tuo, un modo fanciullesco che si chiama profondo, perché d'un tratto, senza farci scendere a uno a uno i gradini del pensiero, ci trasporta nell'abisso della verità...

the most ingenious similarities and relations among things. He adapts the name of the bigger thing to the smaller and vice versa. And he is moved to do this by wonder, rather than by ignorance, and by curiosity, rather than mere loquacity: he makes things small in order to see them, he makes things big in order to admire them. And his language is never imperfect, like that of one who can say things only half-way, rather it is generous, like the language of one who gives two thoughts with each word. And for each mood he gives a sign, a sound, a color, by which to recognize forever what he saw once. Is there, then, someone who has never felt any of all this? Maybe the Child is silent in you, professor, because you frown too much. And you, banker, do not hear him, amidst your assiduous and invisible counting. He sulks in you, farmer, as you dig and hoe and can never stop to look around a while; he sleeps, fists clenched, in you, laborer, who must stay closed up all day long in a noisy and sunless factory.

But he is in everyone, I want to believe this.

Let the laborers, the farmers, the bankers, the professors be in a church at the celebration of a feast; let the poor and the rich, the weary and the annoyed, be gathered in a theater, listening to beautiful music: there will come, also, all their little Children at the window of their soul, lit up by a smile or a tear shining in the eyes of their unknowing hosts; there the Eternal Children will gather, and recognize each other, from the poor ragged curtains of their hovels to the balconies of their palaces, contemplating a common memory and a common dream.

IV

If he is in everyone, then, the *fanciullino* is also in me. And since, from the time in which we were children together I have lived a life to which not even grief, which was plentiful, has given great definition, I have almost never lost him from sight or hearing. Actually, since I have not changed those first feelings of mine, sometimes I even ask whether or not I have lived. And I say yes, because more life is there where there is less death, while others may say no, believing the contrary. At any rate, I often speak to the Child within me, as he at times speaks to me, and to him I say:

— Child, who can only reason in your own way, a childlike way which we call deep, because suddenly, without making us go down the steps of thought one at a time, you plunge us into the abyss of truth...

Oh! non credo io che da te vengano, semplice fanciullo, certe filze di sillogismi, sebbene siano esposte in un linguaggio che somiglia al tuo, e disposte secondo ritmi che sono i tuoi! Forse quei ritmi ce le fanno meglio seguire, quelle filze, e quel linguaggio ce lo fa meglio capire, quel ragionamento; o forse no, ché l'uno, abbagliando, ci distrae, e gli altri, cullando, ci astraggono; sì che il fine del ragionatore non è ottenuto come sarebbe senza quelle immagini e senza quella cadenza. Ma mettiamo che sia: ora il tuo fine non è, credo, mai questo, che si dica: "Tu mi hai convinto di cosa che non era nel mio pensiero". E nemmeno quest'altro: "Tu mi hai persuaso a cosa che non era nella mia volontà". Tu non pretendi tanto, o fanciullo. Tu dici in un tuo modo schietto e semplice cose che vedi e senti in un tuo modo limpido e immediato, e sei pago del tuo dire, quando chi ti ode esclama: "Anch'io vedo *ora*, *ora* sento ciò che tu dici e che era, certo, anche prima, fuori e dentro di me, e non lo sapeva io affatto o non così bene come *ora*! Soltanto questo tu vuoi, seppure qualche cosa vuoi dal diletto in fuori che tu stesso ricavi da quella visione e da quel sentimento. E come potresti aspirare ad operazioni così grandi tu con così piccoli strumenti? Perché tu non devi lasciarti sedurre da una certa somiglianza che è, per esempio, tra il tuo linguaggio e quello degli oratori. Sì: anch'essi, gli oratori, ingrandiscono e impicioliscono ciò che loro piaccia, e adoperano, quando loro piace, una parola che dipinga invece di un'altra che indichi. Ma la differenza è che essi fanno ciò appunto quando loro piace e di quello che loro piaccia. Tu no, fanciullo: tu dici sempre quello che vedi come lo vedi. Essi lo fanno a malizia! Tu non sapresti come dire altrimenti; ed essi dicono altrimenti da quello che sanno che si dice. Tu illumini la cosa, essi abbagliano gli occhi. Tu vuoi che si veda meglio, essi vogliono che non si veda più. Il loro insomma è il linguaggio artifiziato d'uomini scaltriti, che si propongono di rubare la volontà ad altri uomini non meno scaltriti; il tuo è il linguaggio nativo di fanciullo ingenuo, che tripudiando o lamentando parli ad altri ingenui fanciulli.

Non è così?...

Fanciullo, dunque, che non ragioni se non a modo tuo, dicendo di quando in quando le sentenze più comuni e più sublimi, più chiare e più inaspettate, tu puoi per altro, in ciò che ti riguarda più da presso, e intendere la mia e dire la tua ragione. Per questo ti parlo con più gravità che

Oh! I do not believe that from you, a naive Child, come some strings of syllogisms, even though they may be expressed in a language that resembles yours, and arranged according to rhythms which are yours! Maybe those rhythms enable us better to follow those fabrications, and that language lets us understand the reasoning better; or maybe not, since the language, by its dazzling, distracts us, and the rhythms, in their lulling effect, lead us astray; so that the objective of the logician is not attained as it would be without those images and without that rhythm. But let us suppose it is so. Now, your aim, I believe, is not that it may be said: "You have convinced me of something that was not in my mind." Nor: "You have persuaded me of something that was against my will." You do not claim so much, Child! You say, in your own way open and simple things that you see and feel in your own way clear and immediate, and you are satisfied with what you say, when whoever listens to you exclaims: "I also see *now. Now* I hear what you are saying and what was, certainly, outside and inside of me, even previously, even though I was not at all aware of it or not as well as I am now!" This is all you want, if you want anything at all, other than the delight you yourself gain from that vision and that feeling. And how could you aspire, in fact, to such great actions, you with your simple devices? For you must not allow yourself to be seduced by a certain resemblance which exists, for example, between your language and that of orators. Yes indeed: the orators too make things bigger and smaller, as they like, and use, when it pleases them, a word that represents rather than one that denotes. But the difference is that they do so, precisely when they please and of what pleases them. Not you, Child: you always say what you see as you see it. They do it with artifice! You would not know how to say it in a different way, while they say it in a way that is purposely different. You shed light on the object, they dazzle the eyes. You want people to see better, they want people not to see more. In sum, theirs is the artificial language of clever men, who seek to steal the will of others no less clever than themselves; yours is the inborn language of the naive child, who, laughing or crying, speaks to other naive children.

Is it not so?...

Child, then, you who reason only in your own way, stating from time to time the most common opinions and the most sublime, the clearest and the most unexpected, you can, moreover, in things that concern you most closely, listen to my opinion and speak your own mind. This is why I am talking to you more seriously than is my habit, and, from you, I would like an answer less... how should I put it? childish?... poetic, than is your habit.

io non soglia, e vorrei avere da te una risposta meno... come ho da dire? infantile?... poetica, che tu non costumi.

V

Tu sai che io ti amo, o mio intimo benefattore, o invisibile coppiere del farmaco *nepenthès* e *acholon*, contro il dolore e l'ira, o trovatore e custode d'un segreto tesoro di lagrime e sorrisi! E sai ancora che io non ti credo, come fanciullo, così irragionevole, né stimo un perditempo l'ascoltarti quando detti dentro. Oh! no, molto ci corre. Sebbene qualche volta, a vedere le tiritere isosillabiche e omeoteleute (non ti spaventare! è come dire "versi rimati") con le quali certi orecchianti vogliono far credere di far l'arte tua, anch'io rischio di pensare, come molti, che codesto parlare cadenzato e sonoro non sia naturale né ragionevole. Ma è un momento. Dimentico quelle tiritere, e dico a te che per quel momento mi fissi tra spaurito e malcontento con codesti occhi che vedono con maraviglia; dico a te:

"No no: non temere. Tu sei il fanciullo eterno, che vede tutto con maraviglia, tutto come per la prima volta. L'uomo le cose interne ed esterne, non le vede come le vedi tu: egli sa tanti particolari che tu non sai. Egli ha studiato e ha fatto suo pro' degli studi degli altri. Sì che l'uomo dei nostri tempi sa più che quello dei tempi scorsi, e, a mano a mano che si risale, molto più e sempre più. I primi uomini non sapevano niente; sapevano quello che sai tu, fanciullo.

Certo ti assomigliavano, perché in loro il fanciullo intimo si fondeva, per così dire, con tutto l'uomo quanto egli era. Maravigliavano essi, con tutto il loro essere indistinto, di tutto; ché era veramente allora nuovo tutto, né solo per il fanciullo, ma per l'uomo. Maravigliavano con sentimento misto ora di gioia ora di tristezza ora di speranza ora di timore. Se poi tale commovimento volevano esprimere a sé e ad altri, essi traevano fuori dalla faretra, per dirla con te, certi preziosi e numerosi strali di cui non si doveva far gettito.

Pronunziavano essi, i primi uomini, con lentezza uniforme, con misurata gravità, la difficile parola che stupivano volasse e splendesse e sonasse, e fosse loro e diventasse d'altri, e recasse attorno l'anima di chi la emetteva dopo la lunga silenziosa meditazione. Oh! non le gettavano essi come cose vili che soprabbondano, le parole pur mo nate, legate coi più

V

You do know that I love you, my intimate benefactor, invisible cup-bearer of *nepenthès* and *acholon* against pain and anger, finder and keeper of a secret treasure of tears and smiles! And you know, furthermore, that I do not consider you, as a child, unreasonable, nor do I think it a waste of time to listen to you when you speak within. Oh! no, far from it. Even though, sometimes, when I see those isosyllabic and homeoteleuthic rigmaroles (do not be scared! it is the same as saying "verses in rhyme") with which certain dabblers playing by ear pretend to do your art, I too risk thinking, as many do, that such cadenced and resonant speech is not natural or reasonable. But it is only for a moment. I forget those rigmaroles and I say to you, who in that moment look at me scared and unhappy, with those eyes which see in wonder; I say to you:

"No, no: do not fear. You are the Eternal Child, who sees everything with a sense of wonder, everything as if for the first time. The adult man does not see the inward and outward things as you see them: he knows many details that you do not. He has studied and has taken advantage of other peoples' studies. So that the man of our time knows more than the man of time past, and even more, much more if we go farther back in time. The first men knew nothing; they knew what you know, Child.

Surely they resembled you, because in them the inner Child blended, so to speak, with the whole man. They marveled, with all their indistinct being, at everything; because, at that time, everything was really new, and not only for the child, but for the man. They stood in wonder with mixed feelings of joy and sadness, of hope and fear. And if, then, they wanted to express such deep feelings to themselves and to others, they would, to put it as you do, take out of their quiver some special arrows, precious and numerous, which were not for tossing.

They, the first men, pronounced with uniform slowness, with measured gravity, that difficult word which they marveled could fly and shine and sound, could belong to them and could belong to others and carry the soul of the one who emitted it after long, silent meditation. Oh! they did not throw them around, as vile things in excess, those words just born, bound with the slightest of knots, stamped with the sharpest markings, wrought in the most ingenious niello designs! They would

sottili nodi, segnate con le più vive impronte, lavorate coi più ingegnosi nielli! Ne vedevano essi tutti i pregi, e il peso e il timbro del loro metallo, e il suono col quale in principio rompevano dalle labbra schiudentisi, e quello col quale in fine ronzavano nelle orecchie aperte. Or tu, fanciullo, fai come loro, perché sei come loro.

Fai come tutti i bambini i quali non solo, quando sono un po' sollevati, giocano e saltano con certe loro cantilene ben ritmate, ma quando sono ancora poppanti, e fanno la boschereccia, con misura e cadenza balbettano tra sé, e sé le loro file di *pa pa* e *ma ma*.

E in ciò è ragione perché è natura. Tu sei ancora in presenza del mondo novello, e adoperi a significarlo la novella parola. Il mondo nasce per ognun che nasce al mondo. E in ciò è il mistero della tua essenza e della tua funzione. Tu sei antichissimo, o fanciullo! E vecchissimo è il mondo che tu vedi nuovamente! E primitivo il ritmo (non questo o quello, ma il ritmo in generale) col quale tu, in certo modo, lo culli o lo danzi! Come sono stolti quelli che vogliono ribellarsi o all'una o all'altra di queste due necessità che paiono cozzare tra loro: veder nuovo e veder da antico, e dire ciò che non s'è mai detto e dirlo come sempre si è detto e si dirà! E si ribellano, gli uni con gli schifi gesti di pedanti: "Questa metafora non è in ..." (e qui il nome d'un poeta a mano a mano più recente); gli altri con pugnaci atteggiamenti di novatori: "Questo non è assai inaudito e inaudibile!" Quelli sono in generale vecchi che nella vecchiaia credono riposta ogni autorità e questi, giovani che nella giovinezza imaginano insita ogni forza; più noiosi questi di quelli, perché l'un vanto è sempre con impertinenza, e l'altro non è mai senza tristezza, e perché se gli uni non intendono più, per senile sordità l'arguto chiacchiericcio del fanciullo, gli altri non lo intendono ancora, per quello schiamazzare che fanno, miseramente orgoglioso, intorno al loro *io* giovane. E, in verità giovani non sono, ché d'essere, se fossero, non si accorgerebbero. D'essere vecchio uno s'accorge sì, qualche volta, e allora si veste, si tinge, grida a giovane. E forse il caso di voi, vecchiastri?

A ogni modo, pace. Sappiate che per la poesia la giovinezza non basta: la fanciullezza ci vuole!

recognize all their qualities, and the weight and tone of their metal and the sound with which they first broke forth from their parted lips, and the sound which finally resounded in their open ears. Now you, Child, do as they did because you are like them.

You sing like all children who jump and play at some well timed sing-song of theirs, not only when they are somewhat grown, but even when they are still nursing and making wild woodland sounds, and babble to themselves in measured rhythm their long strings of *pa pa* and *ma ma*.

And in this lies reason because in this lies nature. You are still in front of the world in its newness, and you use words that are new to give meaning to it. The world is born to everyone who is born to the world. And herein is the mystery of your essence and of your function. You are most ancient, Child! And very old is the world which you see ever new! And primitive is the rhythm (not this or that one, in particular, but rhythm in general) with which somehow you rock it or make it dance! How silly are those who wish to rebel against one or the other of these two necessities, which seem to clash with one another: to see things anew and to see them as an old person; to say what has never been said and to say it as it always was and will be said. And they protest. Some with the fastidious gestures of the pedant: "This metaphor is not in..." (and out comes the name of a poet ever closer in time); others with the bellicose attitude of the innovator: "This is not strange and unbelievable enough!" The first are generally old men who believe all authority rests in old age; and the second are the young who imagine all power to reside in youth; and the latter are more annoying than the former, because their boast is always insolent, while the others' is never without sadness, and because if the former ones, due to elderly deafness, no longer hear the clever chatter of the Child, the others do not hear it yet, because of all that pitiable proud cackling they stir up around their young ego. And, in truth, young they are not, because if they were, they would not notice. One becomes aware, yes, at times, of being old, and then one dresses up, and puts on make-up and shouts youthfully. Is this your case, crotchety old men?

At any rate, peace. Know that for poetry youth is not enough: you need childhood!

VI

Tu sei savio e mi contento. Non vuoi né ripetere il già detto né trovare l'indicibile, non vuoi essere né un'inutilità né una vanità. Vuoi il nuovo, ma sai che nelle cose è il nuovo, per chi sa vederlo, e non t'indurrai a trovarlo, affatturando e sofisticando. Il nuovo non s'inventa: si scopre. Mi contento dunque, a dirla tra noi, vale a dire, tra *me*... Ma intendiamoci subito: di ciò non ti attribuisco gran lode, perché non ci vedo gran merito. Come? Aspetta e sii paziente, ché mi conviene andar per le lunghe. E prima vorrei farti una domanda. Un fine, l'hai tu? Fuori, s'intende, di quello appunto di dire o dittare? E puoi dirmi, quale? Ho bisogno di saperlo. Non rispondi? Pensi? esiti? dubiti? Imagino che codesto fine non sia, per esempio, quello di dare un po' d'aiuto, di fornire un poco d'oro al tuo vecchio ospite, che ne ha tanto bisogno. Imagino, anzi so che tu non conosci altro oro che metaforico, cioè che non si spende. Ridi? Intendiamoci. So per certo che tu non credi di procacciarmi direttamente un utile materiale, ma sospetto che ti figuri di procacciarmelo indirettamente, aggiungendo non saprei che favore alla mia povera persona e che pregio alle mie umili virtù, sì che l'industria, che sai che esercito, mi profitti qualche cosa più. Ebbene, ti ingannaresti. Sappi che è il contrario; e che è ragionevole che sia il contrario. Tu sei un fanciullo: ora non tutti sanno distinguere te fanciullo da me vecchio, e perché mi sentono e vedono bamboleggiare qualche volta, credono volentieri che io bamboleggi sempre, anche quando lavoro sul serio, per guadagnarmi la vita. Per ciò essi meno apprezzano quei lavori serii, e io minor utile ne ricavo. E hanno torto. Sempre? Sappi che non hanno torto sempre. Hanno, per esempio, ragione (né parlo soltanto di me, ma di molti altri), quando tra i miei ragionamenti, che non dovrebbero essere se non giusti e chiari, vedono comparire i tuoi sorrisi e le tue grida. Vedi: i passeri sono graziosi uccelli (anch'essi: perché no?); ma nei seminati i contadini non ce li vogliono, per graziosi che siano. Le spadacciole sono bellissimi fiori; ma tra il grano sarebbe molto meglio che non ce ne fosse. Ma fanno così bel vedere! Non nego che possano dilettare qualcuno: non dilettano però colui che spera l'utile di quel grano. Capisci? Se anche c'è qualcuno a cui piacciono i tuoi frulli e i tuoi lampeggiamenti in mezzo a un ragionare che avrebbe a essere serio, ai più non può essere che non dispiaccia. E sai che cosa succede? Questi,

VI

You are wise and I am satisfied. You wish neither to repeat what has been said already, nor to find what cannot be expressed; you do not want to be either useless or vain. You want the new, but you know that the new is in the things themselves, for those who can see it, and you will not force yourself to find it with enchantments and sophistication(s). The new is not to be invented, it is to be discovered. I am satisfied, then, to state the matter between us, that is, between myself... But let us understand each other straightway: I do not give you much praise for this, since I do not see much merit in it. What? Wait, and be patient, because I will go on at some length. And, first, I should like to ask you a question. Do you have a purpose? Besides, that is, that of telling or dictating? And can you tell me what this purpose is? I need to know. You do not answer? Are you thinking? Hesitating? Doubting? I imagine that this purpose of yours is not, for example, that of giving a little help, of providing a little gold for your old host who needs it so. I imagine, indeed I know, that you are aware only of metaphorical gold, that is, gold that cannot be spent. You laugh? Let us be clear. I know for a fact that you do not believe you are supplying me directly with a material benefit, but I suspect you think you are providing it indirectly, adding some sort of favor to my poor person, some sort of merit to my humble virtues, so that the business you know I practice, could profit me somewhat more. Well, you would be mistaken. Rest assured that it is the opposite; and it is reasonable that it be the opposite. You are a Child: now, not everybody is able to distinguish you, the Child, from me, the adult; and since they see me and they hear me act and talk like a Child, they are glad to believe that I am always childish, even when I work in earnest, to earn my living. Because of this, they appreciate less my serious work, and I earn even less from it. And they are wrong. Always? Rest assured that they are not always wrong. For instance they are right (and I do not speak only of myself, but of many others), when amidst my arguments, which should be only direct and clear, they note the appearance of your smiles and your shouts. You see: the sparrows are graceful birds (they too: why not?); but the farmers do not want them in their fields, no matter how graceful they are. Gladioli are very beautiful flowers; but it would be much better if they were not among the wheat. But they look so beautiful! I do not deny they may delight someone: they do not, however, delight the one who hopes to make a profit from that wheat. Do you understand? Even if there is someone who may like your fluttering and your sparkling in the midst of some reasoned discourse that should be serious, it cannot help but

trovandoti così fuori di posto, non pensano che tu sia il fanciullo dalla voce argentina, ma credono sentire in te l'uomo roco, l'uomo che parla per ingannare: e gridano: *Retorica!* Ora per evitare tale scambio a te e tale danno a me, non sarebbe male che quando io bado ai fatti miei, tu te ne andassi lontano e dormissi nei profondi boschi d'Idalia e tra l'odoroso cespuglio dell'amaraco. Se tu conoscessi Platone, ti direi che come egli ha ragione nel volere che i poeti facciano *mythous* e non *logous*, favole e non ragionamenti, così non ho torto io nel pretendere che i ragionatori facciano *logous* e non *mythous*.[9] Ma purtroppo è difficile trovare chi si contenti di far solo quello che deve. E Platone stesso... Ma egli era Platone.

Tornando a noi, dunque, nessun utile né diretto né indiretto mi viene da te, o fanciullo. Checché, tu possa dire, nessuno. Quale invero sarebbe? Parla! —

VII

IL FANCIULLO

A te né le gemme né gli ori
fornisco, o dolce ospite: è vero;
ma fo che ti bastino i fiori
che cogli nel verde sentiero,
nel muro, su le umide crepe,
su l'ispida siepe.

Non reco al tuo desco lo spicchio
fumante di pingue vitella;
ma fo che ti piaccia il radicchio
non senza la sua selvastrella,
con l'ovo che a te mattutina
cantò la gallina.

---

[9] PLAT., *Phaed.* III B.

displease the majority. And do you know what happens? These people, finding you so much out of place, do not think you are the Child with the silvery voice, but believe, rather, they are listening to the gruff-voiced man, the man who speaks to deceive: and they shout: *Rhetoric!*

Now, to spare you of such a charge and myself of such injury, it would not be a bad idea if, when I am looking after my affairs, you were to go faraway and sleep in the deep Idalian woods amidst the sweet-smelling marjoram. If you knew Plato, I would tell you that he is right when he insists that poets create *mythos* and not *logos*, tales and not discursive speech. Therefore, I am not wrong in expecting discoursers to engage in *logos* and not in *mythos*.[9] But unfortunately it is hard to find those who are happy to do only what they should. And Plato himself... But he was Plato.

Returning to what we were saying, then, no benefit comes to me directly or indirectly from you, Child. No matter what you may say, none. In truth, what could it be? Speak! —

VII

THE CHILD

For you neither jewels nor gold
I provide, my sweet host: it is true;
but I so plan that the flowers suffice you
that you pick in green paths,
in the wall, on the damp crevices,
on the bristly hedge.

I bring not to your table the smoking
hind quarter of fine veal;
but I so plan that your chicory
with a pimpernel dash may be pleasing to you
and the egg that the chicken
announced early this morning.

---

[9] Plato, *Phaedo*, III B.

Per me tu non ari, o poeta,
né vigne sassose, né grasse
maggesi; ma dimmi se più
di vigne e maggesi s'allieta
quel cupo signore, od il passero
garrulo e tu!

Non fragili coppe di Cina,
la lampada d'oro t'irradia;
ma tu la tua scabra cucina
tu ami e la provvida madia;
la fiamma che lustra, tu ami,
sui nitidi rami.

Non hai che dal ciglio ti penda,
né paggio né florida ancella;
ma lieta, ma grata sfaccenda
per te la tua dolce sorella;
che cinge il grembiule, e sorride;
lo scinge e s'asside

con te... E per letto di morte,
che a tutti è sì duro e sì grave,
che cosa ti serbo, sai tu?
Oh! rose per letto di morte,
cadute dal pruno: il soave
dolore che fu!

VIII

— Bene! Tu hai cantato e detto: hai cantato strofe e detto verità. E mi viene in mente che oltre codeste verità, diremo così, usuali, di cui io ti sono testimone, ci sia sotto il tuo dire una verità più riposta e meno comune, a cui però la coscienza di tutti risponda con subito assenso. Quale? Questa: che la poesia, in quanto è poesia, la poesia senza aggettivo, ha una suprema utilità morale e sociale. E tu non hai mica ragionato, per rivelare a

For me you do not plow, oh poet,
in stony vineyards, or in fertile
fallow land; but tell me if that gloomy master
takes more joy in vineyards and fields
than the garrulous
sparrow and you!

The golden lamp does not light up
fragile China cups for you;
but you love your rugged kitchen
and generous cupboard;
you love the light that glistens
on the smooth branches.

You do not have a page boy or a buxom handmaid
hanging on your every look;
but happily, but gladly, about you
bustles your sister so sweet;
who ties on her apron, and smiles;
she unties it and sits

next to you... And for your deathbed,
that for all is so hard and so grievous,
do you know what I am saving you, do you?
Oh! Roses for your deathbed,
fallen from the thorn-bush: that sweet
pain that once was!

VIII

Fine! You have sung and you have spoken: you have sung verses and spoken truths. And it comes to my mind that, besides those truths, that are, shall we say, the usual, to which I bear witness for you, beneath all that, there is a deeper and less common truth, to which, however, the conscience of all responds with immediate assent. What is it? This: that poetry, insofar as it is poetry, poetry unqualified, has a supreme moral and social usefulness. And you certainly have not discoursed in order to reveal your

me il tuo fine. Tu hai detto quel che vedi e senti. E dicendo questo, hai forse espresso quale è il fine proprio della poesia. Ora tocca a me ragionarci sopra. Chi ben consideri, comprende che è il sentimento poetico il quale fa pago il pastore della sua capanna, il borghesuccio del suo appartamentino ammobigliato sia pur senza buon gusto ma con molta pazienza e diligenza; e vai dicendo. O è il contrario? E il pastore che, parando le pecore, sogna una bottega da avviare nel borgo vicino, e il borghesuccio che fantastica d'un palazzo in città grande e rumoreggiante, sono, essi sì, poeti fantasiosi e sognatori, e gli altri no? Già, per me, altro è sentimento poetico, altro è fantasia; la quale può essere bensì mossa e animata da quel sentimento, ma può anche non essere. Poesia è trovare nelle cose, come ho a dire? il loro sorriso e la loro lacrima; e ciò si fa da due occhi infantili che guardano semplicemente e serenamente di tra l'oscuro tumulto della nostra anima.

A volte, non ravvisando essi nulla di luminoso e di bello nelle cose che li circondano, si chiudono a sognare e a cercare lontano. Ma pur nelle cose vicine era quello che cercavano e non avervelo trovato, fu difetto non di poesia nelle cose, ma di vista negli occhi. Direte voi (non parlo a te, ora, o fanciullo, ma a cotali fanciulloni), direte voi che il sentimento poetico abbondi più in chi, torcendo o alzando gli occhi dalla realtà presente, trovi solo belli e degni del suo canto i fiori delle agavi americane, o in chi ammiri e faccia ammirare anche le minime nappine, color gridellino, della pimpinella, sul greppo in cui siede? E non voglio dire che non abbondi nel primo, quel sentimento, e non si trovi anzi unito ad altre virtù di scienza e di fantasia che lo facciano giustamente ammirabile; sebbene, come più agevolmente muove, così più presto annoia il suo lettore, e, a ogni modo, poiché le cose assenti, o non viste mai, sono sempre a tutti meravigliose, egli fa come l'uomo che pretende d'aver rallegrato con sue novellette l'uditore che, pure ascoltando, abbia bevuto largamente del vino letificante. Egli è stato, forse, arguto e festevole; ma chi rallegra con la parola sua schietta, senza bisogno di calici, ha maggior merito.

Or dunque intenso il sentimento poetico è di chi trova la poesia in ciò che lo circonda, e in ciò che altri soglia spregiare, non di chi non la trova lì e deve fare sforzi per cercarla altrove. E sommamente benefico è tale sentimento, che pone un soave e leggiero freno all'instancabile desiderio, il

purpose to me. You have said what you see and hear. And in so doing you have perhaps expressed what is the proper aim of poetry. Now it is my turn to reflect on it. If one thinks carefully, one understands that it is the poetic feeling that makes the shepherd content with his hut; the *petit bourgeois* happy with his small apartment, furnished, perhaps without much taste, but with much patience and diligence; and so on. Or is it by chance the opposite? And the shepherd who, while caring for his sheep, dreams of a little shop he might set up in the nearby village, and the little white-collar worker who daydreams about a palace in a big noisy city, they, they are the imaginative, dreaming poets, and others are not? Certainly, to my mind, poetic feeling is one thing, and imagination is quite another; and the latter may very well be inspired by that feeling, but it also may not. Poetry is to find in things, how shall I say?, their smiles and their tears; and this is done through the two little eyes of the Child that look out simply and serenely from within the dark turmoil of our soul.

At times, not perceiving anything bright and beautiful in the things around them, those eyes close up to dream and to search far away. And yet, what they were looking for, was in the very things that were near, and not to have found it there was not due to lack of poetry in the things but to lack of vision in the eyes. Will you say (I am not speaking now to you, Child, but to those big children), will you say that there is more poetic feeling in the one who, turning or lifting his eyes from the surrounding reality, finds beautiful and worthy of his song only the flowers of the American agave, or in the one who admires and causes others to admire even the tiny red blossoms of the pimpernel on the grassy slope where he sits? I certainly do not want to say that feeling does not abound in the first one, where it is actually joined with other virtues of knowledge and imagination which make him rightfully admirable; even though, just as he moves more easily, he annoys his reader all the sooner. At any rate, since what is far away, or never seen, is always an object of fascination for everyone, he is like the man who is sure that his little stories have cheered his listener who, while listening, has drunk deeply of some gladdening wine. He may well have been clever and funny; but greater merit belongs to the one who spreads cheer with his words alone, without the help of the drinking cup.

In sum, then, intense is the poetic feeling of the one who finds poetry in what is near at hand and others are likely to scorn, not of the one who does not find it there and must endeavor to look for it somewhere

quale ci fa perpetuamente correre con infelice ansia per la via della felicità. Oh! chi sapesse rafforzarlo in quelli che l'hanno, fermarlo in quelli che sono per perderlo, insinuarlo in quelli che ne mancano, non farebbe per la vita umana opera più utile di qualunque più ingegnoso trovatore di comodità e medicine? E non so dire quanto la comunione degli uomini ne sarebbe avvantaggiata; specialmente in questi tempi in cui la corsa verso l'impossibile felicità è con tanto fulmineo disprezzo in chi va avanti, con tanta disperata invidia in chi resta addietro. Già in altri tempi vide un Poeta (io non sono degno nemmeno di pronunziare il tuo santo nome, o *Parthenias*!), vide rotolare per il vano circolo della passione le quadriglie vertiginose; e quei tempi erano simili a questi, e balenava all'orizzonte la conflagrazione del mondo in una guerra di tutti contro tutti e d'ognuno contro ognuno; e quel Poeta sentì che sopra le fiere e i mostri aveva ancor più potere la cetra di Orfeo che la clava d'Ercole. E fece poesia, senza pensare ad altro, senza darsi arie di consigliatore, di ammonitore, di profeta del buono e del mal augurio: cantò, per cantare. E io non so misurare qual fosse l'effetto del suo canto, ma grande fu certo, se dura sino ad oggidì, vibrando con dolcezza nelle nostre anime irrequiete. O rimatori di frasi tribunizie, o verseggiatori di teoriche sociali, che escludete dall'ora presente ogni poesia che non sia la vostra, vale a dire, escludete la POESIA, ditemi: Era o non era al suo posto, nel secolo d'Augusto, il cantore delle Georgiche? Sì, non è vero? Egli insegnava ad amare la vita in cui non fosse lo spettacolo né doloroso della miseria né invidioso della ricchezza: egli voleva abolire la lotta tra le classi e la guerra tra i popoli. Che volete voi, o poeti socialisti, che dite cose tanto diverse e le dite tanto diversamente da lui?

IX

Dei due fraterni poeti Augustei (ché non si può parlare di Virgilio senza soggiungere Orazio) voi direte che fu la filosofia che li addusse a quella ragione sana e pia di considerare la società e la vita. E no: fu il fanciullino che li portò per mano, dicendo: "Vi dirò io dove è nel tempo stesso la poesia e la virtù". Fu il fanciullino che, se mai, fece che trascegliessero tra le opinioni dei filosofi quelle che confermavano il loro sentimento.

else. And exceedingly beneficial is this feeling, which sets a light and gentle restraint on the unremitting desire that makes us perpetually run, full of wretched longing, in search of happiness. Oh! the poet who could strengthen such feeling in those who have it, firm it up in those who are about to lose it, impart it to those who are deprived of it. Would he not do for human life something more useful than any highly ingenious discoverer of conveniences and medicines? And I cannot begin to tell how much the consortium of men would benefit from it; especially in our time when the search for an impossible happiness is mixed with such violent contempt in those who get ahead, and with such desperate envy in those who are left behind. Long ago, in different times a Poet (and I am not worthy of pronouncing your sacred name, Parthenias!), saw the warring chariots hurtling down the vain circle of passion; and those times were similar to these, and on the horizon loomed the conflagration of the world in a war of all against all and of each against each; and that Poet sensed that Orpheus' lyre had more power than Hercules' club over the wild animals and monsters. And he made poetry, not thinking of anything else, not putting on the airs of the counselor, of the admonisher, of the prophet of good and bad omen: he sang just to sing. And I cannot gauge the effect of his song, but surely it was great, if it has lasted up to now, vibrating sweetly in our restless souls. O rhymers of authoritarian pronouncements, o versifiers of social theories, who exclude from the present hour all poetry that is not yours, that is to say, you exclude POETRY, tell me: was he or was he not in his rightful place, in the century of Augustus, that singer of the Georgics? Yes, is it not so? He taught how to love the kind of life in which there might be neither the painful spectacle of wretched poverty nor the offensive spectacle of wealth: he wanted to abolish class struggles and wars. What do you want, oh socialist poets, who say such different things and in a way so different from his?

IX

Of the two fraternal poets of the Augustean age (for we cannot speak of Vergil without immediately adding Horace) you may say that it was philosophy that guided them to that sound and pious way of considering life and society. But no: it was the Eternal Child who took them by the hand saying: "I will tell you where poetry and virtue reside together." And it was the Eternal Child, if anything, who made them choose, from among the opinions of the philosophers, the ones that supported their feeling.

Considerate. Catone e Varrone scrissero di agricoltura prima di Virgilio. Erano uomini di molto giudizio e sapere, essi. Per esempio, Catone, suggerendo al *pater familias* che cosa deve dire e fare, quando si reca alla villa, conclude: "Venda l'olio, se si vende bene; il vino, il frumento che avanzi, lo venda. I buoi incaschiti, le fattrici non più buone, così le pecore, la lana, le pelli, un barroccio vecchio, ferramenti vecchi, uno schiavo attempato, uno schiavo ammalazzito, e altra roba che ci sia di troppo, la venda. Un padre di famiglia deve tirare a vendere, non a comprare".[10] Quegli schiavi, tra la ferraglia vecchia e l'altra roba d'avanzo, a noi fanno un certo senso; eppure era naturale che si nominassero a quel punto. Varrone in fatti riferisce questa elegante distinzione delle cose con le quali si coltivano i campi: "Altri le dividono in tre generi: strumento vocale, semivocale e muto; vocale, in cui sono gli schiavi, semivocale in cui sono i bovi, muto in cui sono i carri."[11] È naturale, s'intende, che Virgilio scrivendo di proposito sull'agricoltura, in versi bensì ma non a fantasia, in versi ma dopo avere studiato l'argomento anche sui libri degli altri, parlasse a ogni momento, oltre che dei plaustri e dei bovi, di quello strumento precipuo della coltivazione che erano gli schiavi. Noi, per esempio, dobbiamo aspettarci che come insegna quale profenda dare, erbe in fiore e biada, al polledro da razza,[12] e ai manzi in tanto che si domano, non sola erba e frasche di salcio e paleo di palude, ma anche piantine di grano appena nato;[13] così ammaestri il buon massaio sul pane e companatico, vino e vestimenta, da fornirsi alla *familia*. Parlando di olive, è certo che egli penserà al *pulmentarium familiae*. Catone, gran maestro, dice pure:[14] "Indolcisci quanto più puoi, di olive caschereccie. Quindi le olive anche buone, da cui non possa uscire che poco olio, indolciscile: e fanne grande risparmio, perché durino il più possibile. Quando le olive saranno mangiate, dà *allec* e aceto". Tornava bene, mi pare, discorrere di codeste olive da riporre per gli schiavi, e così anche dei vestimenti; ché poteva cadere in taglio, a proposito della lana, fare per esempio un'osservazione di tal genere: "quando a uno schiavo dài una tunica o un pastrano nuovo, prima ritira il

---

[10] CAT., *De Agricultura*, 2, 7. *Armenta delicula, oves deliculas.* Traduco così scostandomi dal Keil. Cfr. per il significato di *armenta* VERG., *Georg.*, 3, 129.
[11] VARR., *Rerum Rusticarum*, I, 17.
[12] *Georg.* 3, 126 sgg.
[13] Ib. 174 sgg.
[14] CAT. *a. c.* 58 e leggi 56, 57 e 59.

Consider this. Cato and Varro wrote about agriculture before Vergil. They were indeed men of much wisdom and knowledge. Cato, for example, advising the *pater familias* on what to do and say when he goes to the village, concludes: "Let him sell the oil, if it sells well; let him sell any leftover wine and wheat. The oxen decrepit with age and the cows no longer fertile, likewise the sheep, the wool, the hides, an old cart, old iron tools, an aged slave, a sickly slave, and any other superfluous stuff, let him sell. A good family man should aim at selling, not at buying."[10] Surely those slaves, among the rusty ironware and the other refuse, disturb us some; and yet it was natural to mention them in that context. Varro, in fact, relates this elegant distinction among things used in farming: "Some divide them into three kinds: vocal, semi-vocal and dumb instruments; among the vocal are the slaves, among the semi-vocal the oxen, among the dumb the carts."[11] It is natural, of course, that Vergil, writing specifically on agriculture, — in verse, yes, though not out of whim, in verse, but after studying the subject in books by others as well — should speak constantly not only of oxen and ox-carts, but also of that principal means of farming that were the slaves. We, for example, should certainly expect that, as he teaches what fodder to give to the thoroughbred colt:[12] flowering grasses and grain; and to the steers that are being tamed, not just meadow grass and willow boughs and sweet marsh grass but also tender wheat sprouts[13] — he should likewise teach the good husbandman about the food, wine, and clothing to provide to his *familia*. Speaking of olives he will surely think of the *pulmentarium familiae*. Cato, a great teacher, also says:[14] "Sweeten as much as possible the wind-fallen olives. And even the good ones that cannot give much oil, sweeten them: and save a lot of them, so that they last as long as possible. When the olives are eaten, add *allec* [a highly esteemed fish-sauce prepared originally from the garus but later chiefly from scomber or mackerel] and vinegar." It was appropriate, I think, to talk about those olives to be put aside for the slaves, and also about the clothes; because it could always be pertinent, when talking about wool, to make an observation such as this, for example: "when you give a slave a new tunic or a new coat, first take

---

[10] Cato, *De Agricultura*, 2, 7. *Armenta delicula, oves deliculas*. I translate this way and not according to Keil. For this meaning of armenta see Vergil, *Georgicae* 3, 129.

[11] Varro, *Rerum Rusticarum* 1, 17.

[12] Vergil, *Georg.*, 3, 126 ff.

[13] Vergil, *ibidem*. 174 ff.

[14] Cato, a.c. 58 and read 56, 57 and 59.

vecchio, per farne casacche a toppe (*centones*)". Insomma queste e simili provvidenze erano buone a mettersi in bei versi con quel tanto garbo del poeta che sa parlare con solennità e gravità di umili cose.

Oh! Sì! Non ci sono schiavi per Virgilio. Nei suoi poemi non c'è mai nemmeno la parola *servus*; c'è *serva* due volte e a proposito di altri tempi e di altri costumi:[15] tempi e costumi in cui il poeta vede bensì i re serviti da molti schiavi; eppur chiama questi *famuli* e *ministri* non servi.[16] Ma i suoi campi, quelli che esso insegnava a coltivare, quelli che arava e seminava con i suoi dolci versi, quelli non hanno gente incatenata e compedita. Il poeta che nella prima delle ecloghe pastorali mette sé, in persona d'uno schiavo liberato, ha proclamato nelle campagne italiche quella parola che con tanta enfasi suona dalla sua bocca di Titiro: LIBERTAS.[17] Gli agricoli di Virgilio né sono schiavi né mercenari. Essi sono di quelli di cui parla Varrone,[18] che coltivano la terra da sé, come tanti possidentucci con la loro figliolanza. Questi ha in mente Virgilio, quando esclama che sarebbero tanto felici, se conoscessero la loro felicità, con tanta pace, con tanto fruttato, tra tanto bello, senza il rodio o della miseria o della soverchianza altrui, lavorando alla sua stagione, godendosi la famiglia in casa e le care feste fuori.[19] Di gente che lavori per altri, nemmeno una traccia. L'ideale del poeta è quel vecchiettino Cilice, trapiantato dalla sua patria nei dintorni di Taranto. Aveva avuto pochi iugeri di terra non buona né a grano né a prato né a vigna: una grillaia, uno scopiccio. Ebbene il bravo vecchiettino ne aveva fatto un orto, con non solo i suoi cavoli, ma anche gigli e rose, e alberi da frutta, e bugni d'api, e vivai di piante.[20] Sì: il poco e il piccolo era il sogno dei due grandi fraterni poeti. Virgilio diceva: "Loda la campagna grande, e

---

[15] *Aen.* 5, 284; è data come premio a Sergesto, Foloe, una cretese, esperta nel tessere, con due gemellini alla poppa. Ed è imitazione di OMERO: *Il.* 23, 263. Anche è *serva* , in 9, 546, Licinnia che diede al re dei Lidi un figlio, Elenore. E anche questo è omerico. Inoltre Andromaca partorisce *servitio* : *Aen.* 3, 327. E c'è l'idea e la parola di *servitium* a proposito di giovenchi in *Georg.* 3, 168, e di se stesso, cioè di TITIRO in *Ecl.* I, 41.

[16] *Aen.*, 1, 701 sgg. 705; 5, 391; 8, 411, 584.

[17] *Ecl.*, 1, 28.

[18] *Rerum Rusticarum*, I, 17: *ipsi colunt, ut plerique pauperculi cum sua progenie.*

[19] *Georg.*, 2, 458 sgg ; 1, 300 sgg. e altrove.

[20] *Georg.*, 4, 125 sgg.

back the old one, to make patchwork jackets (*centones*) out of them." In short it was good to put these and similar provisions in fine verses with that special grace of the poet who can speak with solemnity and gravity of humble things.

Oh! Yes! There are no slaves for Vergil. In his poems there never appears even the word *servus*; twice we find *serva* but referring to other times and other customs:[15] times and customs, however, in which the poet sees kings, to be sure, served by many slaves, but he does not call them *servi*, rather, *famuli* and *ministri*.[16] But his own fields, those that he taught how to cultivate, those that he ploughed and sowed with his sweet verse, those do not have any people chained and restrained there. The poet who, in the first of his pastoral eclogues places himself in the shoes of a freed slave, proclaimed in the Italian countryside the word which rings out so emphatically from the mouth of Tytirus: LIBERTAS.[17] Vergil's farmers are neither slaves nor mercenaries. They are of the kind Varro[18] describes, who cultivate the land themselves, with their children, as many small owners do. These are the ones Vergil has in mind when he exclaims that they would be so happy if they recognized their happiness, with so much peace, with so many fruits, in such beauty, far from the biting bitterness of their poverty or of oppression at the hands of others, working according to the season, enjoying their family at home and celebrating their dear holidays outside.[19] Not even a hint of people working for others. The poet's ideal is that little old man Cilicius, transplanted from his own birthplace in the vicinity of Taranto. He had obtained a few jugers of land not good for wheat or meadowland or vineyard: a barren spot, a sterile moor. Well, the fine old fellow had turned it into a garden, and not only with cabbage but also lilies and roses, and fruit trees, and beehives, and greenhouses.[20] Yes: the little and the small was the dream of the two great brother poets. Vergil used to

---

[15] Vergil, *Aeneid* 5, 284; Pholoe, a young girl from Crete, expert in weaving, with two suckling twins at her breast, is given as a prize to Sergestus. It is an imitation from Homer, *Iliad* 23, 263. It is also serva in 9, 546 Lycinnia who gave a son, Elenore, to the king of the Lydians. This, too, is from Homer. Furthermore, Andromache gives birth *servitio: Aeneid* 3, 327. And the idea and the word of *servitium* appears in *Georgicae* 3, 168 referring to some bull-calves, and to himself, that is, to Tytirus, in *Aeclogae* 1, 41.

[16] Vergil, *Aeneid*, 1, 701 and 705; 5, 391; 8, 411 and 584

[17] Vergil, *Aeclogae*, 1, 28

[18] Varro, *Rerum Rusticarum*, 1, 17 *is coolant, UT plaque pauperculi cum sua progenie.*

[19] Vergil, *Georgicae*, 2, 458 ff.; 1, 300 ff.; and elsewhere.

[20] Vergil, *ibidem.*, 4, 125 ff.

tienti alla piccina."[21] E Orazio: "Questo era il mio voto: un campicello non tanto grande, con l'orto, con una fonte, e per giunta un po' di selvetta."[22] Chi non dovrebbe preferire la campagna grande alla piccola, quando non toccasse di coltivarla a lui? Ma ai due poeti, quando erano poeti, non si presentava al pensiero questa considerazione così semplice. A dir meglio, il fanciullo che era in loro, preferiva, come tutti i fanciulli, ciò che è piccolo: il cavallino, la carrozzina, l'aiolina. Oh! c'è chi ha rimproverato a Orazio quest'amor della mediocrità! Ma esser poeta della mediocrità, non vuol dire davvero essere poeta mediocre. Il contrario, anzi, è vero. Non ama, chi dice di amare un serraglio di donne. Non è poeta, chi non si fissa in una visione che i suoi occhi possano misurare. E le cose grandi, le cose ricche, le cose sublimi non riescono poetiche, se non sono sentite e dette in persona di chi stupisce avanti loro, perché appunto esso è piccolo, è povero, è umile. Il poeta è il poverello dell'umanità, spesso anche cieco e vecchio. E se tale non sembra, se anzi è gran signore e giovane e felice, ebbene vuol dire che se è ricco lui, è *pauperculus* però il fanciullino che è in lui; cioè si è conservato povero, come a dire fanciullo. Perché poverino è sempre il bimbo, sia pur nato in una culla d'oro, e tende sempre la mano a tutto e a tutti, come non avesse niente e desidera il boccon di pan duro del suo compagno trito, e vorrebbe fare il duro lavoro del suo compagno tribolato. Per questo non Virgilio proprio, ma il fanciullo che egli aveva in cuore, non voleva gli schiavi nei campi. Diremo noi che Virgilio attingesse dai libri di qualche filosofo o di qualche profeta questa legge di libertà? No: egli stesso ne era forse inconsapevole, di questa libertà che proclamava. Era la sua poesia che aboliva la servitù, perché la servitù non era poetica. Non era poetica, e il divino fanciullo che non vede se non ciò che è poetico, non la vedeva. Tanto che noi, se non avessimo dei tempi di Virgilio altro testimone che Virgilio, dovremmo credere che non esistesse allora più questa miseria e vergogna che non è cessata nemmeno ai nostri, di tempi. Oh! dovremmo credere che il Cristo non anco nato ispirasse al poeta contadino dell'Esperia, come il vaticinio del suo avvento, così il presentimento della grande fratellanza umana! Non c'è la schiavitù nell'Italia Virgiliana: nemmeno c'è il salariato, nemmeno il mezzadro!

---

[21] *Georg.*, 2, 412 sgg.
[22] *Serm.*, 2, 6, 1 sgg.

say: "Praise the large land property but keep to the small."[21] And Horace: "This was my wish: a nice little field, not too large, with a vegetable garden, with a spring, and in addition a patch of woods."[22] Who would not prefer a large piece of land to a small one if he were not the one to have to work it? But so simple a consideration never came to the mind of the two poets, when they were poets. Or rather, the Child who was in them, preferred, as all children do, that which is small: the little horse, the little cart, the little flower-bed. Oh! There are those who have criticized Horace for this love of mediocrity! But to be the poet of mediocrity does not mean at all to be a mediocre poet. The contrary is actually true. He does not love who professes to love a harem of women. He is not a poet who does not set himself in a vision that his eyes can measure. And big things, rich things, sublime things are not poetic if they are not felt and said by one who stands in wonder before them, precisely because he is small, is poor, is humble. The poet is the beggar of mankind, often he is also blind and old. And if he does not look it, if he is, in fact, a rich man, and young, and happy, well, then, it means that though he himself may be rich: *pauperculus*, however, is the Child within him; that is, he has remained poor, that is to say he has remained a child. Because the child is always somewhat poor, even though he be born in a golden cradle, and he always stretches out his hand to everything and everyone, as if he had nothing and he wants the morsel of hard bread of his down-trodden companion, and would like to do the hard work of his afflicted friend. That is why, not Vergil himself, but the child in his heart, did not want slaves in the fields. Shall we say that Vergil got this law of freedom from the books of some philosopher or of some prophet? No, he himself was probably unaware of the freedom he proclaimed. It was his poetry that abolished slavery, because slavery was not poetic. It was not poetic, and the divine Child who sees only what is poetic did not see it. So that if we had of Vergil's time no other witness but Vergil, we would have to believe that the wretchedness and shame that has not yet ceased even in our day, did not exist in his. Oh! we would have to believe that Christ yet unborn inspired in the farmer-poet of Hesperia both the prophecy of His advent and the presentiment of great human brotherhood! There is no slavery in the Italy of Vergil: and there is not even a wage-earner, not even a share-cropper!

---

[21] Vergil, *ibidem.*, 2, 412 ff.
[22] Horace, *Sermones*, 2, 6, 1 ff.

X

Così il poeta vero, senza farlo apposta e senza addarsene, portando, per dirla con Dante, il lume dietro, anzi no, dentro, dentro la cara anima portando lo splendore e ardore della lampada che è la poesia; è, come si dice oggi, socialista, o come si avrebbe a dire, umano. Così la poesia, non ad altro intonata che a poesia, è quella che migliora e rigenera l'umanità, escludendone, non di proposito il male, ma naturalmente l'*impoetico*. Ora si trova a mano a mano che impoetico è ciò che la morale riconosce cattivo e ciò che l'estetica proclama brutto. Ma di ciò che è cattivo e brutto non giudica, nel nostro caso, il barbato filosofo. È il fanciullo interiore che ne ha schifo. Il quale come narrando le imprese dei suoi eroi, e dicendo tutto di loro, e, oltre le battaglie e i discorsi, anche i pasti e i sonni, e figurando a noi, per esempio, i loro cavalli, e ridicendo che brucavano e sudavano e spumavano, pur non dice mai (tu vedi che procuro quanto posso, che tu non torca il niffolo) non dice mai che stallavano; così della nostra anima non racconta che il buono e della nostra visione non ricorda che il bello. Ché per cantare il male bisogna fare uno sforzo continuo su se stesso, a meno che non si tratti di pazzia. E in questo caso, la pazzia sta appunto in questo, di pensar da buoni e cantar da cattivi.

Così, caro fanciullo, hanno gran torto coloro che attribuiscono, per ciò che tu non vedi se non il buono, qualche merito di bontà a colui che ti ospita. Il quale può essere anche un masnadiero, e aver dentro sé un fanciullo che gli canti le delizie della pace e dell'innocenza, e la casa dove non deve più riposare, e la chiesa dove non sa più pregare.

XI

Il poeta, se è e quando è veramente poeta, cioè tale che significhi solo ciò che il fanciullo detta dentro, riesce perciò ispiratore di buoni e civili costumi, d'amor patrio e familiare e umano. Quindi la credenza e il fatto, che il suon della cetra adunasse le pietre a far le mura della città, e animasse le piante e ammansasse le fiere della selva primordiale; e che i cantori guidassero e educassero i popoli. Le pietre, le piante, le fiere, i popoli primi,

X

And so the true poet, without doing so intentionally, and without going far away, bearing, as Dante would say, the lamp behind him, or rather, within himself, bearing within his dear soul the splendor and the heat of the light that is poetry, is, as we say today, a socialist, or, as it should be said, human. Thus poetry, attuned only to poetry, is what improves and renews humanity, excluding from it, not intentionally what is evil, but naturally what is *unpoetic*. Now, little by little, one finds that unpoetic is what morality considers bad and aesthetics proclaims ugly. But in our case it is not the bearded philosopher who judges what is ugly and bad. It is the Child inside who finds it repulsive. He is the one who, as he narrates his heroes' adventures, and tells us everything about them, their battles and their discourse, and also their meals and their dreams, and as he represents for us, for example, their horses while grazing and sweating and foaming, still never says (you see I try my best in order for you not to turn up your nose) that they were defecating; in the same way, he says only what is good about our soul and he remembers only what is beautiful about our vision. Because to sing about evil we must put ourselves under a continual strain, unless we are dealing with madness. And in this case the madness lies precisely in this: to be thinking like a good person and to sing like a bad one.

Thus, my dear Child, very wrong are those who, just because you see only what is good, attribute some merit of goodness to the person in whom you dwell. Such a person could be even a bandit and have within him a Child who sings to him the delights of peace and of innocence, and a house where he must not rest any longer, and a church where he can no longer pray.

XI

The poet, if and when he is truly a poet, that is, such a one that signifies only what the Child dictates within, is therefore an inspirer of good and civil customs, of love of country, family and mankind. Hence the belief and the fact that it was the sound of the lyre that gathered the stones to build the walls of the city, and gave life to the plants and tamed the wild animals of the primordial forest; and that the singers guided and educated

seguivano la voce dell'eterno fanciullo, d'un dio giovinetto, del più piccolo e tenero che fosse nella tribù d'uomini salvatici. I quali, in verità, s'ingentilivano contemplando e ascoltando la loro infanzia. Così Omero, in tempi feroci, a noi presenta nel più feroce degli eroi, cioè nel più vero e poetico, in Achille, un tipo di tal perfezione morale, che poté servire di modello a Socrate, quando preferiva al male la morte. Così Virgilio, in tempi più gentili, avendo la mira soltanto al poetico, ci mostra lo spettacolo tanto anticipato, ahimè! d'un'umanità buona, felice, tutta al lavoro e alle pure gioie dei figli, senza guerre e senza schiavi. Gli uomini, al suo tempo, parrebbe che avessero impetrato, ciò che è ancora il desiderio inadempiuto de' nostri operai, le otto ore di lavoro per ogni otto di sonno e altre otto di svago. — Oh! qualche volta presso lui il contadino aggiunge la notte al giorno! — Sì: ma che dolcezza di lavoro, quella, tra l'uomo che col pennato fa il capo a spiga a suoi rami di pino, che hanno a essere fiaccole, e la donna che o tesse la tela o schiuma il paiolo cantando.[23] E nell'Eneide Virgilio canta guerre e battaglie; eppure tutto il senso della mirabile epopea è in quel cinguettio mattutino di rondini o passeri, che sveglia Evandro nella sua capanna, là dove avevano da sorgere i palazzi imperiali di Roma![24]

Ma Omero, ma Virgilio, non lo facevano apposta. Ma il poeta non deve farlo apposta. Il poeta è poeta, non oratore o predicatore, non filosofo, non istorico, non maestro, non tribuno o demagogo, non uomo di stato o di corte. E nemmeno è, sia con pace del Maestro, un artiere che foggi spada e scudi e vomeri; e nemmeno con pace di tanti altri, un artista che nielli e ceselli l'oro che altri gli porga. A costituire il poeta vale infinitamente più il suo sentimento e la sua visione, che il modo col quale agli altri trasmette l'uno e l'altra. Egli, anzi quando li trasmette, pur essendo in cospetto d'un pubblico, parla piuttosto tra sé, che a quello. Del pubblico, non pare che si accorga. Parla forte (ma non tanto!) più per udir meglio esso, che per farsi intendere da altrui. E, per usare imagini che sono presenti ora al mio spirito, è, sì, per quanto possa spiacere il dirlo, un ortolano; un ortolano, sì, o un giardiniere, che fa nascere e crescere fiori o cavolfiori. Sapete che cosa non è? Non è cuoco e non è fiorista, che i cavolfiori serva in bei piatti, con buoni intingoli, che i fiori intrecci in mazzetti o in ghirlandette. Egli non sa se non levare al cavolo qualche foglia

---

[23] PLAT., *Apol.*, 28 B. sgg., *Georg.*, I, 291 sgg.
[24] *Aen.*, 8, 155 sgg.

the people. Stones, plants, beasts, primitive people, followed the voice of the Eternal Child, of an adolescent god, of the youngest and most tender in the tribe of savages. And they, in truth, became gentler, contemplating and listening to their childhood. Thus, Homer, in savage times, presents us in the fiercest of his heroes, that is in the truest and most poetic of his heroes, in Achilles, a human type of such moral perfection that he could serve as a model to Socrates when he preferred death to evil. Thus, Vergil, in gentler times, aiming only at the poetic, displays for us the spectacle — alas how long awaited! — of a humanity good, happy, fully given to work and to the pure joys of their children, without wars and without slaves. It would seem that, in his times, men had demanded and obtained what is still the unfulfilled desire of our workers today: eight hours of work for every eight hours of sleep and every eight hours of relaxation. — Oh! sometimes, in his poems, the farmer adds night to day! — Yes, but what sweet work is that of the man who clips the branches of his pine trees that are to be made into torches, and that of the woman weaving her cloth or skimming the pot as she sings.[23] And in the *Aeneid*, Vergil sings of battles and wars; and yet all the meaning of the wonderful epic is in the morning chirping of swallows or sparrows, which awakens Evander in his hut, right there where would eventually rise the imperial palaces of Rome! [24]

But Homer, but Vergil, did not do what they did deliberately. The poet must not make poetry to some purpose. The poet is a poet, not an orator or a preacher, not a philosopher, not a historian, not a teacher, not a tribune or demagogue, not a statesman or courtier. And he is not even, be it by leave of the Teacher, [i.e., Giosuè Carducci] an artisan who fashions swords and shields and ploughs; and not even, by leave of many others, an artist who decorates and chisels the gold others may offer him. To make a poet, his feeling and his vision count much more than the way in which he transmits them to others. Moreover, when the poet transmits them, even before an audience, he speaks more to himself, than to it. Of the audience he does not seem to be aware. He speaks loudly (but not too loudly!) more to hear himself better, than to be heard by others. And, to use images now present to my spirit, he is, however unpleasant it may be to say so, a vegetable-grower; a vegetable-grower, yes, or a gardener who cultivates flowers or cauliflower. Do you know what he is not? He is not a cook who serves the cauliflower in pretty dishes, with tasty sauces, and he is not a florist who weaves the flowers in little bouquets and pretty garlands. He

---

[23] Plato, *The Apology of Socrates*, 28 B et al. Vergil, *Georgicae* 1, 291 ff.

[24] Vergil, *Aeneid*, 8, 155 ff.

marcia o bacata, e legare i fiori alla meglio, con un torchietto che strappa lì per lì a un salcio: come a dire, unisce i suoi pensieri con quel ritmo nativo, che è nell'anima del bimbo che poppa e del monello che ruzza.

Ora il poeta sarà invece un autore di provvidenze civili e sociali? Senza accorgersene, se mai. Si trova esso tra la folla; e vede passar le bandiere e sonar le trombe. Getta la sua parola, la quale tutti gli altri, appena esso l'ha pronunziata, sentono che è quella che avrebbero pronunziata loro. Si trova ancora tra la folla: vede buttare in istrada le masserizie di una famiglia povera. Ed esso dice la parola, che si trova subito piena delle lagrime di tutti.

Il poeta è colui che esprime la parola che tutti avevano sulle labbra e che nessuno avrebbe detta. Ma non è lui che sale su una sedia o su un tavolo, ad arringare. Egli non trascina, ma è trascinato; non persuade, ma è persuaso.

Perché pensi alla patria e alla società bisogna proprio che sia un momento che tutti intorno a lui ci pensino. Se no, è un guaio serio. Quello per la mamma, è il più soave degli affetti. Ma che direste voi d'uno che facesse la cronaca, giorno per giorno, di sua mamma? "Stamane s'è levata, cara mamma! Io l'ho guardata, povera mamma! M'ha dato il caffè e latte, povera cara mamma!" Costui è un imbecille, quando non è uno che finga e abbia bisogno di darsi l'aria di amare quella che è così facile amare! Oh! la madre è malata, la madre è lontana, la madre è morta! Ecco che allora ci si pensa, alla mamma, e ci si strugge. Oppure la mamma ha una gran consolazione; e noi siamo più che consolati, e ci sentiamo invasi da un impeto di canto. Così per la patria. Non ci accorgiamo di lei, se non nelle sue feste e nelle sue — nostre! — disgrazie. E allora prorompe anche dal cuore del fanciullo il grido di gioia e il grido di dolore; ed è grido che ha subito mille echi. Ma il bambino non è un bambino che s'impanchi a far lezione quotidiana d'amor patrio o d'amor paterno e materno ai suoi fratellini, e anzi ai suoi zii e nonni. Chi pretende che faccia questo, vuole che il vispo fanciullo sia un vecchio noioso; vuole, insomma, che non esista la poesia. Perché la poesia, costretta a essere poesia sociale, poesia civile, poesia patriottica, intristisce su libri, avvizzisce nell'aria chiusa della scuola, e finalmente ammala di retorica, e muore. E noi di questa pseudopoesia ne abbiamo tanta, sin da quando, morto Virgilio, invecchiando Orazio, chiusa

knows only how to remove from the cauliflower some rotten or worm-eaten leaves, and to tie his flowers, as best he can with a binding strip plucked then and there from a willow: that is to say, he connects his thoughts with that inborn rhythm which is in the soul of a suckling babe and of a carefree urchin.

Now will the poet instead be an author of civil and social measures? Without being aware of it, maybe. He finds himself in a crowd and he sees flags go by and trumpets play. He casts out his word, and all the other people, as soon as he utters it, know it is the very same word they would have uttered. He is still in the midst of the crowd and he sees the belongings of a poor family being thrown into the street. And he speaks and his words are immediately drowned in the tears of all.

The poet is the one who expresses the word everyone had on his lips and no one would utter. But he is not one to climb on a chair or a table, to make a public speech. He does not sway but is swayed; he does not persuade, but is persuaded.

For the poet to think about country and society, it has to be the precise moment when all around him are thinking about it. Otherwise, there is trouble to pay. Love for one's mother is the sweetest of feelings. But what would you say of someone who gave us a day-by-day report on his mother? "This morning she got up, dear mommy! I looked at her, poor mommy! She gave me *café au lait*, poor dear mommy!" He is an imbecile, unless he is one who needs to make outward display of loving the person it is so easy to love! Oh! Mother is ill, mother is far away, mother is dead! And suddenly then, we think of our mother, and we pine away. Or else the mother receives some great consolation, and we are more than comforted, we feel an overwhelming urge to sing. The same holds true for the motherland. We are not consciously aware of her except on her holidays and in her — and our! — misfortunes. And then the cry of joy and the cry of grief bursts out even from the hearts of children, and it is a cry that is immediately echoed a thousand times over. But the child is not a child who sets himself up to give daily lessons on love of country or of father and mother to his little brothers, or indeed, to his uncles and aunts and grandparents. The one who expects him to do so, wants the bright youngster to be a boring old man; in a word, he wants to inhibit poetry. For poetry that is forced to be social poetry, civic poetry, patriotic poetry, languishes in the books, withers in the closed atmosphere of the school, and finally becomes ill with rhetoric, and dies. And of this pseudo-poetry we have had a great deal ever since the time when — Vergil dead, Horace aging — the great revolution was concluded that had begun and ended, we

la grande rivoluzione che cominciò, si può dire, e finì con la morte di due
donne, di Giulia e di Cleopatra, la figlia e l'amante di Cesare; ebbene i corvi,
quali Pindaro li avrebbe chiamati, si gettarono gracchiando sull'immenso
campo di battaglia, per beccare non occhi di uccisi, ma semi di poesia. E
che facevano essi? Raccontavano un fatto storico, di quelli ultimi: lo
condivano con declamazioni, esclamazioni, maledizioni; e lo mettevano in
esametri. Ma anch'essi capivano che non bastano i versi a far poesia: e
perciò incorniciavano la loro storia verseggiata e declamata con una
descrizione di alba e un'altra di tramonto; e il poema era fatto.[25] Ecco
Giulio Montano. Questi era un poeta come tant'altri. A ogni tratto inseriva
albe e tramonti. Pertanto, poiché un tale s'era seccato ch'egli avesse recitato
per tutto un giorno, e diceva che non si doveva andare alle sue recite; Natta
Pinario esclamò: "O che io posso essere più condiscendente con lui? Io
sono pronto a starlo a sentire da un'alba a un tramonto!" Voleva dire, il
buon Natta, che la seccaggine sarebbe durata poco, e che dopo due o tre
versi esso poteva andare pei fatti suoi.[26] È inutile. Già Orazio ammoniva
che non bastavano le descrizioncelle, le digressioncelle, le belle toppe rosse
e gialle, per far di prosa poesia.[27] Bisogna che il fatto storico, se vuol divenir
poetico, filtri attraverso la maraviglia e l'ingenuità della nostra anima
fanciulla, se la conserviamo ancora. Bisogna allontanare il fatto vicino
allontanandocene noi.[28] Volete una prova a cui distinguere la poesia dalla
pseudopoesia, in siffatto genere storico? Se la narrazione, che il
verseggiatore vi fa, vi commuove meno che la stessa, fatta in prosa, dallo

---

[25] SEN. *Ep.*, 122, II: cfr. *Apoc.* 2.

[26] SEN. *Ep.*, 122, II. E continua a leggere il fattarello che segue. Montano avendo
subito cominciato con un'alba: "Febo comincia a metter fuori le ardenti fiamme, e il
dì rosseggiante a spargersi per la terra; e già la rondine triste comincia a recare ai
garruli nidi il cibo, con assiduo va e vieni, e a somministrarlo bene scompartito col
molle becco"; un tal Varo esclama: "E l'ora che Buta va a letto. Perché Buta era un
fuggi-luce, un vivi-al-lume-di-lucerna, uno insomma, che faceva di notte giorno."
Di lì a poco, Montano declamava: "Già i pastori ricoverarono nella stalla i loro
armenti; già la notte cominciava a dare il nero silenzio alle terre assopite." E Varo:
"Che dice? E già notte. Andrò a fare la salutazione mattinale a Buta."

[27] *A P.* 15 sgg.

[28] "Avete un binocolo? Puntatelo verso una campagna, verso una casa, verso un
borgo. Guardate per il suo verso: ecco la prosa. Guardate all'incontrario: ecco la
poesia. Più particolari nella prima e meglio distinti. Più visione nella seconda e più
… poesia. Provate!"

could say, with the death of two women: Julia and Cleopatra, Caesar's daughter and Caesar's lover; well, then, the ravens, as Pindar would have called them, threw themselves, croaking, over the immense battlefield, to peck not at the eyes of the slain, but at the seeds of poetry. And what did they do? They would narrate a recent historical event: seasoning it with declamations, exclamations, maledictions; and they would cast it in hexameters. But even they understood that verses are not enough to make poetry: and that is why they began their story set in verse and well-declaimed with a description of a sunrise and then another of a sunset; and the poem was done.[25] There is the case of Julius Montanus. He was a poet like so many others. At intervals he would insert dawns and sunsets. Consequently, when a certain man tired of listening to a recitation for a whole day said that nobody should go to his recitals, Natta Pinarius exclaimed: "Could I ever be more condescending with him? I am ready to listen to him from a sunrise to a sunset!" What good Natta meant was that the boredom would last only a short time and that after a few lines he could simply go about his own business.[26] It is no good. Horace was already warning that cute little descriptions and nice little digressions and red and yellow patches were not enough to make poetry out of prose.[27] To become poetic, the historical fact must be filtered through the wonder and the candor of our childlike soul, if we still have it intact. We have to gain perspective on a near event by distancing ourselves from it.[28] Do you want a test by which to tell poetry from pseudo-poetry in such a historical genre? If the narration done by the versifier moves you less than the same thing

---

[25] Seneca, *Ep.*, 122, II; see Apoc. 2.

[26] Seneca, Ep., 122, II. And he continues to read the following anecdote: Montanus having started right away with a dawn; "Phoebus begins to put forth his bright flames, and the reddish day to spread over the earth; and the sad swallow already begins to bring food to the garrulous nests, assiduously going back and forth, and meting it out to them, dividing it with her soft beak"; a certain Varus exclaims: "It is the hour Buta goes to bed." Because Buta was a shunner of the light, a night owl, in short, one who made day of the night. A while later Montanus would declaim: "Already the shepherds had brought their herd back to the stables; already the night had begun to bring black silence over the sleepy lands." And Varus: "What is he saying? It is night already, I will go and bring my morning greetings to Buta."

[27] Horace, *Ars Poetica*, 15 ff.

[28] "Do you have a pair of binoculars? Point them at a landscape, at a house, at a village. Look through them the right way: that is prose. Look through the opposite end: that is poetry. More details in the first and more distinct. More vision in the second and more ... poetry. Try it!"

storico e dal cronista, dite pure che il verseggiatore ha tradotto, e male; non ha poetato. E ha perduto il suo tempo e ha fatto perdere a noi il nostro.

Xll

Ma in Italia la pseudopoesia si desidera, si domanda, s'ingiunge. In Italia noi siamo vittime della storia letteraria! Per vero, né in Italia soltanto, mi pare che delle lettere si sia ingenerato un concetto falso. Le lettere sono gli strumenti delle idee, e le idee fanno di sé tanti gruppi che si chiamano scienze. Ma noi, fissati sugli strumenti, abbiamo finalmente dimenticato i fini. Siamo agricoltori che non pensano se non alle vanghe e non parlano se non di aratri, e più delle loro bellurie che delle loro utilità. Delle semente, della terra, dei concimi, non ci curiamo più. Quindi avviene che abbiamo, come fisici, filosofi, storici, matematici, così letterati; modo di dire, come coltivatori di canapa, di viti, di grano e d'ulivi, così periti di vanghe e d'aratri, i quali non s'occupano di altro, e credono che non ci si debba occupar d'altro, e stimano, io vedo, che la loro sia la più nobile delle occupazioni. E almeno li facessero essi, codesti strumenti: no, li "giudicano" e li "collezionano". Codest'ozio noi chiamiamo ora critica e storia letteraria. E ognuno può vedere che ci sono cose molto più utili e belle da fare: cioè coltivare e seminare. Ma c'è pure, tra le tante branche della letteratura, la poesia che sta a sé, la poesia che comprende in sé tutto ciò che si dice e scrive per diletto, amaro o dolce, suo o altrui. Questa non è rispetto alle scienze quello che lo strumento rispetto al fine. È una coltivazione, poniamo, anch'essa, ma d'altro ordine e specie. È, poniamo, la coltivazione, affatto nativa, della psiche primordiale e perenne. Ma noi la mettiamo insieme con l'altra letteratura "strumentale", e ne ragioniamo allo stesso modo. La dividiamo per secoli e scuole, la chiamiamo arcadica, romantica, classica, veristica, naturalistica, idealistica, e via dicendo. Affermiamo che progredisce, che decade, che nasce, che muore, che risorge, che rimuore. In verità la poesia è tal maraviglia che se voi fate ora una vera poesia, ella sarà della stessa qualità che una vera poesia di quattromila anni sono. Come mai? Così: l'uomo impara a parlare tanto diverso o tanto meglio, di anno in anno, di secolo in secolo, di millennio in

done in prose by the historian or the chronicler, you can just say that the versifier has only translated, and badly; he has not made poetry. He has wasted his time and caused us to waste ours.

XII

But in Italy pseudo-poetry is desired, is demanded, is dictated. In Italy we are the victims of literary history! In truth, and not in Italy only, it seems that a false concept of letters has been generated. Letters are the instrument of ideas, and ideas form many groups that are called sciences. But we, obsessed with the means, have ultimately forgotten the ends. We are farmers who think only of spades, who talk only of ploughs, and more about their fine appearance than about their usefulness. We no longer pay attention to seeds, soil, fertilizers. And so it comes about that, just as we have physicists, philosophers, historians, mathematicians, we have men of letters; which is to say, together with the growers of hemp, and the growers of grape vines, and wheat, and olives, we also have experts on spades and ploughs who do not deal with anything else, and they believe that one should not be concerned about anything else, and, it is clear to me, they consider theirs to be the noblest of occupations. And if only they were at least the ones to make those instruments! But no, they "judge" them and they "collect" them. We now call such idleness literary criticism and literary history. And everyone can see that there are much more beautiful and useful things to do: such as to sow and to cultivate. But, among the various branches of literature, there is also poetry which stands on its own, poetry which embraces within itself all that is said and written for pleasure, sweet or bitter, to oneself or to others. Poetry does not bear the same relation to the sciences as the instrument bears to its end. It, too, is a cultivation, we submit, but of a different order and species. It is, we submit, the cultivation, entirely innate, of the primordial and everlasting psyche. Yet we place it together with the other "instrumental" literature and we talk about it in the same way. We divide it by centuries and by schools, we call it Arcadian, Romantic, Classic, Realistic, Naturalistic, Idealistic, and so on. We affirm that it progresses, that it decays, that it is born, that it dies, that it rises again, that it dies again. In truth, poetry is such a wonder that if you compose a true poem now, it will have the same quality as a true poem of four thousand years ago. How come? In the following way: man learns to speak so differently and so much better, from year to year, from century to century, from millennium to millennium; but in all times and places he

millennio; ma comincia con far gli stessi vagiti e guaiti in tutti i tempi e luoghi. La sostanza psichica è uguale nei fanciulli di tutti i popoli. Un fanciullo è fanciullo allo stesso modo da per tutto. E quindi, né c'è poesia arcadica, romantica, classica, né poesia italiana, greca, sanscrita; ma poesia soltanto, soltanto poesia, e... non poesia. Sì: c'è la contraffazione, la sofisticazione, l'imitazione della poesia, e codesta ha tanti nomi. Ci sono persone che fanno il verso agli uccelli, e al fischio sembrano uccelli; e non sono uccelli, sì uccellatori. Ora io non so dire quanta vanità sia la storia di codesti ozi. Eccola in due parole. Un poeta emette un dolce canto. Per un secolo, o giù di lì, mille altri lo ripetono fiorettandolo e guastandolo; finché viene a noia. E allora un altro poeta fa risonare un altro bel canto. E per un secolo, o più o meno, mille altri ci fanno su le loro variazioni. Qualche volta il canto iniziale non è né bello né dolce; e allora peggio che mai!

Ma in Italia, e altrove, non stiamo paghi a questo compendio. Ragioniamo e distinguiamo troppo. Quella scuola era migliore, questa peggiore. A quella bisogna tornare, a questa rinunziare. No: le scuole di poesia sono tutte peggio, e a nessuna bisogna addirsi. Non c'è poesia che la poesia. Quando poi gli intendenti, perché uno fa, ad esempio, una vera poesia su un gregge di pecore, pronunziano che quel vero poeta è un arcade; e perché un altro, in una vera poesia, ingrandisce straordinariamente una parvenza, proclamano che quell'altro vero poeta pecca di secentismo; ecco gl'intendenti scioccheggiano e pedanteggiano nello stesso tempo. Qualunque soggetto può essere contemplato, dagli occhi profondi del fanciullo interiore: qualunque tenue cosa può a quelli occhi parere grandissima.

Voi dovete soltanto giudicare (se avete questa mania di giudicare) se furono quelli occhi che videro; e lasciar da parte secento e Arcadia. La poesia non si evolve e involve, non cresce o diminuisce; è una luce o un fuoco che è sempre quella luce e quel fuoco: i quali, quando appariscono, illuminano e scaldano ora come una volta, e in quel modo stesso.

Solamente s'ha a dire che raramente appariscono. Sì: la poesia, detta e scritta, è rara. Proprio rara la poesia pura. Ma c'è la poesia "applicata". La poesia "applicata" è dei grandi poemi, dei grandi drammi, dei grandi romanzi. Ora molto ci corre che questi siano tutta poesia. Immaginate che siano un gran mare, ognuno. Nel mare sono le perle; ma quante? Ben poche; però in quale più, in quale meno. Occorre anche dire che in essi poemi, drammi, romanzi, la poesia pura di rado si trova pura.

begins with the same whining and whimpering. The psychic make-up is the same in the children of all peoples. A child is a child in the same way everywhere. And so there is no Arcadian, Romantic, or Classic poetry, no Italian, Greek or Sanskrit poetry; but just poetry, only poetry, and ... non-poetry. Yes, there is the counterfeiting, the adulteration, the imitation of poetry, and that has many names. There are people who imitate birds, and as they whistle, they sound like birds; but they are not birds, rather, they are bird-catchers. Now I cannot begin to say how vain is the history of such pointless things. Here it is in just a few words. A poet comes out with a sweet song. For a century, or thereabouts, a thousand others repeat it, adorning it and spoiling it; until it becomes a bore. Then another poet brings forth the sound of another beautiful song. And for a century, more or less, a thousand others work up variations on it. Sometimes the initial song itself is neither beautiful nor sweet; and then it is worse than ever!

But in Italy, and elsewhere, we are not satisfied with this compendium. We reason and distinguish too much. That school was better, this one worse. We must go back to that one and give this one up. No: the schools of poetry are all bad and we must not commit ourselves to any of them. There is only poetry. And when the experts, just because one writes, for example, a true poem on a flock of sheep, decree that that true poet is an Arcadian; and because another, in a true poem, makes extraordinarily much out of something commonplace, they declare this other true poet guilty of "preciosity;" here is where we have the experts becoming silly and pedantic at the same time. Any subject whatsoever can be contemplated by the deeply penetrating gaze of the inner Child: any slightest thing can to those eyes appear immense.

You must only judge (if you have this mania of judging) if those were eyes that did indeed see; and leave aside the seventeenth century and the Arcadia. Poetry does not expand and contract, does not grow or diminish; it is a light or a flame which is always that light and that flame: and these, when they appear, brighten and warm us, now as they did then, and in the very same way.

Only it must be said that they appear rarely. Yes: poetry, recited and written, is rare. Very rare is pure poetry. But there is "applied" poetry. "Applied" poetry we associate with the great epic poems, with great dramas, with great novels. Now these are far from being entirely poetry. Imagine each one of them to be a great sea. In the sea there are pearls; but how many? Very few, and yet more in one and fewer in another. It must be said also that in those epics, dramas, and novels pure poetry is rarely pure.

Faccio un esempio. Una di queste perle, nel grande oceano perlifero che è la divina Comedia, diremo la campana della sera:

Era già l'ora che volge il disio
ai naviganti, e intenerisce il core
lo dì ch'han detto ai dolci amici addio;

e che lo nuovo peregrin d'amore
punge, se ode squilla di lontano
che paia il giorno pianger che si muore.

In questa rappresentazione, che di più poetiche non se ne può trovare (Dante ci rappresenta l'ora in cui ridiveniamo per un momento fanciulli!), il tocco più poetico è l'ultimo. È l'ultimo; sebbene la squilla lontana che piange il giorno che muore, sia di quei tocchi che noi verseggiatori abbiamo fatti tornare a noia, a forza di ripeterli. E così quel suono di squilla può essere stinto e fioco per alcuno, assordato da tanti doppi. Ma tant'è. Orbene: il poeta ha dovuto mettere, per la necessità dell'arte, un pochino di lega nel suo oro puro. Quale? Quel "paia". L'ha dovuto mettere, perché egli racconta un sentimento poetico altrui, sebbene anche di sé. E allora ha detto che la squilla pare piangere, non piange veramente. A un tratto il fanciullo (qui un poco, e molto altrove, molto presso altri), il fanciullo a mezza via si riscuote, e par che si vergogni d'esser fanciullo e di parlar fanciullesco, e si corregge. "Pare, non è, intendiamoci." Ma caro bimbo, lo sapevamo da noi, che la campana non piange, ma par che pianga: anche però il giorno par che muoia, e non muore.[29]

---

[29] È superfluo aggiungere che per quanto non tutto nella Comedia sia poesia, e non tutta la poesia che v'è, sia pura, per altro quel poema è nella sua concezione generale il più "poetico" dei poemi che al mondo sono e saranno. Nulla è più proprio della fanciullezza della nostra anima che la contemplazione dell'invisibile, la peregrinaztone per il mistero, il conversare e piangere e sdegnarsi e godere coi morti.

Let me give an example. One of these pearls, in the vast pearl-laden ocean that is the *Divine Comedy*, we may call the evening bell:

> *It was now the hour that moves the longing*
> *of sailing men, and makes their heart grow tender*
> *the day they bid their good friends farewell*
>
> *and that the pilgrim newly on his way*
> *pierces with love, when he hears afar*
> *the bell that seems to mourn the dying day.*

In this representation — and a more poetic one could not be found (Dante is representing for us the hour in which, we become momentarily children again!) — the most poetic touch is the last one. It is the last one, even though the distant bell which mourns the dying day is one of those touches we verse-makers have used to the point of boredom, by dint of repeating them over and over. And so, that bell sound may be faded and faint for some grown deaf by hearing it so many times. But that is how it is. Well then: the poet, due to the demands of his art had to put a little alloy in his pure gold. What is that? That word "seems." He had to put it in, because he is narrating someone else's poetic feeling, though it is his own too. And so he said that the bell "seems" to weep, it does not really weep. Suddenly the child (here only a little, and a great deal elsewhere, and a great deal more with other poets), the child rouses himself half way, and he seems to be ashamed of being a child and of speaking like a child, and he corrects himself. "It seems, not is, let us be clear." But, dear child, we knew on our own that the bell is not weeping, but it sounds as if it is weeping: the day also, moreover, seems to be dying, and it is not really dying. [29]

---

[29] It is unnecessary to add that even though not everything in the Comedia is poetry, and not all of the poetry is pure poetry, nevertheless that poem is in its general conception the most "poetic" of the poems that are and that will ever be in the world. Nothing is more proper to the childhood of our soul than the contemplation of the invisible, the pilgrimage through mystery, the talking and crying and being angry and taking joy with the dead.

XIII

La poesia benefica di per sé, la poesia che di per sé, ci fa meglio amare la patria, la famiglia, l'umanità, è, dunque, la poesia pura, la quale di rado si trova. In Italia poi, che è la mia patria (non la tua, o fanciullo: tu sei del mondo, non sei d'ora ma di sempre), in Italia è più rara che altrove. Invero non mai da noi fu amata la poesia elementare e spontanea. Come in genere la nostra letteratura, così in ispecie la nostra poesia ha avuto innanzi sé, dei modelli. Noi abbiamo specchiato il nostro stile nell'arte latina, come i latini avevano fatto coi greci. Ciò può aver giovato a dare concretezza e maestà alle nostre scritture; ma quanto a poesia, ciò l'ha soffocata; la poesia non si fa sui libri. Poi amiamo troppo l'ornamentazione; e questo gusto lo dimostriamo specialmente in ciò che meno lo comporta: nella poesia. Il fanciullino italico non ruzza che ben vestito e ben pettinato: le noci con le quali fa a filetto, devono essere coperte di carta d'oro e d'argento. Noi vogliamo farci sempre onore: invece di badare al giuoco, badiamo a noi: ci stiamo a sentire e ammicchiamo alla nostra ombra. E anche più che a noi, badiamo al pubblico: guardiamo con la coda dell'occhio i grandi che stanno a vederci; e così facciamo tutto senza garbo e senza scioltezza. E siccome, particolarmente ai nostri giorni, tutto da noi si fa a concorso e tutto si dà all'asta e tutto si conclude con la aggiudicazione e la premiazione, così ci proponiamo, più che altro, di sopraffare l'un l'altro e di conquistarci con qualche grazietta il favore dei giudici. Nei giochi dei nostri fanciulli, c'entra per molta parte la gherminella che è cosa da attempati. Sono troppo scaltriti, i nostri fanciulli, e cercano meglio di essere primi, che di esser loro. Perciò la nostra poesia (per chiamarla così) è per lo più d'imitazione, anzi di collezione, e sa di lucerna, non di guazza e d'erba fresca. Noi studiamo troppo, per poetare; ed è superfluo aggiungere che, per sapere, studiamo troppo poco. Mettiamo lo studio ove non c'entra.

Come? Non c'entra nel poetare lo studio? Sí, ma diretto al fine, che Dante mostrò. Virgilio, che è lo studio, conduce Dante a Matelda che è l'arte; l'arte in genere e in ispecie. L'arte di Dante è appunto la poesia. Dunque lo studio condusse Dante alla poesia. Ebbene, Matelda, o la poesia, è nel giardino dell'innocenza, sceglie cantando fior da fiore, ha gli occhi luminosi, purifica nei fiumi dell'oblio e della buona volontà. Ossia, il poeta,

XIII

Poetry that is truly beneficial, poetry that, in and of itself, makes us better love country, family, and mankind, is, well, pure poetry, and it is rarely found. In Italy, moreover, which is my country (not yours, Child: you are of the world, you are not of now, but of always), in Italy it is more rare than anywhere else. Indeed we have never loved simple and spontaneous poetry. Like our literature in general, our poetry in particular has had before itself a number of models. We have mirrored our style on Latin art, as the Latins had done with the Greeks. This fact may have helped to give solidity and majesty to our writings; but, insofar as poetry is concerned, it has suffocated it. Poetry is not made with books. And then, we love ornamentation too much; and we show this taste just where it is least suited: in poetry. The Italian *fanciullino* romps about only when well-dressed and well-groomed: the walnuts with which he plays *filetto* [a simple *tic-tac-toe* kind of game] must be covered in silver and golden paper. We always want to look good: instead of paying attention to the game, we pay attention to our own looks: we listen to ourselves and wink at our shadows. And even more than ourselves we mind our audience. We look out of the corner of our eye at the grownups who are looking at us; and so we do everything without grace or spontaneity. And since, particularly in our own day, we do everything in competition, and everything is auctioned and everything is concluded with appraisals and prizes, so we endeavor, above all, to outdo one another and to win for ourselves, with the help of some little flourish, the favor of the judges. The artful ruse, which we associate with the elderly, plays a large role in the games of our children. They are too clever, our children, and they strive more to be first, than to be themselves. That is why our poetry (to call it so) is for the most part poetry of imitation, indeed, of compilation, and it smells of the oil-lamp, not of dew and fresh grass. We study too much, to write poetry; and it is superfluous to add that in order to know we study too little. We put the effort where it does not belong.

What? Study does not enter into the making of poetry? Yes, but only if directed toward the end as shown by Dante. Vergil, who represents study, leads Dante to Matelda who is art; art in general and in particular. Dante's art is indeed poetry. So, study led Dante to poetry. Well then, Matelda, or poetry, is in the garden of innocence, she gathers flowers while singing. Her eyes are shining, and she purifies [the man] in the rivers of

mercé lo studio, è riuscito a ritrovare la sua fanciullezza, e puro come è, vede bene e sceglie senza alcuna fatica, sceglie cantando, i fiori che pare spuntino avanti i suoi piedi. Io, senza insistere sul valore morale del mito tanto esatto e bello, dico, interpretando il poeta per il rispetto artistico, che lo studio deve essere diretto a togliere più che ad aggiungere: a togliere la tanta ruggine che il tempo ha depositata sulla nostra anima, in modo che torniamo a specchiarci nella limpidezza di prima; ed essere soli tra noi e noi. Lo studio deve togliere le scorie al puro cristallo che noi troviamo quasi casualmente; e quel cristallo pur con le scorie val più d'un vetro che noi dilatiamo e formiamo soffiando. Lo studio deve rifarci ingenui, insomma, tal quale Dante figura sé come avanti Beatrice così rispetto a Matelda; che se dall'una è sgridato e fatto piangere e vergognare come fanciullo battuto, dall'altra è, come bambino che non vuole o non può fare da sé, preso e tuffato nell'acqua e menato a bere alla fonte. Lo studio deve togliere gli artifizi, e renderci la natura. Così dice Dante. La sua arte è impersonata in Matelda, che è la natura umana primordialmente libera, felice, innocente.

XIV

Ma noi italiani siamo, in fondo, troppo seri e furbi, per essere poeti. Noi imitiamo troppo. E sì, che studiando si deve imparare a far diverso, non lo stesso. Ma noi vogliamo far lo stesso e dare a credere o darci a credere di fare meglio. Perciò sovente ci pare che, incastonando la gemma altrui in un anello nostro, noi abbiamo trovata e magari fatta la gemma; e più sovente ci imaginiamo che, dorando la statua di bronzo, quella statua non solo sia più bella, ma diventi opera nostra.

Noi non gettiamo più il martello contro i blocchi di marmo: ci accontentiamo di pulire e lustrare le statue belle e fatte. Al più al più, noi facciamo l'arte di Giovanni da Udine: eleganti stucchi: ma non ricordiamo quel che Giovanni disse, mi pare, a Pietro Aretino che ne lo ammirava: "Bambocci vogliono essere!"

E le scuole ci legano. Le scuole sono fili sottili di ferro, tesi tra i verdi mai della foresta di Matelda: noi, facendo i fiori, temiamo a ogni tratto d'inciampare e cadere. L'ho già detto: se uno si abbandona alle delizie della campagna, teme che lo chiamino arcade; se un altro si vede avanti

oblivion and of good will. This means that the poet, through study, has succeeded in finding his childhood again, and, pure as he now is, sees clearly and selects without effort, he selects, while singing, the flowers that appear to sprout before his feet. Without insisting on the moral value of such a precise and beautiful myth, I say, interpreting the poet from an artistic standpoint, that study should be aimed at removing rather than adding: at removing all the rust that time has deposited on our soul, so that we may go back to mirroring ourselves in the clarity we once knew; and be alone with ourselves. Study has to remove the slag from the pure crystal we find almost by chance; and that crystal, with all its slag, has more value than the glass we expand and shape by blowing. In short, study has to make us naïve [i.e. children] again, just the way Dante represents himself before Beatrice and so too with Matelda. The one scolds him and makes him cry and feel shame like a beaten child; the other takes him, like a child who does not want to or cannot act on his own, and plunges him into the water and leads him to drink at the spring. Study, then, has to eliminate artifice and bring nature back to us. So Dante says. His art is impersonated in Matelda, who is human nature primordially free, happy, innocent.

XIV

But we Italians are, at bottom, too serious and too clever to be poets. We imitate too much. To be sure, by studying one should learn to do things differently, not in the same way. But we want to do the same thing and have others believe or persuade ourselves that we are doing better. That is why we often think that by mounting someone else's precious stone in a ring of ours, we have found and perhaps even made the gem; and more often we fancy that, by gilding the bronze statue, that statue is not only more beautiful, but becomes our own work.

We do not wield our hammer on blocks of marble any more: we content ourselves with cleaning and polishing statues already made. At the very most, we follow the art of Giovanni da Udine: elegant plaster casts; but we forget what Giovanni said, I believe, to Pietro Aretino who admired him for them: "They are meant to be mere dolls!"

And the schools tie our hands. The schools are thin wire threads, strung among the green boughs of Matelda's forest: while we gather the flowers, at every step we are afraid of stumbling and falling. I have already said: if one abandons himself to singing the delights of the country, it is with the fear they may call him Arcadian; if another is challenged by an

un'antitesi, sta un pezzo tra il sì e il no, temendo d'essere chiamato secentista. Mentre la mandra degli imitatori si butta alla rinfusa dietro qualche ariete maggiore, e tutti si mettono a belare o mugliare a un modo; sì che in certi tempi pare che gl'italiani (giudicandoli da quelli che scrivono in versi) non abbiano che l'amica, in certi altri non abbiano che la mamma; i poeti veri sono pieni del contrario affetto: vogliono cioè non essere imbrancati né nel verismo né nell'idealismo né nel simbolismo. Queste preoccupazioni li rendono troppo circospetti, troppo irresoluti, troppo sforzati. E Matelda si allontana da loro, facendo echeggiare sempre più lunghi il suo dolce salmo che finisce per confondersi con lo stormir delle foglie e col gorgoglio del ruscello, e morire.

Ma poi per la poesia vera e propria, a noi manca, o sembra mancare, la lingua.

La poesia consiste nella visione d'un particolare inavvertito, fuori e dentro noi.

Guardate i ragazzi quando si trastullano seri seri. Voi vedete che hanno sempre alle mani cose trovate per terra, nella loro via, che interessano soltanto loro e che perciò sol essi sembrano vedere: chioccioline, ossiccioli, sassetti. Il poeta fa il medesimo. Ma come chiamare questi lapilli ideali, questi cervi volanti della sua anima? Il nome loro non è fatto, o non è divulgato, o non è comune a tutta la nazione o a tutte le classi del popolo. Pensate ai fiori e agli uccelli, che sono de' fanciulli la gioia più grande e consueta: che nome hanno? S'ha sempre a dire uccelli, sì di quelli che fanno *tottavì* e sì di quelli che fanno *crocro*? Basta dir fiori o fioretti, e aggiungere, magari, vermigli e gialli, e non far distinzione tra un greppo coperto di margherite e un prato gremito di crochi? Ora se vi provate a dire il nome proprio loro, ecco che il nome di Linneo non va, per cento ragioni, e il nome popolare varia, quando c'è, da regione a regione, anzi da contado a contado. Se il popolo italiano badasse a queste tali cose, fiori, piante, uccelli, insetti, rettili, che formano per gran parte la poesia della campagna, il nome che esse hanno in una terra, avrebbe finito per prevalere su quello dominante in altre. Ma gl'italiani, abbarbagliati per lo più dallo sfolgorio dell'elmo di Scipio, non sogliono seguire i tremolii cangianti delle libellule. E così il poeta, se vuol poetare, bisogna che si lasci ogni tanto dire: "E questo che è? che vuol dire? O poeta saccente e seccante!" E tuttavia così il

antithesis, he hesitates at length, fearing he may be called "Baroque." The herd of imitators throw themselves pell mell behind some bigger ram, and they all start to bleat or to bellow in unison; so it would seem that at certain times the Italians (judging by those who write in verse) have only a mistress, and, at certain other times, they have only a mother. True poets, instead, are full of the opposite affect: that is, they do not want to be herded under the label of Realism, or Idealism, or Symbolism. These kinds of worries make them too cautious, too irresolute, too unnatural. And Matelda moves away from them, singing her sweet psalm farther and farther away, until it blends with the rustling of the leaves and the gurgling of the brook, and dies away completely

But then, for poetry true and proper we lack, or we seem to lack, the language.

Poetry consists of the vision of a detail unnoticed, outside and inside ourselves.

Look at children when they are so deeply engrossed at play. You can see that in their hands they always have little things they have found on the ground, in their path. Things that are of interest only to them and so they alone seem to see them: little snails, little bones, pebbles. The poet does the same. But what shall we call these imaginary pebbles, these flying beetles of his soul? Their names are not to be found, or they are not widely known, or they are not common to the whole nation or spread among the different social classes. Think of flowers and birds, which are the usual and greatest joy of children. What are their names? Do we always have to call them birds, both the ones that cry *tottavì* and the ones that go *crocrò*? And is it sufficient to speak of flowers and little flowers, adding, perhaps, red and yellow, and not make any distinction between a knoll covered with daisies and a meadow brimming with crocuses? Now, if you try to use their proper names, you find that the labels of Linnaeus are not right, for a hundred reasons, and the popular name, when there is one, changes from region to region, indeed, from one locale to another. If the Italian people paid attention to things such as these: flowers, plants, birds, insects, reptiles, which form, in large part, the poetry of the countryside, the name they have for them in one place would prevail in the end in other places. But the Italians being, for the most part, dazzled by the flashing of Scipio's helmet, are not given to following the iridescent flickering of the dragonflies. Thus, the poet, if he wants to make poetry, must every so often allow himself to say: "And this, what is it? What does it mean?" Oh, pedantic, annoying

poeta deve fare, e lasciar dire così, sperando, se non altro, che se ne avvantaggino i poeti futuri, i quali troveranno divulgati tanti nomi prima ignoti e perciò chiamati oscuri. In verità non è egli l'Adamo che per primo mette i nomi? Così deve operare, facendo a ogni momento qualche rinunzia d'amor proprio. Perché l'arte del poeta è sempre una rinunzia. Ho detto che deve togliere, non aggiungere: e ciò è rinunzia. Deve fare a meno di tanti ghirigori, così facili a farsi, di tante bellurie, così piacevoli alla vista, di tante dorature, che danno tanta idea della propria ricchezza: e questa è rinunzia. Deve lasciar molto greggio e molto imperfetto. Oh! come è necessaria l'imperfezione per essere perfetti! Lo sapeva anche Marziale che derideva quel Matone che voleva dir tutto *belle*. "Di" egli esclama "qualche volta soltanto bene, anche né ben né male, magari male!" La continua eleganza è sommamente stucchevole. È come quel pranzo descritto dal De Amicis nel Marocco, che tutto vi sapeva di pomata. Questa bellezza in tutto e per tutto è totalmente antipoetica; ché la poesia è ingenuità, e quel fanciullo, che ogni cosa che fa e dice, la fa con una moina e con una smorfietta, e la dice con parolucce smaccate e dolciate; che scapaccioni chiama quel fanciullo consapevole della sua fanciulleria!

XV

Con tutto questo, che speri tu? che fine hai? Ritorno, come vedi, al primo detto. Essere utile a me? No, s'è detto. Recar utile agli altri? S'è detto che, se mai, non lo fai apposta: dunque non è il fine tuo, codesto. Dilettar te stesso? Ecco: se questo fosse il tuo fine, tu chiuderesti dentro te la tua visione, e te la godresti tra te e me, senza quei tanti struggimenti che ci sono per comunicare la visione agli altri. O dunque?

La gloriola...

O povero fanciullo!

Pensa, o fanciullo, quante altre cose potrei fare con maggiore rispondenza a codesto fine. Da condurre un esercito a volare sulla bicicletta, tutto, o quasi tutto, meglio porta alla meta della vittoria e della gloria. Ma poniamo che ci si arrivi anche "sulle ali del canto". Qual disgrazia sarebbe mettersi in questa via, e per te e per me! Prima di tutto, ne andrebbe molto tempo. La gloriola vuole mutui uffici. Io devo conversare,

poet! And yet this is what the poet should do, and let himself say, in the hope that, if nothing else, his effort will be to the benefit of future poets, who will find many names in wide use that before were not known and, for this reason, were termed obscure. In truth, is he not the Adam who first gives names to things? He must operate this way, constantly humbling himself to some extent. For the art of the poet is always a sacrifice. I have said he has to take away not add: and this is renunciation. He must do without many arabesques, so easy to make, without many embellishments, so pleasing to the eye, without much gilding, which gives such an idea of one's own wealth; and this is renunciation. He must leave much that is rough and unfinished. Oh, how necessary imperfection is, in order to be perfect! Martial himself knew it too when he made fun of that fellow Mato, who wanted to call all things *"belle."* "Sometimes just say well," he exclaims "or even neither well nor badly, but indeed badly!" Continuous elegance is exceedingly tedious. It is like that dinner described by De Amicis in Morocco, where everything tasted like pomade. Beauty in everything and everywhere is totally anti-poetic; for poetry is spontaneity; and that child, who, everything he says and does, does it with a bit of wheedling and with a cute mincing look, says it with sickly sweet little words; what a spanking that child invites who is so aware of his own childishness!

XV

All this said and done, what are you hoping for? what is your purpose? I go back, you see, to what I asked at the beginning. To be useful to me? No, we have settled that. To be useful to others? We have already said that, even if you are, you do not do it on purpose: then such cannot be your aim. To please yourself? Well, if this were your goal, you would enclose your vision within yourself, and you would enjoy it solely with me, without all that anguish that comes from trying to communicate the vision to others. Well, then?

Petty fame, *la gloriola...*

Oh, poor Child!

Think, Child, of how many other things I could do that would bring me closer to this end. From leading an army to flying on a bicycle, everything, or almost everything, leads more easily to the goal of victory and glory. But let us assume that one can also reach it "on the wings of song." What a misfortune it would be, for you and for me, to set out on this road! First of all, it would take a lot of time. Petty recognition demands

e per lettere e a voce, sì con quelli che coltivano medesimi campi, e chieder loro e averne notizie sull'efficacia d'un concime che usiamo, e dar loro e riceverne auguri e rallegramenti per un buon raccolto che speriamo d'avere o abbiamo avuto; sì con quelli che professano soltanto di fornir le pianticelle, i semi, i concimi chimici, gli strumenti agricoli, a mano e a vapore. Quanto studio, quanta diligenza e pazienza si richiede per siffatta coltivazione! Bisogna raccattare tutti i cocci, come fanno i contadini, per seminarci e trapiantarci le tante pianticelle; anche i caldani rotti raccattiamo; anche quei vasi, dove cresceva il garofano di Geva contadinella. E star sempre lì ad annaffiare, a mondare, a potare; e sbirciare i vasi del vicino, e struggerci ch'egli abbia papaveri più grandi e girasoli più vistosi, e buttare a lui il malocchio, e contro il malocchio di lui tener molta ruta, e guardare che non ci si secchi.

Ma tu dirai: "Anche il tempo si raccatta!" Bene: parliamo d'altro. Non miete, chi non s'inchina. Ora, per la gloriola, ci s'inchina troppo, tanto umile sovente è la pianticella, e ci s'inchina troppo spesso, tante sono. Voglio dire che la nostra anima (l'anima, intendi!) si deforma, si fa gobba, come è la schiena dei poveri contadini che s'inchinano per il grano. E tu devi essere dritta, serena, semplice, o anima mia! Non c'è forse sentimento al mondo, nemmeno l'avidità del guadagno, che sia tanto contrario all'ingenuità del poeta, quanto questa gola di gloriola, che si risolve in un desiderio di sopraffazione! Quando sei preso da questo morbo, tu (ma tu non c'entri, allora), io, non cerco il poetico, il buono e il bello, ma il sonante e l'abbagliante. Oh! non cerco allora i lapilli, i nicchi, i fiori per la mia via, ma veglio inquieto spiando i quaderni altrui, magari leggendo di sulle spalle dello scrittore ciò che egli scrive. Allora io smetto il mio verso, e mi metto a far quello d'altri: come un merlo noioso che canta, in questo mentre, non le sue arie mattinali di bosco, ma la ritirata: perché, se non per voglia di gloriola, nel suo padrone e forse in lui? O merlo dal becco giallo, tu hai voluto esser troppo furbo! Come puoi credere che il tuo *Io ti vedo!* che risonava tra il cader della guazza, sia peggio di codesto insopportabile *Ritirati cappellon!*? Ma è pur vero che "merlo" vuol dire sì furbo e sì il

reciprocal services. I have to converse, both through letters and in person, with those who cultivate similar fields, questioning them and getting information from them on the effectiveness of a fertilizer we are using, and extending them and receiving from them good wishes and congratulations for a good crop which we hope to have or that we have had. And I must also converse with those who profess they only provide seeds, seedlings, chemical fertilizers, tools and steam-powered machines for farming. How much effort, how much diligence and patience are required for such cultivation! We must pick up all the fragments of pottery, as the peasants do, in order to sow the seeds and to transplant the many seedlings; we also pick up the broken braziers; even those pots in which grew the carnations of the little peasant girl, Geva. And always be there to water, to clean up, to prune. And keep a constant eye on the neighbor's flower pots and torment ourselves over his having larger poppies, and more showy sunflowers. And cast the evil eye on him, and to ward off against his own evil eye, keep plenty of rue on hand and be sure to protect it from drying up.

But you will say: "Time too can be regained, like a dropped stitch!" All right: let us talk about other things. One cannot harvest without bending over. Now, for that small fame we are talking about, we must bend over too much, so low to the ground are often those little plants, and we bend over too frequently, so numerous are they. I mean to say that our soul (the soul, you understand!) becomes deformed, it hunches up, like the back of poor farmers who bend over for their wheat. And you must be straight, serene, simple, o my soul! There perhaps is no sentiment in the world, not even greed for profit, so contrary to the spontaneity of the poet, as this lusting after petty fame, which often turns into a desire for power! When you are taken over by this sickness, you (but then, *you* are not involved here) — *I, I* do not seek the poetic, the good and the beautiful, but the loud and the showy. Oh, I do not look for pebbles, shells, flowers along my road, but I stay up late, restless, poring over someone else's notebooks, or even reading over his shoulder what another author is writing. Then, I stop doing my own verse-making and start doing someone else's: like an annoying *merlo* [blackbird] singing taps, in the meantime, and not its morning sylvan arias: and why? if not for the desire of that *gloriola* present in his master and perhaps in itself? Oh, yellow-beaked blackbird, you wanted to be too smart! How could you believe your *I see you!* which rang out amid the falling of the dew, to be worse than that insufferable *Ritirati*

contrario! O anche, insistiamo troppo su un nostro verso o motivo o vezzo o genere, che sia una volta piaciuto; e riusciamo stucchevoli; non basta, diventiamo falsi. Imitiamo da noi medesimi, col vetro d'un bicchiere, il diamante puro che una volta trovammo. E sempre, pensando o scrivendo, siamo distratti dalla preoccupazione dell'effetto: che ne diranno? vincerò, con questo, il tale o il tal altro? E la tua grazia, che non è grazia se non è spontanea, si perde per sempre. Tu non vedi più giusto e limpido; anzi non guardi più; seppure, ciò che sarebbe peggio, non guardi, come ho detto, negli altri, e non baratti le vesti e magari l'anima con altri, che tu veda o creda più pregiati di te!

XVI

Non pensare alla gloriola, fanciullo: non è cosa da te. Ella è troppo difficile, o facile, a raggiungersi. Difficile: non ho già detto quanto è raro che t'intendano? Tu non fai se non scoprire il nuovo nel vecchio. Gli altri, ossia i tuoi lettori e uditori, non dovrebbero dire o pensare se non: "Come è vero! e io non ci avevo pensato". Ma questo assentimento non ti vien sempre e nemmeno spesso. Gli occhi della gente sono oggi così fissi nell'ombelico della propria persona, che non hanno visto, si può dire, altro. E perché hanno le luci velate dalla catalessi del loro egoismo, dicono che sei tu oscuro. Puoi, quanto tu voglia, descrivere un mattino, per esempio, in campagna: chi non l'ha mai veduto sorgere, il sole, né in campagna né in città, non capisce e non approva nulla di ciò che dici. Sei inoltre oscuro, sovente per un'altra ragione: perché sei chiaro. Sono tanto avvezzi i lettori oggi alle girandole, agli andirivieni, ai viluppi dei pensieri e sentimenti; perché gli autori, attingendo questi e quelli di sui libri, s'ingegnano con gli stucchi e gli ori a dar loro un aspetto nuovo, o fanno come le lepri, le quali, per nascondere al cacciatore le loro tracce, si mettono a girare e pestare su esse; sono i lettori tanto abituati ai misteri o gherminelle degli autori, i quali, troppo comodi, vogliono perpetuamente che s'intenda dagli altri meglio che da lor si ragioni; che quando tu dici nel tuo semplice modo le tue semplici cose, ecco che non ti capiscono più. Essi cercano in te quello che non c'è, e perché non lo trovano, ci rimangono male. E se anche ti capiscono, vale a dire se capiscono che non vuoi dire se non quel che dici, e non sottintendi

cappellon!? [a military call] But then, it is true that *merlo* means both clever and its opposite! And also, we insist too much on a line or motif or set manner or genre which was once found pleasing; and we become boring; worse than that, we become false. We ourselves substitute a piece of glass for the pure diamond we once found. And always, while thinking or writing, we are distracted by worry about the effect: what will they say about it? will I win, with this, over this person or that one? And your charm, which is not charm, unless it is spontaneous, is lost for ever. You do not see clearly and exactly any longer, indeed, you do not observe any more; unless, what would be even worse, you were to look, as I said, at others, and exchange clothes, maybe even your soul, with others, whom you may see or consider more highly regarded than you.

XVI

Do not think about petty fame, child: it is not worthy of you. It is too difficult, or too easy, to achieve. Difficult: have I not already said how rare it is for people to understand you? You only discover the new in the old. Others, that is, your readers and listeners, should not say or think anything but: "How true it is! And I had not thought about that." But this kind of understanding does not always come to you, and certainly not often. Today, the eyes of the people are so set on their own navel, that it can be said that they have not seen anything else. And since their eyes are dimmed by the catalepsy of their own selfishness, they say it is you who are obscure. You may describe as much as you want a morning in the country, for example: the ones who have never seen it rise, the sun, either in the country or in the city, will not understand and will not approve anything you say. You are obscure, moreover, often for another reason: because you are clear. Today's readers are very much used to spinning wheels, mazes, tangles of thoughts and feelings; because authors, drawing on books for this and that, try their best with plastic and gilding to give them a new look, or they do what the hares do, when in order to cover their tracks from the hunter they keep circling back and stamping them out. Today's readers are so used to the mysteries and tricks of authors who, all too conveniently, are forever wanting others to understand beyond what they say, that, when you say in your simple way your simple things, lo! they do not understand you any more. They look in your work for what is not there, and since they do not find it, they are left disappointed. And if they do understand you, which is to say, if they understand that you mean to say only what you are saying,

nulla, e non hai la pretesa, assurda e comune, che il senso, nelle tue cose, ce lo mettano i lettori, allora i più non ti apprezzano. Ai più pare che il bello sia nei fregi e che il poetico sia nella foga oratoria. E infine, quasi tutti, come vuoi che ascoltino lo stormire delle foglie o il gorgoglio del ruscello o il canto dell'usignuolo o il suono della tua avena, se lì presso la banda del villaggio assorda la campagna coi tromboni e i colpi di gran cassa?

No no, fanciullo. La gloria o gloriola si forma con l'assenso di molti, e tu non sei udito, ascoltato, approvato, che dai pochi. È vero che tu ti rivolgi a tutti, ma ricordati: non agli uomini proprio, ma ai fanciulli, come te, che sono negli uomini. Ora codesti fanciulli, dato che in nessuno manchino, in pochi però prestano ascolto. E sai quali sono questi pochi? Sono generalmente poeti. Cioè il loro fanciullo, o ti sta a sentire solo perché anch'esso canta e vuol sapere se tu canti meglio o peggio di lui, o standoti a sentire finisce con cantare anche lui. E che succede? Succede che un giorno o l'altro comincia a fare il tuo verso. Prima fa solo qualche nota, poi qualche battuta, infine tutta la tua canzone. E allora? Allora diventa tuo imitatore. Ebbene? Ebbene l'imitatore è un debitore; e il debitore, presto o tardi, parlerà male del creditore. E così, anche di quei pochi, molti si sottrarranno dal dir le tue lodi, per assicurar le loro. E la tua gloriola o non nascerà o intisichirà appena nata.

XVII

Ma poi ti sentiresti d'accettarla codesta gloriola? Sai com'ella nasce. Nasce in generale dalla affermazione tua stessa. È pensiero giustissimo del nostro Leopardi: "La via forse più diretta di acquistar fama, è di affermare e con sicurezza e pertinacia, e in quanti più modi è possibile, di averla acquistata."[30] E altrove: "Rara è nel nostro secolo quella persona lodata generalmente, le cui lodi non siano cominciate dalla propria bocca... Chi vuole innalzarsi, quantunque per virtù vera, dia bando alla modestia."[31] E tu, fanciullo, vorresti che io da una seggiola o da un palco mi mettessi a gridar le tue lodi o affermare la tua fama? "Questo ragazzo è un ragazzo miracoloso... noto in tutto il mondo..." In questo modo la gloriola sarebbe facile. Ma tu no, non vorresti. Eppure gli uomini non crederanno mai che

---

[30] Pensiero LX.
[31] Pensiero XXIV.

and do not imply anything more, and do not expect, as is commonly and absurdly done, that the readers be the ones to lend meaning to what you write, then the majority do not appreciate you. The majority think that beauty lies in ornamentation, and poetry in oratorical passion. And finally, and for almost all of them, how can you expect them to listen to the rustle of the leaves or the gurgling of the brook or the song of the nightingale, or the sound of your flute, if, right nearby, the village band deafens the countryside with the sound of base-drums and trombones?

No no, child. Glory or petty fame is formed with the approval of the many, and you are heeded and approved only by the few. It is true that you address everybody, but remember: you do not really address the men, but the children, like you, who are in the men. Now, those children, although present in all, listen actively only in the few. And do you know who these few are? They are generally poets. That is, their child either listens to you only because he also sings and wants to know if you sing better or worse than he does, or, listening to you, he also winds up singing. And what happens? It happens that one day or another he begins making your sounds. First he plays only a note or two, then a few bars, finally the whole song. And then? Then he becomes your imitator. So? Well, the imitator is a debtor; and the person indebted will sooner or later speak ill of his creditor. And so, even of those few, many will avoid praising you in order to secure the praise for themselves. And your petty fame either will not sprout at all or will wilt as soon as it has sprouted.

XVII

But then, would you really feel like accepting that petty fame? You do know how it comes into being. Generally it is born from your own declaration. Here is a very accurate thought of our Leopardi: "Perhaps the most direct way to acquire fame is to affirm confidently and obstinately, and in as many ways possible, that you have acquired it already."[30] And elsewhere: "Rare in our century is the person praised widely whose praises did not begin from his own mouth... One who wants to extol himself, however much for genuine merit, should banish all modesty."[31] And you, child, would you want me to sing your praises or affirm your fame from a chair or a platform? "This boy is a miraculous boy... known all over the

---

[30] Pensiero LX.
[31] Pensiero XXIV.

sia grande un merito che non sia tanto grande da vincere persino la modestia di colui che l'ha. Se la tua modestia è grande, contentati d'una grandezza assai modesta. Sarai considerato un poeta mediocre, e poiché mediocre non deve essere il poeta, sarai proclamato non poeta. Ovvero tu, non credendo all'amara considerazione del Leopardi, aspetterai che la tua lode cominci dalle bocche altrui? Perché questa lode sia tale da crearti una vera fama occorre ch'ella possa propagarsi per gran numero di persone; le quali ti loderanno poi a lor volta senza conoscerti, senza averti udito, senza averti letto! Ti loderanno per "suggestione". Oh! il pessimo fatto che sarebbe allora il tuo! Tutto quel che tu facessi, sarebbe ugualmente lodato: ciò che tu sentissi d'aver fatto di meglio, sarebbe pareggiato a ciò che tu conoscessi d'aver fatto di peggio. Persino cosa che non avessi fatto tu, ma comparisse col tuo nome, sarebbe levata alle stelle, e così preferita a quelle che proprio tu avessi fatto e credessi buone e belle! e che ne faresti di tale gloriola?

Tanto più che bisogna vedere da che ti venne quella lode iniziale, che avviò tutte quell'altre lodi. Da che? Da qualche cosa più atta delle altre ad accecare, ad inebbriare, a far delirare la gente. Dalla politica, per esempio: dal partito o dalla setta. Badaci, ragazzo. È il fatto di qualcuno che vuol procacciarsi la popolarità mettendo la cannella a una botte, e che tutti bevano. La gran botte è la politica, il vino che ognuno ne beve, è il proprio sentimento che si riscalda alla botte comune: la sbornia generale è la tua gloria!

O gloriola indegna del tuo desiderio! E poi è amara. Sai che siamo al tempo dei concorsi; al tempo delle classificazioni e premiazioni. Il divertimento più grande che si diano gli uomini, è quello di giudicare. In Atene fu in altri tempi una consimile mania di seder nell' Elièa e deporre le sue pietruzze. Oggi non c'è più solo qualche pazzo, ma molti; e non giudicano, in mancanza d'altro, i cani e i gatti di casa, ma gli scrittori e i poeti di casa e fuori. Giudicano e classificano: questo è il primo, quello il secondo, l'altro il terzo, e vai dicendo. Ahimè! tu fanciullo, fai il tuo discorsino, esprimi un tuo sentimento, esponi il tuo pensiero, mostri un tuo sorriso, versi una tua lagrima, senza riguardarti, senza saperlo, si può dire, senza perché, al primo venuto, sfogando il cuore, quasi fuori di te: a mezzo le tue parole, al tuo riso, al tuo pianto, ecco senti che il tuo uditore piglia appunti, pesa le frasi che dici, disegna, col pollice, in aria la linea del tuo

world..." In this way the *gloriola* would come easily. But no, you would not want this. And yet men will never believe a merit to be very great if it does not overcome even the modesty of the one who possesses it. If your modesty is great, be happy with a quite modest greatness. You will be considered a mediocre poet, and since the poet must not be mediocre, you will be proclaimed a non-poet. Or, not believing in Leopardi's bitter thinking on the matter, will you wait for your praise to begin on someone else's lips? For this praise to be such as to create a real reputation for you it is necessary that it be propagated by a great number of people; who then will praise you, in their turn, without knowing you, without having heard you, without having read you! They will praise you out of "suggestion." Oh, what a terrible thing it would be for you! All that you might do, would be equally praised, what you might feel to be your best would be equated to what you knew to be your worst. Even something that you had not done yourself but might appear with your name, would be raised to the stars, and so, preferred over things you might have done and considered good and beautiful! What would you ever do with such *gloriola*?

Not to mention that we have to see whence came that initial praise which started all the others. From what? From something better suited than other things to blind, to excite, to make people rave. From politics for example, from the party or the sect. Be careful, child. It is a matter of someone wanting to gain popularity for himself by putting a spigot to the barrel, for everybody to drink. The great barrel is politics, the wine everyone drinks from it is one's own sentiment warming up at that common source: the general inebriation is your glory!

O petty fame unworthy of your desire! And it is bitter too. You know we live in times of contests; in times of classifications and the awarding of prizes. The greatest amusement men have found for themselves is that of judging. In other times there was in Athens a similar mania for sitting in the Eliea and putting down one's pebbles. Today there are not just a few madmen, but many; and they do not judge, for lack of anything else, house cats and dogs, but writers and poets, domestic and foreign. They judge and classify: first, second, third, and so on. Alas! Child, you make your little speech, express your feeling, state your thought, show your smile, shed a tear, carelessly, without thinking, one can say without any specific reason; opening your heart, almost beside yourself, to the first comer: and amid your words, your laughter, your tears, there now, you sense that your listener is taking notes, is weighing the sentences you speak, outlining with his thumb in the air the shape of your smile, analyzing the water and the crystal of your tears; and murmuring: "Not bad! Rather well!

sorriso, esamina l'acqua e il cristallo della tua lagrima; e mormora: "Non c'è male! Benino! Bene! Benissimo! Peggio però del tale! Anche meglio del tal altro! Primo! Secondo! Terzo! Poeta maggiore! Poeta minore!" Certo tu, se non sei un vanarello o un frignone, cancelli il sorriso, ribevi la lagrima, e te ne vai. Forse giuri in quel momento di non andare più da altri, e godere o piangere tra te, un'altra volta. Ma sei fanciullo, e torni sempre da capo, trovando però ogni volta che per i fanciulli non c'è più luogo in questo mondo! Il fatto è che, oltre la noia di quel sentirti sempre paragonato, come se tu facessi un esercizio scolastico, puoi provare anche l'amarezza d'essere posposto, con giudizio spiccio o maligno, e anche d'essere preposto, a tali che tu non ti sogni nemmeno di emulare, a tali a cui tu non pensavi nemmeno, a cui non dovevi, non potevi pensare, assorto come eri nel tuo piacere o nel tuo dolore. Ti paragoneranno con gli altri e anche con te stesso. Ti conteranno gli anni e le rughe agli occhi, e i capelli bianchi e non vedono l'ora di dirti che decadi, che rimbecillisci, che muori. Bella carità! E un bel giorno ti butteranno in un canto, dimenticandosi di te, e a torto. A torto sempre, perché ciò che hai fatto di buono, non deve essere annullato da ciò che poi faccia di men buono; e perché non può nascere mai un portento tale da far dimenticare quelli che prima di lui trovarono pur una mica di poesia. Sia grande quanto si voglia il poeta che si aggiunge al canone, egli deve sedere su una seggiola, o vogliam dire trono, sola: non ha bisogno di due o di tutte, e che un altro o tutti gli altri si rizzino e se ne vadano.

La gloriola non è per te fanciullo! La poesia pura, quando si legge, fa che il lettore volgare dica: "Come si potrebbe far meglio e più!" È vero che codesta è illusione d'ornatista... E io penso ai panforti fiorati che sono tanto più belli, e si contemplano così a lungo; ma finalmente gli ornati si gettano e si mangia il panforte solo.

Tuttavia ricordati, anche per via di questo esempio fanciullesco del panforte fiorato, che generalmente si ammira e loda quel che sta sopra, non quello ch'è sotto. Ricordati che la poesia vera fa battere, se mai, il cuore, non mai le mani.

Well done! Fine! Worse, however, than so and so! Also better than such and such! First! Second! Third! Major poet! Minor poet!" Surely, unless you are quite vain or a whiner, you wipe off your smile, swallow your tears, and go away. Maybe, at that moment, you swear not to go and talk to others any more, and to laugh or cry by yourself once more. But you are a child and always do it all over again, even though each time you find that there is no more place for children in this world! The fact is that, besides the nuisance of hearing yourself always being compared to others, as if you were doing a classroom exercise, you may feel even the bitterness of being put behind, with quick or nasty judgment, or even of being put ahead of some you do not even dream of emulating, some you never even thought about, some about whom you should not, you could not have thought, absorbed as you were in your pleasure or in your pain. They will compare you with others and even with yourself. They will count your years and the wrinkles around your eyes, and your white hair, and they cannot wait to tell you that you are declining, that you are growing stupid, that you are dying. Fine charity! And some day they will cast you aside, forgetting you, and unjustly! Always unjustly, because the good that you have done should not be nullified by the less good you may do after; and because no prodigy can ever be born such as to make us forget those who before him found a merest crumb of poetry. Great as may be the poet who is added to the canon, he must still sit only on one chair, or throne perhaps, but he has no need for two or all of them, nor does he need for one or all the others to get up and leave.

This petty fame is not for you, child! Pure poetry, when it is read, makes the common reader say: "How much more, how much better one could do!" It is true that such is the illusion of the decorator... And I think of the prettily decorated fruitcakes which are so very beautiful, and are looked at for so long: but in the end the ornaments are thrown away and only the cake itself is eaten. At any rate, remember, even through this childlike example of the decorated fruitcake, that generally what is on top, and not what is underneath, is admired and praised. And remember that true poetry makes your heart beat, perhaps, but it never makes your hands clap.

XVIII

Dunque... Ma intendo. Tu non aspiri alla gloriola, ma alla gloria; e così distingui, come se la gloriola fosse tra i vivi, e la gloria dopo morte. Non voglio dirti (le tue illusioni mi sono care), non voglio dirti che dopo morte non sentiremo nulla, di ciò che si dice di noi. Sentirò o almeno sentirai: non rabbuiarti. Ma sentirai belle cose? Qui sta il punto. Prima di tutto: diranno nulla? Si ha fretta, ai nostri giorni, di vivere; e le visite ai camposanti fanno perder tempo. Ci si assorda, ai nostri giorni, con la nostra vita; e non è possibile udire lo stridio leggiero delle ombre. I morti, ai nostri giorni, non contano più. Un poeta disse che il dì della morte era il dì della lode; ma il detto, pochi anni dopo che fu detto, non era più vero; e il Prati stesso lo sa, se nel sepolcro qualcosa si sa! E questo oblio che preme subito i morti, non è, quanto ai letterati, senza ragione e senza giustizia. Noi letterati vogliamo in vita occupar troppo il mondo di noi. Se stessimo nel nostro angolo, se non ci sbracciassimo tanto nel mezzo della gente, se non vociassimo tanto, non avverrebbe questo compenso di silenzio dopo morte. Dunque, diranno nulla di te? E se mai, diranno bene e giusto? O credi che allora sarà cessata la mania della classificazione, l'artifizio della suggestione, la cecità del partito e della setta? Vedi: spesso i morti sono disturbati nel loro riposo, e tratti fuori per dare addosso ai vivi. Spessissimo. L'invidia sai in che forma si esercita per lo più. Tu dài a uno la debita lode in presenza d'alcuno. Questi conferma breve: poi a lungo si volta a lodare un altro, il quale può essere inferiore o superiore al tuo lodato, ma quasi sempre è morto. Ora tu, fanciullo, vorresti essere disseppellito a questo fine? Poiché sarai un'ombra, avresti piacere d'esser adoperato a far ombra a qualche buon fanciullo saldo, che viva e canti? Questo non ti piacerebbe: meglio dormire dimenticato. È meglio esser morto tutto, che continuare a comparire avanti i tribunali ad essere giudicato e classificato: tanto più, che i giudici si trasmettono, cursori che stanno eternamente fermi, le fiaccole de' loro giudizi.

Tu non vuoi giudizi: vuoi commozione, vuoi assenso, vuoi amore; e non per te, ma per la tua poesia. Ebbene morto che tu sia, se la tua voce fu pura, se fu la voce dell'anima e delle cose, non l'eco, o più fioca o più forte, d'altrui voce; ebbene codesta voce sarà inavvertita, quando non sia dimenticata. In vero se è spesso ripetuta, come forse è ragione, si fonderà

XVIII

Well then... But I understand. You do not aspire to petty fame, but to glory; and so you make a distinction, as if petty fame were to be for the living and glory after death. I do not want to tell you (your illusions are dear to me), I do not want to tell you that, after death, we shall not hear a thing of what is said about us. Oh, do not frown, I shall hear, or at least you will hear. But will you hear beautiful things? Here lies the problem. First of all: will they say anything? One is in such a great hurry to live, nowadays; and visits to the cemetery take up too much time. We become deaf, nowadays, with the life we live; and it is not possible to hear the soft whispering of the shadows. Nowadays the dead do not count any more. A poet said that the day of death was the day of praise; but the statement, a few years after it was made, was no longer true; and Prati himself knows it, if indeed anything is known after death! And this oblivion which immediately bears down on the dead, is not without reason or justice when it comes to the literary people. We men of letters, while alive, want too much of the world's attention. If we stayed in our corner, if we did not struggle so much among people, if we did not shout so much, this recompense of silence after death would not take place. So, will they say anything about you? And if so, will they say good and right things? Or do you believe that by that time the mania for classification, the artifice of suggestion, the blindness of party or sect will have ceased to exist? Look: often the dead are disturbed in their rest and called forth to chastise the living. It happens quite often. You know the form envy takes for the most part. You duly praise a person in the presence of somebody. The latter supports you briefly; then he starts to praise at great length somebody else, who may be inferior or superior to the one you praised, but who almost always is dead. Now you, child, would you want to be exhumed for this purpose? Since you will be a shade, would you like to be used to overshadow some good sturdy child, alive and singing? This you would not like: better to sleep, forgotten. It is better to be totally dead, than to continue to appear from time to time before the courts to be judged and classified: especially because the judges, ever unchanging in their office, pass on to one another the torches of their judgments.

You do not want judgments, you want emotion, recognition, love; and not for you, but for your poetry. Well then, after your death, if your voice was pure, if it was the voice of your soul and of things, and not the echo, weaker or stronger, of someone else's voice; well, your voice will go unnoticed if not forgotten. In truth, if it is repeated often, as perhaps it

col tempo, non so se nel silenzio o rumore circostante: come il cinguettio delle rondini sotto la tua grondaia, che quando è un pezzo che lo senti, non lo senti più...

Tu vuoi parlare? Aspetta: non ho finito.

A ogni modo perché dovrebbe essere altrimenti? Che cosa fai tu, veramente, che sia degno di lode e di gloria? Tu ridi, tu piangi: che merito in ciò? Se credi d'averci merito, è segno che ridi e piangi apposta: se lo fai apposta, non è poesia la tua: se non è poesia, non hai diritto a lode. Tu scopri, s'è detto; non inventi: e ciò che scopri, c'era prima di te e ci sarà senza te. Vorresti scriverci il tuo nome su? Ti adiri, che ti vogliano giudicare e anche premiare per quello che non è se non la tua natura e la tua manifestazione di vita. Dunque che importa a te del nome?

XIX

IL FANCIULLO

Il nome? Il nome? L'anima io semino,
ciò ch'è di bianco dentro il nocciolo,
che in terra si perde,
ma nasce il bell'albero verde.

Non lauro e bronzo voglio; ma vivere;
e vita è il sangue, fiume che fluttua
senz'altro rumore,
che un battito, appena, del cuore.

Nei cuori, io voglio, resti un mio palpito,
senz'altro vanto che qual d'un brivido
che trema su l'acque
fa il sasso che in fondo vi giacque.

Nell'aria, io voglio, resti un mio gemito:
se l'assiuolo geme voglio essere
tra i salci del rio
anch'io, nelle tenebre, anch'io.

rightly is, your voice in time will blend, I do not know whether in silence or in the surrounding noise: just like the chirping of the swallows under your roof gutter, which, when you have heard it for a good long while, you do not hear it any more...

You want to speak? Wait, I have not finished.

At any rate, why should it be otherwise? What do you really do that is worthy of praise and glory? You laugh, you cry: what is your merit in this? If you believe there is some merit in it, then it is a sign that you are laughing and crying on purpose; if you do do it on purpose, yours is not poetry; if it is not poetry, you have no claim to praise. You discover, as we said, you do not invent: and what you discover was there before you and will be there without you. You would like to write your name over it? You get upset that they should want to judge you and even praise you for what is nothing but your nature and your manifestation of life. Well, what do you care about the name?

XIX

THE CHILD

A name? A name? The soul I sow, the soul,
that which is white within the fruit pit,
that gets lost in the soil,
but bears the handsome green tree

Neither laurel and bronze do I want; but to live:
and life is the blood, a river that flows
with no other sound,
but the faint beat of the heart.

In people's hearts, I want a throb of mine to linger,
with no other claim, than that of a shiver
rippling over the waters,
made by the stone that fell to the bottom.

In the air, I want a moan of mine to linger:
if the owl moans I want to be
among the willows of the brook,
I too, in the darkness, I too.

Se le campane piangono piangono,
io nelle opache sere invisibile
voglio essere accanto
di quella che piange a quel pianto.

Io poco voglio; pur, molto: accendere
io su le tombe mute la lampada
che irraggi e conforti
la veglia dei poveri morti.

Io tutto voglio; pur, nulla: aggiungere
un punto ai mondi della Via Lattea,
nel cielo infinito;
dar nuova dolvezza al vagito.

Voglio la vita mia lasciar, pendula
ad ogni stelo, sopra ogni petalo,
come una rugiada
ch'esali dal sonno, e ricada

nella nostr'alba breve. Con l'iridi
di mille stille sue nel sole unico
s'annulla e sublima...
lasciando più vita di prima.

XX

— Bene! Dunque riassumo, come uomo serio che sono. La poesia, per ciò stesso che è poesia, senz'essere poesia morale, civile, patriottica sociale, giova alla moralità alla civiltà, alla patria, alla società. Il poeta non deve avere, non ha, altro fine (non dico di ricchezza, non di gloriola o di gloria) che quello di riconfondersi nella natura, donde uscì, lasciando in essa un accento, un raggio, un palpito nuovo, eterno, suo. I poeti hanno abbellito agli occhi, alla memoria, al pensiero degli uomini, la terra, il mare, il cielo, l'amore, il dolore, la virtù; e gli uomini non sanno il loro nome. Ché

If the bells cry out and cry out,
in the inky dark evenings,
I want to be, unseen, near
the woman who weeps at that crying.

Little do I want; and yet much: to light up
on the silent graves, the lamp
that shines forth and comforts
the vigil of the poor departed.

All do I want; and yet nothing: to add
a small speck to the realms of the Milky Way,
in the infinite sky;
to give new sweetness to the primal birthing

I want to leave my life behind; hanging from
every blade of grass, on every petal,
like a dew which
is given off by sleep, and falls back

into our own brief dawning. With the halos
of its thousand droplets in the one sun
it fades off and shines bright...
leaving more life than before.

XX

Fine! Then let me summarize, like the serious man I am. Poetry, for the very fact that it is poetry, without being moral, civic, patriotic, or social poetry, is beneficial to morality, civilization, nation, and society. The poet need not have, does not have, any end other (I do not say of wealth, or petty fame, or glory) than that of blending once more with the nature from which he issued forth, leaving in it an accent, a ray, a throb that is new, eternal, his. Poets have beautified for the eyes of men, for their memory and their thoughts, the earth, the sea, the sky and love and grief and virtue; yet men do not know their names. For the names they say or

i nomi che essi dicono e vantano, sono, sempre o quasi sempre, d'epigoni, d'ingegnosi ripetitori, di ripulitori eleganti, quando non siano nomi senza soggetto. Quando fioriva la vera poesia; quella, voglio dire, che si trova, non si fa, si scopre, non s'inventa; si badava alla poesia e non si guardava al poeta: se era vecchio o giovane, bello o brutto, calvo o capelluto, grasso o magro: dove nato, come cresciuto, quando morto. Siffatte quisquilie intorno alla vita del poeta si cominciarono a narrare a studiare a indagare, quando il poeta stesso volle richiamare sopra sé, l'attenzione e l'ammirazione che è dovuta soltanto alla poesia. E fu male. E il male ingrossa sempre più. I poeti dei nostri tempi sembrano cercare, invece delle gemme che ho detto, e trovare, quella vanità che è la loro persona. Non codesta quei primi. E tu, fanciullo, vorresti fare quello che fecero quei primi, col compenso che quei primi n'ebbero; compenso che tu reputi grande, perché sebbene non nominati, i veri poeti vivono nelle cose le quali, per noi, fecero essi.[32]

È così? —

. . . .

Sì.

---

[32] Il lettore ha già veduto da sé, né tuttavia è inutile che glielo faccia meglio notare io, che questi pensieri sulla poesia, più che una confessione che a volte sarebbe orgogliosa e vanitosa, sono veri e propri moniti a me stesso, che sono ben lontano dal fare ciò che pur credo sia da fare!

vaunt, are, always or almost always, the names of epigones, of clever repeaters, of elegant refiners, when they are not names without substance. When true poetry flourished — I mean to say the kind that is found, not made, discovered, not invented — poetry was what mattered and not the poet. No one cared if he was old or young, handsome or ugly, bald or with a full head of hair, fat or thin: where he was born, how he had grown up, when he died. Such trifling details about the life of the poet began to be told, studied, analyzed when the poet himself sought to draw upon himself the attention and the admiration due only to poetry. And it was bad. And the evil is constantly growing. The poets of our time seem to be seeking, and to find, not the gems I have talked about, but the vanity that is their own self. This was not the case with those first poets. And you, Child, would like to do what those first poets did, with the reward they received for it; a reward that you hold great, because, though unnamed, true poets live in the things they made for us.[32]

Is it not so?

....

Yes.

---

[32] The reader has already noticed on his own, and yet it is not useless for me to bring it even more to his attention, that these thoughts on poetry, more than a confession, which would be, at times, vain and presumptuous, are really admonitions to myself, since I am quite far from doing what, in faith, I truly believe should be done.

THE ETERNAL CHILD

To understand poetry we must be capable
of donning the child's soul like a magic cloak
and of forsaking man's wisdom for the child's.

Johan Huizinga, *Homo Ludens*

Il fanciullino has been read traditionally as Pascoli's intimate testament and a
personal and insightful commentary on his poetry.[1] I would like to present
this essay not only as the outline of a general literary theory, the way the
poet intended it, but also as a delightful accident, free and independent in
spirit and structure, involving the risk as well as the beauty of spontaneous
meditation. Here, Giovanni Pascoli the adult man, the critic, the professor
and scholar of classical and modern letters, encounters Giovanni Pascoli
the poet and his Eternal Child. Each one offers the Child his thoughts and
findings, but it is the Child who ultimately expresses them, responding to
the flight of his own naive imagination and to the power of his sentiments.

Hence, the unusual style of the discourse: a prose that is
unpretentious, unscholarly, obviously not academic, frequently interrupted
by lyrical digressions. There are too many adjectives for a theoretical work
on a topic as ponderous as a formulation of aesthetics, too many
exclamation points, too entreating a tone.[2]

---

[1] This reading is perfectly valid and is corroborated by the poet himself. Pascoli
openly claims that creativity is not a mysterious phenomenon that transcends
rational faculties and defies lucid understanding. On the contrary, it is an activity
consciously pursued like any other human endeavor. As such, he believes that the
artist should be the one best equipped to understand it in himself and to explain it
to others. Obviously, this is not always the case and the original theoretical
principles Pascoli offers us do not always guide his own artistic production when
they are not deliberately disclaimed.

[2] Notwithstanding a distinct flavor of improvisation, which warrants a certain
apprehension about his expertise as theoretician, and as University professor as
well, only a narrow-minded scholarship has prevented the identification of Pascoli's

Poetry, however, or at least what poetry in Pascoli's view should be, is, above all things, illumination and unpredictable dramatization of thoughts and feelings. Thus, we are invited to a two-act play organized around fairly distinct scenes (the essay is divided into twenty chapters) within a very open setting, heedless of the unities of time and space. Actors are the poets of all times and they pass in and out of focus, more or less anonymously. Antagonists are the non-poets of Pascoli's days, the unsympathetic critics incapable of seizing the poet's idea and of sharing his enthusiasm and illusion. The author who is staging the *mise en scène* steps out from an independent clause in chapter III, and, peremptorily, takes over the action, generating an essay-conversation, in the peculiar style of a short, semi-serious Platonic dialogue. A dialogue begins, in fact, in chapter IV and coordinates this mental adventure around three lines of force. Along the first line travels the silvery voice of the Eternal Child; along the second one move the considerations of the adult man. A third tangent connects these two voices to the mind of the implied reader, or listener, who is not a mere product of sentimental clichés and rhetorical devices but a cognitive and intentional necessity completing a pattern of ironic complicity.

In the dialogical structure of the essay,[3] the Child *per se* speaks only in verse and short monosyllables; his responses are often implied, echoed, summarized, and corrected by rhetorical questions: they are acts of

---

many contributions to the field of aesthetics. In other important prose works (namely in some of his discourses: "Il sabato," "La ginestra," "Eco di una notte mitica," "La mia scuola di grammatica"; in the Introductions to his *Anthologies* for the secondary schools; in the Prefaces to his poetic collections and in some of his University lectures) Pascoli reveals penetrating and original intuitions unsuspected and still underestimated. Basic among them are the abandonment of non-specific objectivity, and the restoration of the totality of sensory perceptions in constant and difficult balance with the symbolic.

[3] According to Michael Holquist, who introduces the translation of Bakhtin's *The Dialogic Imagination*, the critic's basic scenario for modeling the plurality of experiences is two people talking to each other in a specific dialogue at a particular time and in a particular space. Each of the two persons, as in much of Pascoli's work, would be a consciousness defining itself through specific choices: "Thus each will seek, by means of intonation, pronunciation, lexical choice, gesture, and so on, to send out a message to the other with a minimum of interference from the otherness constituted by pre-existing meanings (inhering in dictionaries or ideologies) and the otherness of the intentions present in the other person in the dialogue" (XX).

suspension in the stream of thought of the author. On the other hand, the adult man speaks in various modes; in long, meditative monologues and amusing fragments of memory; with tender appeals to the Child in order to find solace and recapture spontaneity; or with the authority, and the irony, of the consummate intellectual. The Child's voice and laughter are, indeed, a significant incentive, but Pascoli's mind is the unmistakable objective of all that follows, as he tells us emphatically: *you seem to me...; it appears to me...; I often speak to the Child within me, as he at times speaks to me, and to him I say...; I am content then, to state the matter between us, that is, between myself....*

Thus, *Il fanciullino* is an essay, part fantasy, part aesthetic inquiry, about the poet's mind meditating on the creative process. It is also a perpetual confession, sincere and, at the same time, contrived and literary. For Pascoli allows us to share with him his own aesthetic beliefs along with his sorrows and his joys. Thus it is obvious that the reflections in the first part of the treatise are meant to provide answers to the nagging ideas presented later on and focused on ambition or the desire for fame and recognition.

This is where we meet another powerful character-theme: Glory, with its effective variation: *gloriola,* the neologism Pascoli creates on a classical Latin pattern. The dialogue is, then, between the person Pascoli is and the person he would like to be, as is often the case of double-ness in literature.[4]

---

[4] The traditional view of man's soul pulled in different directions by its own different faculties, the god-like and the bestial elements everpresent in him, becomes in modern metapsychology the conflict betwen the id and the superego; the conventional double is often some kind of antithetical self: a guardian angel or a tempting devil. Whatever names are used, the artist seems to need such outlet of "polymorphous transformation" as he projects himself into his work. Schiller is often quoted in this connection as saying: "All creatures born by our fantasy, in the last analysis, are nothing but ourselves." And Walt Whitman speaks of the mystery of his own consciousness: "I cannot understand the mystery, but I am always conscious of myself as two." The examples are many and extremely varied since doubling may be subjective or objective, implied or explicit; it may occur by multiplication and division or as a defense mechanism and as allegory; it is born out of narcissism or confused self-identity and, always, for dramatic effect. An interesting and suggestive study privileging a psychoanalytic approach to the topic is Rogers' *The Double in Literature.*

When we begin to read *Il fanciullino*, the first element that attracts our attention is the predilection for the diminutive openly set, right from the start, with the title, and easily traceable all through this and others of Pascoli's prose and poetic works. It is a statement of [aesth]etics by which the author intends to challenge the universal, innate, and eternal obsession for greatness, quantity, and sophistication. In Pascoli's view, a strong ritual of self-imposed obligations binds our esteem to those who achieve positions of strength, success, and exceptional ability while the small, the powerless, or those who show weakness and modesty are ignored and easily forgotten. In such veneration for the powerful we may discern some surrogate of our desire for immortality, a way to hide the terror of inevitable decay and death. To this effect, we invent competitions and engage in activities that postulate victory and humiliation. Cruelty allows us to distance ourselves, emotionally, from loss and destruction.[5] Compassion, on the other hand, lessens the distance and makes us vulnerable. Therefore, we learn to justify every impulse towards growth and enrichment, we avoid all forms of contraction, reject quiet and silence and admire, instead, all excesses and senseless accumulations no matter how irrationally exaggerated. In order to invert such a fundamental axiology one would have to demonstrate that more is not better and that greater strength and greater quantity actually diminish health, efficiency, and duration. A poet like D'Annunzio may proclaim the value of constantly renewed aspirations. Pascoli advocates, instead, the poetics of "modest desires" not so much as an appeal to resignation, evangelically addressed to the humble or the poor in spirit, but rather as a defiant challenge of all forms of oppression and greed. With such intent, his position is clearly stated in the Preface to the *Poemi conviviali*, the most ambitious and elaborate of his poetic collections:

[...] oltre i mali necessari della vita, e che noi quali possiamo appena attenuare, quali nemmeno attenuare, vi sono altri mali che sono i soli veri mali, e questi sì possiamo abolire con somma e pronta facilità. Come? Col contentarci. Ciò che piace è sì il molto; ma il poco è ciò che appaga. Chi ha sete, crede che un'anfora non lo disseterebbe; e una coppa lo disseta. Ora ecco la sventura aggiunta del genere umano: l'assetato, perché crede che un'anfora non basti alla sua sete, sottrae agli altri assetati tutta l'anfora di cui berrà una coppa sola. Peggio ancora: spezza l'anfora, perché altri non beva, se egli non può bere. Peggio che mai, dopo aver

---

[5] The genesis and the dynamics of cruelty are thoroughly analyzed by Becker.

bevuto esso, sperde per terra il liquore perché agli altri cresca la sete e l'odio. E infinitamente peggio: si uccidono tra loro i sitibondi, perché non beva nessuno.

([...] in addition to the necessary hardships of life, some of which we can alleviate in part, some of which we cannot alleviate at all, there are other evils that are true evils, and these we can abolish with immediate and extreme ease. How? By being happy with what we have. Big things, many things are, yes, what we like; but little is enough to satisfy us. The one who is thirsty does not think that a whole jug of water could ever satisfy his thirst, and yet one cup does. Now, here is the evil that we add: the thirsty one, since he believes that a jug may not be enough for his thirst, takes away from all the other thirsty people the jug from which he will be able to drink only one cup. Worse yet: he breaks the jug so that others may not drink if he cannot. And even worse: after he drinks, he pours the liquid on the ground so that thirst and hatred may grow in the heart of others. And infinitely worse: all the people dying of thirst kill each other so that nobody may drink.)

(My translation)

Once they commit themselves to the pursuit of self-aggrandizement and celebrity, men become hopelessly ensnared. It follows that, in Pascoli's opinion, the true poetic feeling is all that can set "a light and gentle restraint on the unremitting desire that makes us perpetually run, full of wretched longing, in search of happiness" (*The Little Child*, VIII).[6] And in poems like "La vite e il cavolo" or "Ida e Maria," he renounces high purpose, lust, and strong passion. Moreover, he clearly sees that the ambitious artist pursuing *gloriola*, petty, pointless fame, covets a special place in the affection of his readers and critics, always afraid someone else may be there, some other younger, smarter, more popular poet. In his opinion, ambition is a hot and corrosive emotion, arising from pride and nourished on resentment; it is the "sickness" that deforms the soul of all those who strive for success. The temptation may be always present but it must be banished with pride. Such a struggle is revealed in the most confusing pages of the *Fanciullino*. In chapter XV, the impulsive switch of the subject pronouns seems to imply an exchange of roles and qualities between the mature poet and the Child, and marks the extent of the author's angry disappointment. Here, Pascoli attributes to the simple Child his own frustrated expectations, the tendency to waste precious time, waiver, and fall into futile endeavors. For a while it seems that all his attempts to replace ambition with self-contented solitude have been as deceptive and

---

[6] From now on, references to Pascoli's treatise will be identified with the initials *L.C.* followed by the roman number of the chapter.

disputable as ambition itself. Quickly, however, the poet eludes this moment of painful deadlock; the "you" becomes "I" again, deliberately repeated, as a suffered *confiteor.*

There perhaps is no sentiment in the world, not even greed for profit, so contrary to the spontaneity of the poet, as this lusting after petty fame, which often turns into a desire for power! When you are taken over by this sickness, you (but then, you are not involved here) — I, I do not seek the poetic, the good and the beautiful, but the loud and the showy. Oh, I do not look for pebbles, shells, and flowers along my road, but I stay up late, restless, poring over someone else's notebooks, or even reading over his shoulder what another author is writing.

(L.C., XV)

True greatness and recognition are another matter entirely. Undoubtedly such aspirations have been the wonderful vainglory of literature, its immense boast against death: I am stronger than death. I can speak about death in poetry, drama, the novel, because I have overcome it, because I am more or less permanent.... Pindar was the first man on record to state: *This poem will be sung when the city, which commissioned it, has ceased to exist.* And Pascoli himself cannot be as unaffected by the desire for immortality as his rational thoughts would lead us to believe. No matter how modestly,

The poet need not have, does not have, any end other [...] than that of blending once more with the nature from which he issued forth, leaving in it an accent, a ray, a throb that is new, eternal, his.

(L.C., XX)

or how proudly stated,

> [...] Ma se alcuno di loro, dallo stento
> della sua giovinezza, a poco a poco
> avesse alzato, oh! Non la fronte e il mento,
>
> ma il cuore! Il cuore! Se dalla sua creta
> insanguinata avesse tratto il fuoco!
> se fosse, quel mendico, ora un poeta!
>
> fosse un consolatore, egli cui niuno
> consolò! Fosse, il derelitto, un forte!
> un grande fosse l'orfano digiuno!...

Io sogno! Io sogno, o muto autor del male!
ma se di quelli che dannasti a morte
col padre loro, fosse, uno, immortale!

("Tra San Mauro e Savignano")[7]

In *The Little Child*, however, even the poet's desire for enduring glory has to remain secondary. What matters is the purity of the artistic inspiration, the joy and total absorption in the creative experience, sacred and important for its own sake.

Only the time of early childhood, not yet aware of death and daily striving, knows games without losers and winners, games that are played for the sheer pleasure of playing. Ambition never enters the contented privacy of the child's world. No thought of advantage to the self, and almost as little of benefiting others, come to disturb the child's imaginative play. How good it would be to attain that feeling again! To forget all about success and outside appreciation, and find pure enjoyment in the vision of a new world, in the charming realization of a new life! This is truly the message of the *Fanciullino* or, at least, the admonition to himself of the mature poet who is conscious that his own creative impulse is controlled, too often, by practical concerns if not by other less than lofty needs. The advice is simple, and not so carefully disguised: only those who forget the Child can be worried or embittered by lack of money, recognition or glory; if they become children again, the *poiein*, the playing will be joyous, serious, and self-rewarding; it will be the only end to itself. In his own case, Pascoli assures us, the Child has accompanied him through the various stages of life in a dynamic relationship that has not been interrupted:

And since, from the time in which we were children together I have lived a life to which not even grief, which was plentiful, has given great definition, I have almost never lost him from sight or hearing. Actually, since I have not changed those first feelings of mine, sometimes I even ask whether or not I have lived.   (*L.C.,* IV)

---

[7] "Between San Mauro and Savignano": "But if, from the hardship of his youth, one of them could, little by little, have lifted, oh not his brow or his chin, but his heart! His heart! If, from his bloody clay, one could have drawn fire! If that beggar were now a poet! if he, who never was consoled, could console others! If the derelict could indeed be strong! If the starving orphan could indeed be great! .... I am dreaming! I am dreaming! O silent perpetrator of evil! But if, among the ones that you damned to death with their father, just one might be immortal!"

Thus, this Child, whose image is never formally elaborated or explicitly fixed, is the result of the poet's continual attention to the world of the very young. There are different reasons at the root of this interest. Some are biographical and psychological, and they deserve critical inquiry. Pascoli was a teacher for most of his life;[8] he remained, throughout his life, a child of his family, a celibate, neurotically attached to his younger sister who was equally devoted to him. What I consider of interest, however, is to recognize the Child as the anthropological principle that sustains the poet's existential utopia as well as his *ars poetica*. From my point of view, the Child is the interpretive model adopted to underline the interaction between the self and the world. Through the Child, Pascoli moves beyond any real, historical, and even literary convention to an archetypal level where everything can begin afresh and new correspondences can be woven between the factual and the mythical. Accordingly, the adult must learn to re-appropriate specific cultural categories, re-organize his cognitive structures, begin anew a process of socialization, and, first and foremost, he must also re-integrate the child's modalities of perception inasmuch as they are more imaginative and more closely bound up with the rhythms of nature and creation. As we shall see, the major innovations of Pascoli's poetic language are modeled specifically after the verbal and attitudinal components of the style of early childhood. These include the creation of repetitive practices, the acute sense of the musicality of word and line, and the special sweetness of tone and timbre.

Through the Child, then, Pascoli proposes to re-create and revive: first the body, then the soul, then the metaphysical order. Such a conviction is firm and clear in his mind since the very beginning of his meditation on the creative process. We know that the earliest elaboration of Pascoli's poetics goes back to his student years at the University of Bologna (1876-80). We find here a first reference to the Child as poetry and as

---

[8] Pascoli dedicates the collection entitled *Nuovi Poemetti* (1909) to his young students of Matera, Massa, Livorno, Messina, Pisa, and Bologna with words that are as serious as they are heartfelt: "To you to whom I owe much more than I have given. Because it is to you that I owe the practice of keeping before me when I write, as I do before me when I speak, youthful souls that is a duty, and a sacred duty, not to let down, not to turn to ice, not to violate. This is how you have blessed me. This is why I am happy to have combined with divine poetry the human activity that is most in accordance with poetry: teaching."

anthropological construct. One passage seems to outline the profile of the ideal poet:

Tutte le poesie hanno un legame tra loro. È *l'enfant du siècle* che si è perduto nella notte dei secoli: sente voci strane e terribili e ad ora ad ora una melodia di lire eolie e di liuti. Tutto gli si vivifica intorno: le nuvole sembrano guerrieri: gli alberi sembrano dèi… Le memorie del passato brulicano per dove passa e le ombre conversano con lui. Egli è oppresso da tanta vitalità esteriore e si lascia trascinare fuori del presente: egli si trova tra un sogno e una visione, tra il passato e l'avvenire: ma la visione è incerta e vaporosa: colora appena d'oro i lembi delle sue meditazioni angosciose. La poesia che ne nasce è perciò soggettiva; ma l'oggettivo per lo più prende il sopravvento. Il poeta non afferma, non scopre, non prova nulla. Egli rende una sensazione che ha subita come l'ha subita; è la malattia dell'astrazione che è comune ai poeti primitivi. Egli astrae dal mondo piccolo-borghese e si lancia come un falco nelle lande misteriose illuminate dalla calma luce crepuscolare.[…] Io astraggo dal mondo d'oggi come astrae chi sogna senza mancare alla verità: rintraccio in certo modo il vecchio uomo, le vecchie vestigia umane, per spiegarmi la natura umana. La mia concezione la ritengo grande in questo: che io non rinnego dell'umanità nemmeno i morti, e che ne raccolgo religiosamente le ceneri, per porle nel vaso cinerario scolpito da fine scalpello nel luminoso alabastro dell'arte.[9]

(All poems have a tie that binds them. It is the *enfant du siècle* who has lost himself in the infinite night of the centuries: he hears voices terrible and strange, and, from time to time, a melody of aeolian lyres and lutes. Everything becomes alive around him: the clouds are warriors: the trees are gods. Memories of the past flock together everywhere he goes, and the shadows converse with him. He is oppressed by such external vitality, and willingly abandons the present: he finds himself between dream and vision, between past and future: but his vision is indefinite and foggy: it only outlines with gold his tormented meditations. The poetry born of them is, thus, subjective but the objective prevails for the most part. The poet does not state, does not discover, does not demonstrate anything. He renders a sensation he has felt just as he felt it; it is the malady of abstraction typical of primitive poets. He abstracts from the petit-bourgeois world and, like a hawk, flings himself into mysterious, barren lands lighted by the calm light of dusk. [...] I abstract from today's world as does one who dreams, without betraying truth: I trace man back to what he was, I find the oldest vestiges of man, in order to understand human nature. I consider my conception great because of this: I do not forsake even the

---

[9] Quoted in C. Salinari, "Momenti della poetica e ideologia pascoliana," in *Studi per il centenario della nascita di Giovanni Pascoli*, published fifty years after the poet's death in Bologna. (101-18). The unpublished notebooks are examined by Schinetti.

dead of humanity; I religiously collect their ashes, and place them in urns carved by fine chisels in the luminous alabaster of art.)

(My translation)

It is noteworthy that one of the notions of Symbolist poetics, here so ornately summarized, will become the foundation of Pascoli's aesthetics and creativity: poetry must be detached from all historical events and all social constraints and transported in the heaven of Platonic ideas. The Things of nature and the Things of the inner mind live forever, for the poets of all times, because they are a reflection of what was before them. The divine gift of the artist, his elusive and uncanny privilege, is to see things in this light. Pascoli quickly rejects, instead, the idea of distant realms and exotic *realia* in favor of the opposite conviction that poetry lies in what is close and familiar to all, and that the poet has to find it there. In fact, he appears convinced that meaning may lie only in the Words that each language uses to name Things and that the very sounds of the words have the power to make things exist and have meaning. Those humble things of everyday life, in their solid and precise location, speak to him in a disquieting mode. Their voices are terrible and strange; they arrive from far off distances of time and space and have roots in an obscure and timeless world.

These ideas constitute a radically new viewpoint on the process of creativity. As a result, Pascoli's poetry grounds abstract thoughts in a concreteness of imagery and experience that is meant to assure them full connection with reality. This reality, however, is uncertain and elusive even when it is forcefully pursued and precisely represented. Such a paradox (which is only an apparent one) is the best way to define Pascoli's effort to reach a new dimension of consciousness; in fact, the crossing or interrelation of the two modes, the abstract and the concrete, should not suggest the creation of a hybrid, evasive medley. On the contrary, it provides the structure for a particular poetry of meditation, where meditation is intended as the imaginative activity that addresses and challenges both the senses and the intellect. This is the reason the study of the Child, linked to an investigation of the mythical origins of culture, becomes part of a resolute project, contradictory and not fully realized — the project of an unconventional epic outlining not the hero's but every man's passage in time. According to such a model, life's journey begins with the perceptual and emotional experiences by which every child comes in touch with his own primary nature, and continues through a process of radical alienation from the world and the self. Latent in the destination of

the journey, and potentially implied through it all, is the encounter with death.

The poet's first and uppermost purpose remains, however, the process of learning and understanding, based firmly on the two formative forces Pascoli recognizes as central in his own life: nature and literature. As he states in the *Fanciullino*, the poet-child is the one who, looking to the most remote beginnings, faces the reality of primal things: the hours of the day, the seasons of the year; hunger and sleep; love and reproduction; sickness and death; solitude and dreams.

The world is born to everyone who is born to the world. And herein is the mystery of your essence and of your function. You are most ancient, Child! And very old is the world which you see ever new

(*L.C.*, V)

Hence the declaration that the poet does not invent or discover; rather, he finds truths that are always the same and always new. Historical events are of secondary importance. Behind them lies the reality of the psyche with the visions that give us a sense of destiny. These are the things that we remember when we want to reconstruct the history of our soul, our own momentous encounters. The symbols that Pascoli deems to be "dictated by the god speaking within" are the ones that make us face the moral significance of our existence, and seal the conquest of our autonomy. They always allude to the psychological realities that give importance to the facts of ordinary life. Small things and modest ambitions presuppose, then, a very different scope. The detail, that little something the poet is able to perceive — "poetry consists of the vision of an unnoticed detail, outside or inside ourselves" (*L.C., XIV*) — is there to throw light on the universal. To this end, every careful observer of the infant and the young child may become a seer and a magic interpreter of what relates to the origins of awareness in the individual and in the species. If he keeps within himself the qualities of the child and the memories of his own childhood, he can be the most eccentric visionary and the most accurate beholder of what surrounds him. His imagination is illumined by colors, made up of sounds, intrigued by movement, and always connected to the simplest and strongest emotions.

Certainly, in the geography of our psyche, the place where life is perceived as a sequence of meaningful events is that of one's own youth.

All the things that happened in youth are good and are remembered as such: the things seen, the sounds heard, the games played, the books read.[10] The antagonist of the child is not the old man, with whom, on the contrary, there is amity and affinity, but the logical and virile adult. Adulthood in general, and especially the adulthood of the poet (when he betrays his childlike nature) is marked by hypocrisy, sterility, and compromise.

Pascoli's little Child, however, is not only an ideal of innocence and purity. On the contrary, it progressively abandons the Romantic and romanticized view of the nineteenth century to reveal a very different dimension of childhood. He still is a reserve of vitality and hope. His outlook on life and his fundamental spontaneity are essential. But openness, resiliency, pleasure-seeking, and trust are not considered only as the capacities that got us started in life; they are survival traits that must be retained within. Curiously enough, in Pascoli's view, consent and obedience to the dreams and visions with which every child develops a prompt and intense familiarity are the only defense against the power of the irrational. The function of the poet, then, is to provide stories to the adult in order to restore the sense of wonder and spontaneity he knew as a child. Even more importantly, Pascoli's Eternal Child is the carrier of elemental memory and the connecting thread to all that was "in the beginning" and that as such we may call "original." Consequently, it should be obvious that whatever Pascoli says about the child and about childhood is not at all about child and childhood. Benedetto Croce grossly misrepresents the poet when he criticizes him for ascribing the data of his own biographical experience to

---

[10] The myth of the child is amply represented in all of Pascoli's work. Not only is the child the myth inspiring Pascoli's aesthetic and critical essays, but the myth is also a physical and symbolic presence of great intensity in his poetry and the implied and intended reader of many poems and stories: "Pin," "La Befana," "La povera piccina," for example. The child is also the direct receiver and the young student of literature, to whom Pascoli dedicates his early Readers (*Sul limitare, Limpido rivo*) and his anthologies: *Epos* and *Lyra*. These works are of great importance to Pascoli, who believes that what is read during the school years remains part of one's soul forever. As suggested as early as 1937 (Manara Valgimigli), Pascoli's anthologies are a strong indication of his poetics since they reflect not only his own predilections and taste but also the reasons for his own way of looking at the things of the world and at the words of the books. Much closer to Croce's ideal critic than Croce himself, Pascoli cares for pure poetry only and reads what he likes because "it speaks to his soul," awakening forgotten emotions.

the ideal childhood of mankind. On the contrary, no matter how vividly personalized his own memories may be, Pascoli uses them, intentionally, as channels of communication with the life of others, and with the things, small and large, of the universe. From this viewpoint, the novel features of this Child anticipate many ideas brought forth later by the speculative investigation of the new sciences.

What is the Child

Modernity claims that the foundation of anthropology be inherently literary. At the end of the nineteenth century, however, mythical themes were revitalized by the contribution of the developing sciences of ethnography and psychoanalysis. In addition, anthropologists and archetypal psychologists began an investigation of the phenomenology of mythical figures that has proven of interest for literary criticism. According to their research, all the gods of classical antiquity personify primordial syndromes that act as mediators between the particular world of the conscious *ego* and the network of instinctual behaviors. Therefore, original myths are links to the unconscious and manifest what cannot be otherwise articulated.[11]

Myths were once the songs and chants that accompanied ritual gestures and dances. As they gradually separated from their immediate connection to ceremonial enactment, they left unexpressed a dimension of the archetype. Jungian hermeneutics identifies an alternate approach to fulfill the enactment of myths in the creative play of the imagination which is the natural language of the soul. A great deal of poetry, indeed of all creativity, seeks to recreate, disguise, or diagram different forms of the mythical or the visionary in order to rediscover the significance of each original model.

The child is one of these models and its archetype follows us like a shadow. It is a mystery based on the wonder of continuing transformation, and, as such, it populates the structures of what we have learned to call the collective unconscious with specific, remarkable, and recognizable images. These images, which are neglected and ignored when we embrace "the armor of maturity," recur with extraordinary precision in Pascoli's theoretical writings and in his poetry. Long before the elaboration of Jung

---

[11] Mircea Eliade confirms the centrality of symbolic thinking in the process of myth-making also from the perspective of the historian of religion. Images, symbols, and myths respond to a need to fill a function that comes well before language and discursive reasoning. Myths bring to light aspects of reality that defy any other means of understanding. All men and women carry within themselves a great deal of the prehistory of humanity.

and Kerényi,[12] Pascoli's *Eternal Child* appears, in fact, as a complex system of meanings that is conceived to be *active in the present* in order to compensate and correct the extravagant uni-dimensionality of the conscious mind. The pre-logical or anthropomorphic language of the child, rich in symbols and analogies, touches the core of the individual personality and connects it to the collective and transcendent meaning of the archetype. Pascoli states this idea with effective simplicity:

Child, who can only reason in your own way, a childlike way which we call deep, because suddenly, without making us go down the steps of thought one at a time, you plunge us into the abyss of truth....

(*L.C.,* IV)

Poetry is, then, the supreme tool of cognition, since emotion and imagination, not reason, are considered the way to higher truths. Implicit in this notion is the belief that once we know how to use our imagination, we become freer, more independent human beings, capable of progressing beyond reality itself in order to face the constant mutability of life.

Some elements of the child archetype lend an uncanny modernity to Pascoli's portrait. According to Jung, the Child is primordially perfect, and therefore does not develop. Every impulse toward transcendence is lived, however, within the family complex. The child is also the innocent and the naïve; it is all that is abandoned and vulnerable, and yet it represents a most mysterious power, which is curiously linked to an idea of poverty considered to be lack of pride and ambition. We remember that, in the same sense, poverty is attributed to Eros in Plato's *Symposium*,[13] and is identified as the prerequisite for eternal salvation in the Christian tradition.

---

[12] See Jung and Kerényi, *Essays on a Science of Mythology.* In *Psychology of the Child Archetype* (1940), Jung states that the "empirical idea 'child' is the means by which we can express a psychic fact that cannot be formulated more exactly. The mythological idea of the child refers to all that is abandoned, exposed, and is, at the same time, divinely powerful; it is the insignificant dubious beginning and the triumphal end [...] It is an imponderable that determines the ultimate worth or worthlessness of a personality" (CW 9,1 # 300).

[13] In the *Symposium*, Eros is the son of poverty and plenty, a mortal and a god: "always poor and far from being sensitive and beautiful, as more people imagine, he is hard and weather-beaten, shoeless and homeless, always sleeping out for want of a bed, on the grounds, on doorsteps, and in the streets" (trans. W. Hamilton, New York: Penguin Books, 1951: 82).

Indeed, if the original sin of man has been his disobedient pride and independence, the child, detached as he is from the mundane values of greed and calculating intellect, becomes also the ideal Christian model. In fact, in the words of the Gospel, the little children are the ones who will enter the kingdom of God by virtue of their weakness, trust, and fragility.

In Pascoli's treatise, we encounter repeatedly the three symbols: Child (i.e., Poetry)-Poverty-Eros and the complex ideas that they exemplify, often appearing together:

The poet is the beggar of mankind, often he is also blind and old. And if he does not look it, if he is, in fact, a rich man, and young, and happy, well, then, it means that though he himself may be rich: *pauperculus*, however, is the Child within him; that is, he has remained poor, that is to say he has remained a child. Because the child is always somewhat poor, even though he be born in a golden cradle, and he always stretches out his hand to everything and everyone, as if he had nothing and he wants the morsel of hard bread of his down-trodden companion, and would like to do the hard work of his afflicted friend.

(*L.C.,* IX)

The Jungian *puer* is also spontaneous and impatient. He does not seem aware of time passing and acts a-synchronically. In his isolation, he develops the narcissistic attitudes of the *ego*, the hermaphroditic and angelic qualities where masculine and feminine are closely entangled. Relations are superfluous, and so is a woman unless she is a magic eternal-child herself, or a maternal figure admiring and loving without conditions and without questions.[14] In childhood, as in every beginning, all things are meaningful and exciting; every child is easily stimulated to questioning, constantly eager for answers. In Pascoli's view, moreover, the child is resolutely linked to the old man:

---

[14] Nothing is ever fixed in the mercurial disposition that dominates the child archetype. On the contrary, everything is in the making and the psychodynamic of natural impulses effects constant changes. The negative *puer* may become frantically active, rebellious, and totally unrelated. Fascinated by all that is new, original, physical, and adventurous, he rejects history, social rules, and commitments. In psychoanalysis the *puer aeternus* complex is cured by a therapy intended to verify intuitions, limit the fantasy life, and direct energy toward productivity and sexuality toward a meaningful relationship. Rather obviously, the negative strength of the *puer* archetype is linked to the particular feebleness and insecurity that marks the beginning and end of every effort (Hillmann, *Senex and Puer*).

If one had to represent Homer, one would have to portray him old and blind, led by the hand of a little child incessantly speaking while looking all around.

(L.C., I)

It is the two figures, *together*, that represent poetry and the term "vecchi fanciulli" ("old children") which finds echoes in Curtius' *puer senilis* or *puer senex* (98-101), recurs frequently in Pascoli's poetry and prose work. In our text, we know that speaking to the Child is the suffering, rational adult, oppressed by duties and held down by his own insecurities and contradictory desires. Accompanying the Child, however, is the wisest old man. The *senex* comes to join the *puer*.[15] In archetypal psychology, the one is personified by young Hermes, playful, immutable, and in love with language; the other by Saturn-Kronos, the benevolent god of nature and agriculture, the ruler of the Golden Age of happiness and abundance, but also the exiled and solitary god who has lost his kingdom, the God of Death and of the Dead.[16] Both aspects of the archetype see the world *sub*

---

[15] In the essay already quoted, Hillmann underlines the importance of the cult of the Mighty Ones in Samothraki: a pair of unequal male figures: a bearded God-figure together with a young boy. They have been imagined to be mortal and immortal, divine and human, initiated and uninitiated, cultural and natural. The pair of the Mighty Ones points directly to a double structure of consciousness.

[16] Saturn is the father of the gods and of men, but he is also the one who devoured his children, the eater of raw flesh. Among the gods of the Greek Olympus he is the one who presents the most disconcerting contradictions. The saturnine attitude presupposes that the basic elements of our character are limited, innate, and subject to destiny. What derives from it is a pessimistic view of the human condition: fatally doomed, imprisoned, and bonded forever, its only wisdom is the capacity for suffering and enduring. His relation with sexuality is also considered double. On the one side, being arid and impotent he is the protector of bachelors and eunuchs; on the other, represented in the dog and the lascivious goat, he is the god of fertility, the god of the productive earth bearing fruits. Saturn, however, is associated mainly with loneliness and lack of relationships; he does not have children or parents, and he presides over births in order to devour the newborn. Totally immutable he devours his own possibilities of change. Psychologically the *senex* governs the final stages of every process. This is why he is often associated with the biological decline of old age and the completion of natural phases: harvest, winter, night, sleep. The archetype, however, goes well beyond such immediate associations and appears as the potential for order, meaning and teleological accomplishment within the psyche. Of greater interest for the present essay is the

specie aeternitatis. One goes through life with the half-hearted and distant gaze of the melancholic; the other observes the world from within, as the divine spark in touch with the essence of all things. Here is then the double presence of *puer-senex* in man: the "I" who knows history and myths, time and space, feelings and actions, as the other "I":

the one who in the daylight dreams or appears to dream, remembering things he has never seen; the one who talks to the animals, the trees, the stones, the clouds, the stars: the one who fills the shadows with ghosts and the sky with gods [...] the one who cries and laughs without cause, at things that escape our senses and our reason.

(*L.C.,* III)

This double presence is indicated by the dramatic quality of the essay, by the structural device of a conversation, at times explicit, at times hidden, between an "I" and a "you," for the most part; but also between a "we" and a "you" in the plural, or an "I" and a "you" in the plural. On discussing the unique "subjectivity," or lack of predetermined referentiality, of the personal pronouns Emile Benveniste underlines their special function in the "reality of discourse":

"I" cannot be defined except in terms of "locution," not in terms of objects as a nominal sign is. "I" signifies "the person who is uttering the present instance of the discourse containing I." [...] it is a fact both original and fundamental that these "pronominal" forms do not refer to "reality" or to "objective" positions in space or time but to the utterance, unique each time, that contains them, and thus they reflect their proper use. The importance of their function will be measured by the nature of the problem they serve to solve, which is none other than that of intersubjective communication. [...] Their role is to provide the instrument of a conversion that one could call the conversion of language into discourse. It is by identifying himself as a unique person pronouncing "I" that each speaker sets himself up in turn as the "subject."[17]

---

assumption, stressed by the psychologists and intuited by Pascoli, that the *senex* is responsible for the creative energy of the individual *only* in connection with the *puer.* As a matter of fact, if the *senex* is separated from the *puer* component, creative isolation turns into paranoid solitude, and attained knowledge becomes the petrified condition of what has no contact with life.

[17] Implicit in all this is the idea that all transcription systems are inadequate to the multiplicity of the meanings they seek to convey. We may think we are expressing

In *The Little Child* and in Pascoli's poetry, the "I" is often, but not always, the poet, as the child who speaks in his heart; it is the artist who can proclaim to be strong and immortal. Conversely, the "you" is man, in his ceaseless and vain pursuit of meaning and ideals. At other times, the "you" in the singular is the wise old man to whose sensibility the world appears once again as it was in early childhood — obscure, troubled, and resplendent. In this case, as in the case of what has been labeled *cosmic poetry*, all oppositions disappear, the child and the old man are truly one in the same bewildered contemplation of the universe, and the poetic word assumes a clarity and a softness that transfigures reality itself. On the aesthetic level, attributes of the child are the spontaneous and immediate expression, the home-oriented sentiments, the lack of reflection and analysis. The little Child is the alogical, deeply instinctual element in man, ingenuous and perennially wondering. When he identifies creativity with originality, imagination, play, and spontaneity, Pascoli responds to the influence of the child as archetype. These gifts, however, can be resurrected to remember and to sing, *after* the great turmoil of the senses, only by the adult poet, who is the result of centuries of culture, discipline, and hard work. In order to eliminate this discrepancy, Pascoli links the two elements together. Moreover, he connects them to the Schillerian categories of the *naïve* and the *sentimental* to create a complex paradigm of the creative process.

In Schiller's essay, *Über naïve und sentimentalische Dichtung*, a *personal I* and a *creative I* live together, harmoniously, only in the childhood of the individual and in the childhood of civilization, that is, in pre-Socratic Greece, while, thereafter, they experience a difficult rapport of emulation, regret, and rejection. The *personal I* is all that is simple, it is nature, and childhood. The *creative I*, on the other hand, is the sentimental, it is culture, and adulthood. The modern poet, as Pascoli well knows, cannot be but sentimental. He has grown up enough to remember his childhood and knows that he has lost its marvelous talents. Inevitably, then, he becomes prey to nostalgia, and starts longing for that state of perfection he deems destroyed by the forces of the intellect.[18] In the view of the poet, we are

---

clear univocal thoughts while we are constantly uttering multiple meanings, some intended, others semi-conscious. See Benveniste, *Problems in General Linguistics*, in particular chapter twenty, "The nature of Pronouns" (217-22).

[18] The Greek word for the specific feeling of nostalgic desire was *pothos*. Plato defines it in the *Cratylus* (420a) as a yearning desire for a distant object. While

always away and beyond what is here-and-now; our being is metaphorical, always on two levels at once as we are the reflection of an invisible other, an image that is attainable only through imagination. Our wandering and our longing is for the very archetypal, imaginal figure that instigates the longing, it is a return towards an archetype.[19] For Pascoli the *child* is our golden primordial self and is all that which explains the intriguing problem of our affinity with beauty. When we abandon the child, we begin our long journey of adaptation to the horizontal world of adulthood. We want worldly recognition, house, family, lust for power and money. Therefore, for Pascoli, true poetry is either the voice of the child immersed in nature, or that of the man immersed in memory, past the stages of youth and virility, safe in the serene senescence of Solon, of old Odysseus, of ancient Vainamoinen. Not surprising, then, is — the same may be observed in the poetry of Wordsworth — the almost complete absence of adult figures. It is as if all that concerns, worries, and delights men and women in the fullest and longest period of their lives did not belong to the realm of poetry. There is nothing poetic in the life of bankers and farmers, of professors and politicians. Their efforts are necessary to push life forward but, to do so, they have to forget the Child. Only the poets, when they are poets, are privileged to stay in contact with him, and their sacrifice is rewarded with the delight of transparent gaze regained.[20]

---

himeros is physical desire for the immediately present and *anteros* is answering love, *pothos* is longing towards the unattainable, never satisfied by actual possession of the object. This is the side of *eros* which mythologizes life. *Pothos* is also a kind of flower connected with death and burial sites, and a climbing plant that never stays in one place and is always seeking new attachments. Alexander the Great is said to have invented the phrase '*seized by pothos*' to account for his eternal longing. *Pothos* was not only a concept or a feeling, it was also a divine personification which has been brought into association with Dyonisos, Apollo, Attis, Hippolytos and with phallic Hermes. For a full account of the Platonic distinction see Hillmann, *Loose Ends*.

[19] All events in the realm of the soul, all psychological events and behaviors have a similarity and likeness to an archetypal pattern. Our lives follow mythical figures: we think, act, and feel only as permitted by patterns established in the imaginal world. All archetypal psychology is based upon the fundamental principle of epistrophé or reversion, which is the assumption that everything belongs somewhere. This Neoplatonic idea is studied in Proclus' *Elements of Theology*, especially proposition 29.

[20] In one of his *poèmes en prose* ("Les Tentations, ou Eros, Plutus et la gloire," no. XXI), Baudelaire envisions the desires for fame, love, and wealth as male and

Perhaps all modern ontologies can be understood within this original experience of loss and separation, in the search for that other place of which Plato speaks in the *Phaedo*. This phenomenon is essentially poetic and reveals the desperate need of an entire culture: it is Europe between the two centuries, impeded in all natural impulses, exhausted by the conflicts of its nations and by the threatened state of its people, who have surrendered their passion and creative vigor. The dream of another order where weariness, confusion, and inconsistencies could be redeemed is the antidote to such a predicament. And Pascoli seeks such order against the fragility of his own consciousness. He does not reject logic or the need for an organic conceptual system; yet, he seems to abandon any confidence in the objects of his own perceptions, any hope of reconciling what he discerns and what he signifies. Man appears to him as a divided unity in a world devoid of gods and purpose; his basic problems and doubts remain those of the child who first formulates his "whys." Therefore, the poet indulges deliberately in perplexities; he questions without providing answers. His modern poetics, in fact, is founded on this double conviction: the necessity and the impossibility of any solution, of a real *Gestalt*. It is a poetics of contradictions and ambiguities so consistent throughout his entire artistic production as to legitimize the idea of a pre-programmed double system of thinking. The split appears patently in the dyads of many titles: "Speranze e memorie"; "Cuore e cielo"; "Morte e sole"; "Tra il dolore e la gioia"; "I due fuchi"; "I due bimbi"; the two sections *Le pene del poeta* and *Le gioie del poeta*; "Ida e Maria"; "I due cugini"; "Piano e monte"; "I due fanciulli"; "I due orfani"; "Le due aquile"; "I due alberi"; "I due girovaghi"; "I gemelli"; and so on. Furthermore, the reader is often summoned to answer and participate in the poet's quest, and many poems address some other or others, in a pattern of unnecessary and unexpected interrogations, suspended periods, parentheses, apostrophes, all the unnerving and often non-poetic signs of a perennial conversation with the self, so typical of the solitary. Pascoli — need it be said? — does not apply to this dichotomy of forces the kind of binary opposition that has proved so important in structuralist linguistics. He recognizes the conditions of an interminable duel between all things, and his language stresses the fragility of all phenomena, the coming and going of all convictions. Indeed, meticulous

---

female devils that come to tempt him in the middle of the night and he pretends to regret the pride that has convinced him to reject their offers in order to remain a poet.

studies of the actual production dates of the single poems and collections of poems show that divergent ideas and opposing creative models coexist. Thus, Pascoli's poetry seems to develop according to a pattern of polarities that are mirrored in specific splits and find an outcome not in opposition, but rather in combination, since they appear always at the same time. We have emphasized already the co-presence of child and old man. But all thoughts, images and emotions enter into a relationship of reciprocal metaphorization, and associations and contrasts play the same role; that is, pain enhances happiness, evil promotes good, shadows give force to light, noise makes the silence more precious, and death is, irredeemably, the twin sister of life. It is such symmetry of emotional nuances together with their pragmatic, unsentimental representations that form the supporting network of Pascoli's *poiein* and constitute its absolute novelty.

In this respect, *Myricae* is the daring philosophical basis of Pascoli's poetics. Each short poem projects the soul of the poet beset by tensions that are extremely varied. To understand such poetic representations we could think of a nature in which two equal forces operate, one that tends towards limitless expansion, while the other strives to contract and set roots in some small part of this earth.[21] These two incentives are taken to be unrestrained and unchangeable. The result of their juxtaposition can be neither peace nor reciprocal annihilation; we are left with one other possibility only: interaction or, even better, coexistence. Pascoli is intrigued

---

[21] A clear example of such tenacious duality is represented in "Il vischio" (*Myricae*). I should like to quote one stanza of this poem, centered on the oxymoron of the motionless escape, typical of Pascoli's insoluble contradictions: "Due anime in te sono, albero. Senti / più la lor pugna, quando mai t'affisi/ nell'ozioso mormorio dei venti? / Quella che aveva lagrime e sorrisi,/ che ti ridea col labbro de' bocciuoli, / che ti piangea dai palmiti recisi,/ e che d'amore abbrividiva ai voli / d'api villose, già se stessa ignora. / Tu vivi l'altra e sempre più t'involi / da te fuggendo immobilmente; ed ora / l'ombra straniera è già di te più forte, / più te. Sei tu, checché gemmasti allora, / ch'ora distilli il glutine di morte." ("The mistletoe": "Two souls live within you, tree. Do you still feel their fighting, whenever you stand motionless, [as now] in the lazy murmuring of the winds? That one that had smiles and tears, that smiled for you with the lips of your early buds, that cried for you from your severed fronds, and quivered with love at the flight of the fuzzy bees, indeed knows not itself. You live the other one, and more and more take flight, fleeting, motionless from yourself; and now the alien shadow is stronger by far than you, more like yourself. Whatever the buds you produced then, now you give forth the glutinous drops of death.")

by the representation of contradictions and it is never sure whether the ideal toward which he strives is indeed a serene sense of self-assurance. Contrasting what he has just affirmed, presenting points of view in opposition, and therefore accepting doubt and internal split is his form of sincerity. He obviously believes that every change is illusory, a sudden swerve in the straight line of our life that is tenaciously intent on simply existing, indifferent of consequences. All relations, acquisitions, and changes, even the impulse to gain glory and reputation; all ideological systems of doctrines and actions; all emotional problems of desires and regrets appear to him to be the fruit of a senseless deception, masks to conceal man's misery. Maybe here is rooted Pascoli's attachment to the earth, to the seasons, to animals and plants, and to the child who, so much better than man, seems to reconcile what is and what appears to be while presenting intrinsic contradictions.

Let us return to the structure of our archetype. The new child is always represented as the hope of mankind, the future hero, or the Messiah. He also embodies, however, the threat of change and conflict. Therefore, the child of the myth is devoured, abandoned, cursed, exiled, and generally condemned to death. The child of reality is also, in a way, quickly removed from childhood, baptized, inoculated, educated; and our relationship with him is guilt-ridden and ambiguous. It is as if we could not altogether trust its nature; and the more we grow in the perception of our rationality, the more inclined we become to separate ourselves from the time of early childhood, to reject spontaneous impulses, to color the special qualities of infancy with the notion of an "otherness" that is recognized as weak, needy, and disagreeable since it evokes too much of what has been left behind and has become associated with the primitive, the mad, the enigmatic.

Pascoli, instead, imparts to the condition of childhood all the value of a philosophical belief. His *Ur-Child* is a theoretical scheme and a necessary tool for organizing and comprehending the opulent diversity of natural phenomena. As such, it has its own epistemological agenda. It is oriented towards experimentation; endowed with elementary defenses of enthusiasm and trust; strengthened by joy and desire; weakened by fear and pain. It is total openness and vulnerability to what happens; and it is inexhaustible vitality. All these properties, which are common to every member of the species, make Pascoli's *fanciullino* the center of an anthropological utopia that is not at all escape, but rather political strategy. This Child who welds nature to history, universality of values to socio-historical specificity is, primarily, autonomous from the usual image of childhood; consequently, he can be the model and the instrument of

renewal. According to Pascoli, the forces that sustain him, play and ethical commitment, are the key elements at the root of existence. Because of them, childhood is the legitimate ground of exploration and experimentation for the birth of a new man who, it seems implicit, cannot emerge only through the mechanisms of a renewed economy or a series of social revolutions.

The sensing and feeling of the child, expressed through *pietas* and laughter (the smile and the tears so frequent in the text of *The Little Child*, the smiles and tears that provide titles to parts of *Myricae*) confirm such democratic aspirations. The poet ostensibly wants to be convinced of it, engaged, as he seems to be, in the pursuit of a deontological exaltation of equality. Whatever the case, the *Eternal Child* is the voice of a moral law that transcends socio-historical determinations privileging the very essence of a Kantian must-be, with an optimism which is certainly unusual. In the *Fanciullino*, the future comes to coincide with the past and the Child, harbinger and model of an anthropological transformation, experiences what is phylogenetically present in all of us. This Child speaks the language of Homer, understands the language of nature. The ancients used to divine the will of the gods by studying the flight of birds, the entrails of sacrificial lambs and oxen. Animals are supposed to be in closest touch with the earth, and they return in Pascoli's poetry, allied to the Child, and with the same functions as the uncorrupted interpreters of the beginnings. Vitality, autonomy and solidarity are the most positive signs of this child insofar as his anthropological role is concerned and represent the most costly loss in the drama that culminates in the conquest of adulthood. They are emphasized, throughout Pascoli's poetic discourse, as the socialistic or, more broadly and correctly speaking, humanitarian nature of the child who is said to be innately fair, compassionate, and conscious of the basic rights of equality for all men. Pascoli accepts in full the ideal of Leopardi's "La ginestra": only charity and human solidarity can prevail against the irremediable evil of life.[22] It is a philanthropic attitude, and certainly sincere, but I do not find that it goes beyond a most generalized Christian ethic, envisioned from a *petit-bourgeois* perspective at that. It is an attitude that

---

[22] "La ginestra" (1836) is Leopardi's final statement on the evil of nature. At the same time, perpetuating the poet's most intimate contradictions, the flower of the desert, like the "nocturnal song of the shepherd," confirms man's tenacious faith in human strength and possibility of survival against all odds.

often weakens the value of a poem ("Il cane," for instance, or "I due fanciulli"); and it is the least impressive element of *Il Fanciullino*.

Traditionally, children's freedom from sins and wickedness has been a common theme of poets. Wordsworth credits the young child with a higher morality and divine intuition present in him already before birth. Chateaubriand extols the child's instinctive piety. In literary tradition, the afflicted child reveals and condemns all crimes, historical, legendary, social, or political. In Pascoli's poetry, the orphan, the sick, the poor, the hungry, the abandoned child, crying in the dark, are various symbols of a suffering humanity, as so many witnesses and judges of the misery and despair of life. Poems like "Ceppo," "Morto," "Orfano," "Abbandonato" are especially representative of this disposition, since they constitute part of the section *Creature*. Equally poignant, however, are "Il morticino," "Il rosicchiolo," "Sogno d'ombra," "Mistero," "Vagito," poems that evoke images resembling many of Picasso's paintings, especially those of the Blue Period where slender, wistful children are barely sketched against a poorly lit background — like candles about to die out — suggesting an awareness of the fragility and loneliness of life. There is the woe of cold and hunger, the misery of despair as a condition understood through experience and compassion. In a few paintings the child is presented with his mother, in shared misery, yet neither able to comfort the other. The child is often there to condemn more severely or to hope beyond hope, and it is always the drama of life that concerns him, that shares with him laughter and tears, dangers and illusions. Like Pascoli, Picasso identifies with the poorest, the most destitute, even the bleakest aspects of life and beholds all with profound stupefaction. For both artists, poverty is more than the indigence caused or tolerated by inadequate political provisions in a climate of social inequalities; it is, rather, an existential state that penetrates the conscience, forcing intense transformations. This is most visible in the little child, who is assumed to be joyful, by nature, and intent only in the happy discovery of the world. Pascoli never dwells, however, on the cruelty inflicted upon children, or on their own acts of malice.[23] Such emotions do not appeal to his interest simply because they are not poetic:

---

[23] It is an interesting fact that the themes of cruelty and exploitation of young children, while by no means absent in the reality of everyday life, do not find much room in Italian letters, especially before Pascoli's time. When they do — I am thinking for example of some episodes and characters of De Amicis' *Cuore*, and, even more, of Verga's poignant short stories "Jeli il pastore" and "Rosso Malpelo"

And so the true poet, without doing so intentionally, and without going far away, [...] is, as we say today, a socialist, or, as it should be said, human. Thus poetry, attuned only to poetry, is what improves and renews humanity, excluding from it, not intentionally what is evil, but naturally what is *unpoetic*. Now, little by little, one finds that unpoetic is what morality considers bad and aesthetics proclaims ugly. But in our case it is not the bearded philosopher who judges what is ugly and bad. It is the Child inside who finds it repulsive.

(*L.C.*, X)

Rousseau had firmly dismissed the belief, originating with Augustine, that moral and spiritual education must subdue and refashion the wild nature of children.[24] On the contrary, he maintained that "toute méhanceté vient de faiblesse; l'enfant n'est méchant que parce qu'il est faible; rendez-le fort, il sera bon; celui qui pourra tout ne feroit jamais de mal" (I, 422) ("all cruelty comes from weakness; the child is bad only because he is feeble; make him strong, he will be good; the one who is capable of doing everything will never do evil"). For Pascoli also, all anti-social feelings and dispositions of envy, selfishness, and vanity that children may manifest in some act of violence, are fleeting and totally unwilled:

— we are presented with a sick behavior that is the result of poverty, injustice, ignorance: all social maladies that are expected to be cured. What is lacking is an interest in cruelty per se, the study of the powerful inclination of the soul to enjoy victimizing the weakest, most defenseless human beings. We have no Dickens, no Balzac, no Lautréamont whose *Chants de Maldoror* present a veritable collection of tortures and torments inflicted on children and adolescents — young human beings who are abandoned, seduced, imprisoned, raped, and tortured with real hatred. Even D'Annunzio, who expertly represents sadistic and sadomasochistic relations, ignores the narrative possibility of physical and psychological abuse of children. I can only think of "La madia" (from *Le novelle della Pescara*) as a most notable example of unexplainable evil in children.

25 La Bruyère (*De l'homme*) gives us a colorful list of children's poor attributes. In his estimation they are: "hautains, dédaigneux, colères, envieux, curieux, intéressés, paresseux, volages, timides, intempérants, menteurs, dissimulés; ils rient et pleurent facilement; ils ont des joies immodérées et des afflictions amères sur des très petits sujets; ils ne veulent point souffrir le mal et aiment à en faire...." ("children [are] haughty, disdainful, angry, envious, curious, self-indulgent, lazy, voluble, shy, intemperate, mendacious, dishonest; they laugh and cry easily; they feel excessive pleasures and bitter afflictions over insignificant things; they do not want to suffer any evil but enjoy inflicting it [on others]"; my trans.)

I due fanciulli (*Primi poemetti*)

Era il tramonto: ai garruli trastulli
erano intenti nella pace d'oro
dell'ombroso viale, i due fanciulli.

Nel gioco, serio al pari d'un lavoro,
corsero a un tratto, con stupor de' tigli,
tra lor parole grandi più di loro.

A sé videro nuovi occhi, cipigli
non più veduti, e l'uno e l'altro, esangue,
ne' tenui diti si trovò gli artigli,

e in cuore un'acre bramosia di sangue,
e lo videro fuori, essi, i fratelli,
l'uno dell'altro per il volto, il sangue!

[...] A letto, il buio li fasciò, gremito
d'ombre più dense: vaghe ombre, che pare
che d'ogni angolo al labbro alzino il dito.

Via via fece più grosse onde e più rare
il lor singhiozzo, per non so che nero
che nel silenzio si sentia passare.

L'uno si volse, e l'altro ancor, leggero:
nel buio udì l'un cuore, non lontano
il calpestio dell'altro passeggero. [...][25]

---

[26] "The Two Little Boys": "The sun was setting. In the golden peace of the shaded walkway, the two boys were absorbed in noisy play. In their playing [which was] as serious as work, to the surprise of the linden trees, there suddenly came between them words bigger than they were. They both saw before them eyes never seen before, scowls yet unknown, and both, now turned pale, found talons in their tender fingers, and in their hearts was a bitter thirst for blood; and the two brothers saw that blood, for real, and on each other's face! [...] In bed, they were engulfed by a darkness teeming with thicker shadows: vague shadows that from every corner

Anger and animosity are rapidly forgotten; and the easy transition to opposite moods, shows that there is never malice or premeditation involved. [26] According to Pascoli, poetry has the power to guide and elevate man by imbuing him with deeper and more conscious feelings of compassion. Such was the ideological certainty of Hugo, Carducci, and

---

seem to raise a finger to their lips. Little by little their sobs came in more prolonged but less frequent waves, because of I do not know what blackness [that was] moving in the silence. [Then] one turned over, as did the other too, softly: and in the darkness, one heart heard, close-by, the light pounding of the other."

[27] As noted by many critics, Pascoli often becomes too emotionally involved in what he is saying. It is the case of many sudden comments – at times entire stanzas, more often parenthetical lines – that are conventional and artificial, coldly reflective or resentful. In "I due fanciulli," for instance, Pascoli wishes for all of mankind the easy transition from evil to peace that characterizes the heart of the child: "Uomini, nella truce ora dei lupi,/ pensate all'ombra del destino ignoto / che ne circonda, e a' silenzi cupi / che regnano oltre il breve suon del moto / vostro e il fragore della vostra guerra, / ronzio d'un'ape dentro il bugno vuoto. / Uomini, pace! Nella prona terra / troppo è il mistero; e solo chi procaccia / d'aver fratelli in suo timor, non erra./ Pace, fratelli! e fate che le braccia / ch'ora o poi tenderete ai più vicini, / non sappiano la lotta e la minaccia / E buoni veda voi dormir nei lini / placidi e bianchi, quando non intesa, /quando non vista, sopra voi si chini / la Morte con la sua lampada accesa." ("Men, in the savage hour of the wolves, think about the shadow of the unknown fate that surrounds us; and [think] about the dark silences that reign beyond the short-lived sound of your movements, beyond the clamor of your wars, buzzing of bees inside an empty hive. Men, peace! On the prostrate earth too great is the mystery; and only the ones who will have brothers fearing it [with them] are not wrong. Peace, brothers! And see that the arms you will extend, sooner or later, towards your closest neighbors engage not in fighting and threats! And [see that] Death find you nicely asleep, in serene white linens, when she comes unheard, unseen, bending over you, with her lamp alit.") As the poet understands so well in *The Little Child*, the explanation of antithetical ideas, the clarification of conceptual processes are obstacles that disrupt the flow of the imagination. Barberi-Squarotti sketches a general pattern for such poetic structure. An image, an event, or a memory presents itself, freely, to the poet who wants to re-present it in its freedom, independent of rules of syntax, meter, logic or spatial and temporal sequences. Colors, sounds, and thoughts melt into each other, forming a seemingly confused block, that is strikingly beautiful. The last lines of the poem usually pick up one of these elements, betraying the poet's anxious, sentimental side, full of generalized ethical aspirations, strictly connected to contemporary values. (See Barberi Squarotti, *Simboli e strutture della poesia del Pascoli*.)

Tolstoj, which Pascoli too accepts sincerely. But even the ideological taste for moderation, the proclaimed goal of satisfaction and self-contentment, cannot hide his tendency toward a form of individualistic anarchism. His pessimism is tied to the theme of an impossible escape-liberation; it is never exclusively tragic, but it reveals a conception of existence that is fundamentally bitter and disenchanted. The presence of evil in the world is pervasive and dramatic; furthermore, evil is conceived as an absolute in life. Therefore, the problem of children's badness and its origins cannot be but marginal in his poetic discourse; it does not disturb or interfere with the core of his vision of childhood.

On the other hand, it is in creativity that Pascoli establishes the most important aspect of the child's mind. Through creative activity, the soul — the word, which returns hauntingly in all poetry of the turn of the century — convinces the mind to welcome, or at least to take into account, that which is not factual, real, or demonstrable. Creativity proceeds, in fact, from the known to the unknown, through a process of analogies and contamination's that help fabricate new images and renew old ones in order to control and possess one's own world. It is given with life itself, with speech and communication; thus Pascoli claims that it belongs to us all, and that it inspires our formulation of precise aesthetic and philosophical hypotheses. Pascoli's assumptions are organized along the converging lines of scientific, philosophic, and literary supports that can be reconstructed. The roots lie in the Romantic view of fantasy and imagination — in Novalis' *Fantastica*; in German idealism from Kant to Hegel, and more specifically in the concept of productive imagination; in Schiller's principles of aesthetic education. As to literary and poetic antecedents, together with the classics, especially Vergil and Horace, from whom Pascoli learns the interplay of different registers, the grandiose design of the epic genre, the ability to listen to the sounds of the woods and to the voices of the streets are Vico and the early Romantic poets of Europe and America.

A Matter of Sources

In an essay by Giorgio Agamben which serves as preface to the latest edition of *Il fanciullino* (Feltrinelli, 1982), the origins of Pascoli's poetics are traced back to the religious writings of early Christianity, Paul's first letter to the Corinthians (13-14), Augustine's *De Trinitate*, and the eleventh century logicians. Agamben's observations are important in relation to the particular quality of Pascoli's language. In *Il fanciullino* language is viewed, indeed, as a depository of objects that were once alive and are now waiting to be re-animated by the work of the poet; words are signs that exist before and beyond any concrete advent of meaning. The renewal of language is the major ambition of all "decadent" poets, who see themselves moving in ambiguity, enmeshed in enigmatic experiences, and trying to use language as the only access to significance. Language itself becomes, therefore, necessarily ambiguous; and poetry takes on the features of an occult experiment based on the creation of a special rhetoric, with new synonyms, new phonic sequences altered through suffixes and prefixes, a new musicality. Agamben's conclusions, however, are not equally convincing about the sources of Pascoli's abstract conception of childhood, or his elaboration of this theme. These, I believe, follow a genealogical line that goes from Plato to Vico, and find support in the theoretical and poetic texts of early Romanticism, which identify poetic inspiration with the special mode of feeling, thinking, and reminiscing that is characteristic of the child.[27]

---

[27] Freud at first believes that repressed memories causing neuroses were forgotten emotions and distorted scenes from actual childhood. Later he realizes that a fantasy child is at work, and places in childhood events that never happened. His approach to childhood remains, however, unclear and his child merges with a Neoplatonic, Rousseauian child who is psychologically a different thing from an adult: "Childhood has its own ways of seeing, thinking and feeling; nothing is more foolish than to try to substitute our ways" — Rousseau claimed (*Emile* II), and Freud elaborates: "The difference lies in the child's special way of reminiscing: A child catches hold on [...] phylogenetic experience where his own experience fails him. He fills in the gaps in individual truth with prehistorical truth; he replaces occurrences in his own life by occurrences in the life of his ancestors" (*The History of an Infantile Neurosis*, 1918, CP III, 577-78).

Infancy may well have appeared as a privileged condition that enjoyed the seal of approval of the Scriptures[28] and was praised in the writings of the early Christian Fathers and through mediaeval Latin, Renaissance, and post-Renaissance literature, as Agamben points out. But in all these texts, whenever a child is mentioned, it is for the most part an especially gifted child, a child unlike most other children. Otherwise, the condition of early youth is simply a negligible stage in the formation of the one who deserves the attention of artists and philosophers: the young hero, the adult man. At best, what may be attractive in the child is what foretells the future adult. This is surely the object and function of childhood memories in the eighteenth-century *Autobiographies* of Vico, Goldoni, and Alfieri. What is recollected with apparent accuracy and clarity is not to be trusted. Such memories are not a faithful reproduction of the incidents of childhood; rather, they are altered by the image of themselves the authors had, or wanted to have, and constitute an attempt to assimilate and understand the early self through the modifying influence of the later self.

Even from a strictly socio-historical perspective the response to the problems and poignancy of childhood may have been prepared by the reorganization of the social and intellectual life of the late Renaissance up until the years of the French Revolution. The re-evaluation of the condition

---

[28] We find in George Boas, *The Cult of Childhood* a few quotes taken from the Scriptures, prophecies, and similar texts extolling the wisdom of a given child and mentioning the child-like nature as something wonderful. For example, we read in Psalm 8:2: "Out of the mouths of babes and sucklings hast thou ordained strength, because of thine enemies; that thou mightest still the enemy and the avenger." And in the so-called Messianic prophecy of Isaiah (7:15) the child Immanuel "must eat butter and honey in order to refuse evil and choose good." But this refers only to the exceptional child, not to children in general. So does the story of Jesus preaching to the Doctors in the Temple (Luke 2:42-50). On the other hand Matthew (18:3) might well have been used by the anti-intellectualist: "Except ye be converted and become as little children, ye shall not enter into the kingdom of heaven." But again, Boas points out, the Evangelist does not say in what respect one should become like little children. He might indeed be referring to the concept of a spiritual rebirth. In contrast to this lesson is the famous statement of St. Paul (1 *Corinthians* 13:11): "When I was a child, I spake as a child, I understood as a child, I thought as a child; but when I became a man I put away childish things." According to Boas, the cult of the child is a symptom of a loss, a need, a crisis. It is also a therapy intended to heal and promote alternatives to reevaluate the models of our culture and our personal lives.

of childhood, however, is commonly linked to the works of Rousseau. It is with him that childhood begins to be recognized as a precious and distinct age, with its own autonomous behavior, its own models and a specific centrality of meaning. Only then, children, who never had appeared to need particular attention or care, become deserving of an increasingly privileged status. Humanists, pedagogues, and government officials alike concur on the need for intensive periods of discipline and supervision in special schools, which now multiply in the course of the eighteenth century with curiously ambivalent results. It is the time when new educational methods, sustained by the social and epistemological tenets of the Industrial Revolution, are developed, differentiated, and codified according to socio-economic criteria. It is also the time of unchecked, universal enthusiasm for science and early technology, the time when the nuclear family assumes a primary and exclusive role within the social structure.[29] This leads to the weakening of the broader aspects of associative behavior and the enclosing of children in smaller and smaller units. Incidentally, a similar process of differentiation and separation takes place in the treatment of beggars, vagrants, epileptics, the mentally retarded and the madmen, all the "poor of humanity" who begin to be confined to the first mental asylums, since they are considered different and unaccountable, or in any event disturbing for the proper functioning of the social system.[30] Between the eighteenth and the nineteenth centuries, literature and art also confirmed, through observation and theorizing, the importance of childhood as a myth and as a distinct normative category within our culture.

It is a common-sense observation that as long as the intellectual feels himself in agreement with the views and forces of his social group, he will not look for models and existential paradigms among children, primitives, or fools. They would be considered imperfect states, unworthy of interest. It is only when orthodox authority is questioned that the primitive becomes an important figure, defensible against civilized man in virtue of his innocent and spontaneous nature, and, in literature at least, innocence and spontaneity are often synonymous with all moral virtues. New speculative reflections about the true nature of man, new utopias, new

---

[29] On the subject, see the monumental work of Ariès, *L'Enfant et la vie familiale sous l'Ancient Régim.*

[30] Fundamental is Foucault's *Folie et Déraison: Histoire de la folie a l'age classique.* Foucault himself defines madness as "une sorte d'enfance chronologique et sociale, psychologique et organique de l'homme" (621).

plans for the pursuit of happiness on earth all find nourishment in a sense of nostalgia for something that has been lost and is now perceived as better. The very strangeness that had been looked upon with scorn and superiority becomes a desired quality hitherto wrongly oppressed and victimized. And new ideas assume new literary identities. Among them, appear the faces of young children, not just as pathetic or picturesque pauses in the narrative, but as central icons, as models for the soul. Rousseau's ideal of a return to nature includes a reversion to the infant as primordial beauty, issuing virginally from the hands of its maker, unmarred by man's awkward touch. His child is not only defined as in opposition to the adult, but as obviously superior to him. More importantly for our specific interest at hand, the child is one with the spirit of the poet and the artist. In point of fact, Rousseau's observations on the nature of man were not validated by later social developments, but they found faithful echo in the Romantic idea of childhood. Analogously, his *Emile*, the recognized *incipit* of the theme, remained more a case study than a child; but, following in Rousseau's steps, the poets of the nineteenth century discovered the grace of childhood and made the child the symbol of a deeper understanding of the world and its order. The substantial ambiguity of their poetry[31] reproposed the absolute chaos and infinite association of meanings that, according to Friedrich Schlegel (*Fragmente*, 1803), are typical of the fairy-tale. Thus, poetry and make-believe stories became the mirror of a transfigured reality where vagueness and disorder were considered positive forces and were taken to be the only narrative pattern likely to dramatize existential experiences.

   In general, the Romantic poet chose to focus on some specific qualities proper to childhood: cheerfulness, naturalness, grace, total innocence. The writings of Hugo, Sainte-Beuve, and Lamartine, of Wordsworth, Coleridge and the Lake poets, and, earlier, of Goethe and Bernardin de Saint-Pierre come to mind. In the first pages of his *Werther*, for example, Goethe presents a vision of complete and virtuous bliss where children have an important role. Here, as in Foscolo's *Le ultime lettere di Jacopo Ortis*, the childhood motif is intimately connected with the image of the beloved. We recall that Charlotte appears for the first time in the famous scene in which she serves dinner to her little brothers and sisters; in *Ortis*, Teresa's little sister incarnates the same feelings of tenderness,

---

[31] See the analysis of Romantic poetry in the work by Béguin.

turbulent joy, and spontaneous love which conquer the hero.[32] Chateaubriand offers the immortal image of the young child running, hair in the wind, in a solitary wood, to capture "le grand secret de mélancholie que la lune raconte aux chenes et aux rivages de la mer"; he is perfectly in touch with the melancholy of the whole universe. Wordsworth's young boy stands alone: "Beneath the trees, or by the glimmering lake;/ And there with fingers interwoven, both hands / Pressed closely palm to palm and to his mouth / Uplifted, he, as through an instrument,/ Blew mimic hootings to the silent owls, / That they might answer him." The examples are endless, and yet, notwithstanding significant individual variations,[33] the child of the Romantics is consistently the symbol of the past, and the guide toward a new happiness. Often, he appears as a radiant creature, loving and compassionate, in full communion with nature and with all things, because he has not been touched by evil. The hypothesis of the angelic nature of the child and its beauty and function as mediator between man and what mysteriously remains beyond man, develops, throughout the century, into a strong literary convention rooted in the collective conscience and sharply contrasting not only with real babies and children as we know them, but also with the children represented in previous literary works. Such an image is the result of a combination of factors, along with the appropriate expression of particular philosophical ideas and literary conventions. Primarily, the century witnesses a general resurgence of mysticism which often takes on neo-platonic features: the world is but an image of the eternal truth; the soul, exiled on earth, longs for its origins and recognizes in some privileged beings the messengers of the transcendent. The young child, like the woman of medieval poetry, falls under a superior reality.[34] Therefore, together with vitality and joy in the senses, the nature of childhood takes on the metaphysical attributes of a condition not entirely

----

[32] A different and more interesting anticipation of Pascoli's views is the suggestion contained in Foscolo's "A Zacinto," the sonnet in which the image of the little child (*fanciulletto*) is tied to that of the mother, the maternal land, and the enduring appeal of Homer's poetry .

[33] For an extensive investigation of the theme, see Coveney.

34 Childhood then is not regret, but hope, hope that is somewhat tied to the coming of the Kingdom into which will be admitted only those who will have made themselves like children. In *Revelation* at the moment of understanding and death it will be the child who will give his hand to the old man and guide him, seeing for him.

of this world. Even the high incidence of child mortality contributes to this vision of childhood, and in the iconography of the time, in paintings, and on tombstones, the child is frequently represented as a little angel. Actually, he is so often perceived from the perspective of death, that death itself becomes one of his major traits: the Romantic child is the one who dies young.[35] In reality and in memory, the experience of childhood assumes the significance of a privileged journey toward authenticity and wisdom. The poet knows that the child's splendid vision, where all common things *have the glory and the freshness of a dream*, is destined to become opaque and tarnished in adulthood, and he knows that rust will come to coat both the voice and the soul of the grown man. *"We grow up and let our voices roughen, while, in spite of everything, he always makes us hear his chimes, tinkling like a little bell."* (*L.C.*, I). As such, Pascoli's Child reminds us of the figure that is the center of one of the best known and loved poems of all times:

> Our birth is but a sleep and a forgetting
> The soul that rises with it, our life's star
> Hath had elsewhere its setting
> And cometh from afar:
> Not in entire forgetfulness
> And not in utter nakedness
> But trailing clouds of glory do we come
> From God who is our home
> Heaven lies about us in our infancy![36]

This child remembers life before life, and is therefore in harmony with the heavens. His shining eyes are still full of divine mystery. More than a glorification of the angelic nature of the child, however, the beautiful metaphors of the *Ode* are evidence of a belief in the anterior life of the universal soul. The child, like the poet, is the one who perceives all the voices and resonances of the world as the ongoing notes of a musical score previously heard:

> There was a time when meadow, grass and stream
> The earth and every common sight
> To me did seem

---

[35] See Ferrucci, "The Dead Child: A Romantic Myth."
[36] William Wordsworth, "Ode: Intimations of Immortality," *The Prelude*.

> Apparelled in celestial light
> The glory and the freshness of a dream ...

Even more interestingly, Wordsworth's *Ode* is part of a long meditation on creativity and on the relation between the first sensory perceptions and the image of the world built upon them. This is also what is at the heart of Pascoli's interest and inspiration. Exploring his own memories as far back as possible, the poet becomes aware of his own beginning, of cognitive mechanisms, of patterns of understanding.

And here we can begin to trace yet another genealogy. Writing about the *Fanciullino*, Barberi Squarotti points out that Pascoli takes his lead from an old Vichian myth, subsequently renewed by Leopardi ("Il fanciullino e la poetica pascoliana"). According to this conception, the infancy of every man recapitulates the entire history of mankind and so can be proposed as the way to see and represent the world as it was in Homer's time. Already clear, in Vico, is the Schillerian distinction between the poets of the first age who were "fantastic" by nature and the poets of modern times who become such by art and work — that is with the effort of losing the memory of specific words, of forgetting philosophy, of filling the mind with childish and common propensities, of imprisoning it in shackles, forcing themselves, among other things, to the use of rhyme. For Vico, however, poetry came into being not out of whim or pleasure, but out of natural necessity and it was so far from superfluous or dispensable that, without it, there would be no thinking. The subsequent distinction between poetic wisdom and rational thought is maintained throughout the *New Science* and the philosopher strongly reiterates that poetry was never meant to be a means to divulge metaphysical concepts for "it plunged the mind into the senses" and "delighted in giving body to the spirit." Poetry is simply the maternal language of humanity, and it expresses the primitive reality of things. Accordingly, it can be stated that poetry is of all times, it is an ideal category and not a historical event for it is rooted in the intuitive vision of reality: "men at first feel without perceiving, then they perceive with a troubled and agitated spirit, finally they reflect with a clear mind" (*New Science*, LIII, 218).[37] In Vico's conception, feelings engage the memory of sensory perceptions in the play of fantasy; and through fantasy the human infant finds it possible to proceed from the sensory to the abstract,

---

[37] All quotations from Vico appear in the translation by Thomas Goddard Bergin and Max Harold Fisch.

from the physical to the psychological. It is sufficient to recall some of the most significant *degnità* or axioms of the *New Science* in order to re-discover their modernity, and their vital presence in Pascoli's poetics:[38]

Poetic sentences are formed by feelings of passion and emotion, whereas philosophic sentences are formed by reflection and reasoning. The more the latter rise toward universals, the closer they approach the truth; the more the former descend to particulars, the more certain they become.   (N.S. LIII, 219)

Abstract sentences are the work of philosophers, because they contain universals, and reflections on the passions are the work of false and frigid poets. (N.S. II, 704)

The most sublime labor of poetry is to give sense and passion to insensate things; and it is characteristic of children to take inanimate things in their hands, and talk to them in play as if they were living persons.   (N.S., XXXVII, 186)

Imagination [...] is nothing but the springing up again of reminiscences, and ingenuity or invention is nothing but the working over of what is remembered. Now, since the human mind at the time we are considering had not been refined by any art of writing or spiritualized by any practice of counting or reckoning, and had not developed its powers of abstraction by the many abstract terms in which languages now abound, it exercised all its force in these three excellent faculties (here Vico is referring to the head, the breast, and the heart mentioned in the beginning of the paragraph) which came to it from the body. [...] it was fitting that the infancy of the world should concern itself with the first operation of the human mind, for the world then had need of all inventions for the necessities and utilities of life, all of which had been provided before the philosophers appeared [...]
(N.S. II, 699).

In children memory is extremely vigorous; and, therefore, exceedingly vivid is their imagination which is nothing but expanded or compounded memory.
(N.S., L, 211).

The equivalence child-poet, and the link between memory and imagination recur many times and with distinct clarity in Leopardi who also considers memory the magic potion that allows the poet to recreate the past the way it was. Simple sense perception is not enough; the true poet contemplates

---

[38] It has not been noted that Vico's work begins with a reference to that seemingly uninteresting character who returns, I believe intentionally, in the first few lines of *Il fanciullino*: Cebes the Theban from Plato's *Phaedo* and *Crito*.

not the object itself but the memory of the object thanks to his imagination:[39]

... la massima parte delle immagini e sensazioni indefinite che noi proviamo pure dopo la fanciul-lezza e nel resto della vita, non sono altro che una rimembranza della fanciullezza, si riferiscono a lei, sono come un influsso e una conseguenza di lei; [...] proviamo quella tal sensazione, idea, piacere ec., perché ci ricordiamo e ci si rappresenta alla fantasia quella stessa sensazione immagine ec. provata da fanciulli, e come la provammo in quelle stesse circostanze. Così che la sensazione presente non deriva immediatamente dalle cose, non è un'immagine degli oggetti, ma della immagine fanciullesca, una ricordanza, una ripetizione, una ripercussione o riflesso della immagine antica. (16 Gennaio 1821)

(... the greatest part of the images and indefinite sensations we feel after childhood and through the rest of our lives, are but a remembrance of childhood, they refer to childhood, are the influence and consequence of it; [...] we experience that sensation, idea, pleasure, etc., because we remember and that sensation, image, etc. we felt as children returns to our imagination, and in the same way we felt them in those same circumstances. So that the present sensation does not come directly from things, it is not an image of objects, but of our childish imagination, a remembrance, a repetition, a repercussion, or impression of the old image.) (January 16, 1821)   (My trans.)

Such feelings are considered propitious to the creation of poetry:

All'uomo sensibile e immaginoso, che viva, come io sono vissuto gran tempo, sentendo di continuo ed imaginando, il mondo e gli oggetti sono in certo modo doppi. Egli vedrà cogli occhi una torre, una campagna; udrà cogli orecchi un suono d'una campana; e nel tempo stesso coll'immaginazione vedrà un'altra torre, un'altra campagna, udrà un altro suono. In questo secondo genere di obbietti sta tutto il bello e il piacevole delle cose. Triste quella vita (ed è pur tale la vita comunemente) che non vede, non ode, non sente se non che oggetti semplici, quelli soli di cui gli occhi, gli orecchi e gli altri sentimenti ricevono la sensazione. (30 novembre 1828)

---

[39] In *Il fanciullino* Pascoli claims that it is difficult "for the Italians" to create true poetry because they read too much, write too poorly and remember too little. And in the Preface to *Primi poemetti* he writes: "Memory is like a painting, a picture of the event: a beautiful painting, if well impressed in a good soul, even of things that are not beautiful. Memory is poetry and poetry is nothing but memory." This poetry in which memory evoked by sense perceptions re-presents or re-opens the emotions once felt allowing them to blossom again is original with Pascoli and it will be widely accepted and developed in our century. On the subject see Garboli.

(To the sensitive and imaginative man who may live, as I have lived for so long a time, continuously sensing and imagining, the world and the objects of the world appear in some way double. He will see a tower, a field with his eyes; he will hear the sound of a bell with his ears; and at the same time with his imagination he will see another tower, another field, he will hear another sound. In this second type of objects resides all the beauty, all the pleasure of things. Sad is the life (and yet it is life as it is commonly lived) that does not see, hear, feel other than objects plain and simple, those alone of which the eyes, the ears and the other senses receive the impression. (30 November 1828)

(My translation)

Poetry is then rooted in all those fragments of reality that belong to the past, in a mental and physical landscape intimately known, yet indistinct, where every object becomes magically *double*. Here, Leopardi is stating a general, psychological truth. He does not say that poetry consists in looking at life through the eyes of the child, the way Pascoli maintains throughout his *Fanciullino*. The similarities, however, are obvious and of particular interest, especially in view of the fact that Leopardi's philosophical and aesthetic reflections belong to the *Zibaldone*, a collection of thoughts that was still unpublished at the time of Pascoli's theoretical exposition. We therefore face an intricate problem of chronology. We know that in 1896 Carducci has the manuscript of Leopardi's work, which he distributes to friends and colleagues before its publication. Pascoli was not officially on the reading committee, yet, he could easily have gained access to the content of Leopardi's observations, which were widely discussed among the friends and colleagues of his circle.[40] This fact might partially explain the rushed publication of the unfinished *Fanciullino* in 1897. Furthermore, the splendid page of the poetic childhood of humanity, which appears to

---

[40] On pages 442-23 of Volume XX of Carducci's *Opere* (Edizione Nazionale, Zanichelli, 1937) a note on the "Manuscripts of Giacomo Leopardi" states: "Carducci was nominated President of a Committee appointed to examine and study the manuscripts of Leopardi kept in Naples, with a letter of Minister Codronchi, dated October 14, 1897. The members of the Committee were Senator Mariotti, Professor D'Ovidio, Librarian Vito Fornari, the Honorable Professor Mestica, Hon. Martini and Dr. Marino, Attorney at law." The Committee concluded its work on December 20, 1897 and, on December 30, Carducci presented his *Report* which was published, with the same date, in the *Bollettino Ufficiale del Ministero della Pubblica Istruzione*. The text of the *Report* can be found on pp. 209-14 of the same volume.

anticipate, to the letter, themes and motifs of Pascoli's *Eternal Child*, belongs to the *Discorso di un italiano sulla poesia romantica*, written by Leopardi in 1818, but published only in 1906. Are these the images Pascoli adds to the final version of his own treatise for the 1907 edition in *Pensieri e discorsi?* It could be challenging and surely not without purpose to ascertain some direct influence, or to find, in such episodes, evidence for a theory of unconscious and deep rooted "correspondences." Not only Pascoli, but Petrarch, Machiavelli, and Foscolo envision and express the peculiar phenomenon of making the words, the thoughts, the visions of those they deem of the same spiritual family one's own blood and bones, the skin of one's own body, thereby creating, in some way, one's own precursors. What is important is to see how Pascoli reads the texts, what changes he makes, what contribution he himself hands down to his successors.

Pascoli knows and loves Leopardi; he considers the unhappy Romantic poet his twin in spirit and fortune.[41] He also shares Leopardi's incisive conviction that to grow means to grow nostalgic, but to very different ends.

As already noted, the concept that it may be possible to recapture, at least in one's memory, the primal age of newness and wonderment, together with the sense of a real thrust towards the future, had gained significance at the end of the eighteenth century, with the later Goethe and with Schiller. Theirs is the vision of the child at play, serious and ever-questioning; intent at building and destroying what he has built, like life itself; creating fantasies and pretending to find in them the explanation for everything. Schiller envies the spontaneity of childhood but knows that it is impossible to return to such a state of playfulness and awe. Like Vico, he proposes the recovery of such gifts through sophisticated culture and philosophical maturity: if the poet cannot any longer be as *simple* as the child, he might best be *sentimental*. Leopardi declares the same aesthetic conviction and, like Schiller, denies the possibility of a return to childhood, breaking the circle outlined in Vico's axiom 37.[42] In his *Discorso* this is how Leopardi describes the poetic childhood of the world:

---

[41] See also the two essays Pascoli dedicates to Leopardi: "Il sabato" and "La ginestra," both in *Pensieri e discorsi. Prose*, vol. 1, Mondadori, 1946.

[42] Leopardi had certainly read Vico — in the *Zibaldone* he quotes *The New Science* in reference to the Homeric question — and it is conceivable that he may have had knowledge of Schiller's polarity of simple and sentimental poetry. There is another thought in the *Zibaldone*, dated 3 August 1821, that could prove this point: "È vero

... quello che furono gli antichi, siamo stati noi tutti, e quello che fu il mondo per qualche secolo siamo stati noi per qualche anno, dico fanciulli e partecipi di quella ignoranza e di quei timori e di quei diletti e di quelle credenze e di quella sterminata operazione della fantasia; quando il tuono e il vento e il sole e gli astri e gli animali e le piante e le mura de'nostri alberghi, ogni cosa ci appariva o amica o nemica nostra, indifferente nessuna, insensata nessuna; quando ciascun oggetto che vedevamo ci pareva che in certo modo accennando, quasi mostrasse di volerci favellare; quando in nessun luogo soli, interrogavamo le immagini e le pareti e gli alberi e i fiori e le nuvole e abbracciavamo sassi e legni, e quasi ingiuriati malmenavamo e quasi beneficati carezzavamo cose incapaci d'ingiuria e di benefizio; quando la maraviglia tanto grata a noi che spessissimo desideriamo di poter credere per poterci maravigliare, continuamente ci possedeva; quando i colori delle cose quando la luce quando le stelle quando il fuoco quando il volo degli insetti quando il canto degli uccelli quando la chiarezza dei fonti tutto ci era nuovo e disusato, né trascuravamo nessun accidente come ordinario, né sapevamo il perché di nessuna cosa e ce lo fingevamo a talento nostro.... Ma qual'era in quel tempo la fantasia nostra, come spesso e facilmente si infiammava, come libera e senza freno, impetuosa e instancabile spaziava, come ingrandiva le cose piccole, e ornava le disadorne, e illuminava le oscure. ... [43]

che la poesia propria de' nostri tempi è la *sentimentale*. Pure un uomo di genio, giunto a una certa età, quando ha il cuor disseccato dall'esperienza e dal sapere, può più facilmente scriver belle poesie *d'immaginazione* che di *sentimento*, perché quella si può in qualche modo comandare, questo no, o molto meno. E se il poeta scrivendo non è riscaldato dall'immaginazione, può felicemente fingerlo, aiutandosi della rimembranza di quando lo era, e richiamando, raccogliendo, e dipingendo le sue fantasie passate. Non così facilmente quanto alla passione. E generalmente io credo che *il poeta vecchio sia meglio adattato alla poesia d'immaginazione, che a quella di sentimento proprio,* [...] perché *l'immaginazione è propria de' fanciulli, e il sentimento degli adulti.*" (It is true that the poetry of our times is *sentimental*. Even a man of genius, once he reaches a certain age, and his heart is burned out from learning and experience, can more easily write beautiful poems of *imagination* than of *sentiment*, because the former can be somewhat directed, but not the latter, or much less so. And if the poet while writing is not excited by imagination, he can successfully pretend to be, with the help of the memory of a time when he was, and recalling, and collecting, and representing his old fantasies. It is not so easy when it comes to passion. And generally I believe that *the old poet is more attuned to poetry of imagination than to poetry of sentiment proper,* [...] because *imagination belongs to childhood and sentiment to adulthood*.) (Italics and translation mine)

[43] Leopardi, *Discorso di un italiano intorno alla poesia romantica* 20-21.

(... we all have been what the ancients were, and we all have been for a few years what the world was for a few centuries: children I say, and part of that ignorance, those fears, those delights, and those beliefs, and of that infinite operation of fantasy that is the human imagination; when thunder and wind and sun and stars and animals and plants and the walls of our houses, and all things appeared to us as our friends or our enemies, not one of them lifeless, not one indifferent. When every thing we saw seemed, somehow, to indicate a desire to speak to us. When, never feeling alone anywhere, we questioned images and walls and trees and flowers and clouds, and embraced stones and woods. When, as if injured, we mistreated, and, as if benefited, we caressed things incapable of injury or benefit. When the sense of wonder, so dear to us that we often wish we could believe in order to feel wonder again, was constantly with us; when the colors of things, when the light, when the stars, when fire, when the flight of insects, when the song of birds, when the clarity of the springs, when everything was new to us or unfamiliar, and we did not consider any occurrence as ordinary, and we did not know the cause of anything and we figured it all out according to our own desire [...] Oh but what was our imagination in those times, how often and how easily it took fire, how freely and boundlessly, impetuously and tirelessly it moved about, how it could enlarge the little things, adorn the simple, illuminate the obscure. [...])

(My translation)

Curiously, this most Romantic of pages seeks to reclaim the classical against the modern and to emphasize the values of harmonious imagination against the turbulent fantastic championed by the Romantics. However, the proclaimed need for imagination (*la fantasia*) suggests primarily a return to classical antiquity as to the everlasting storehouse of creative passions. That special ancient time is equated with childhood and the feelings of early youth become the poetic feeling by definition. Before his hero who is identified with the eternal, youthful vigor of the romantic genius (*Death of Empedocles*), Hölderlin expresses a desperate awareness of inadequacy. Equally persuasive is the message of Keats' *Endymion* who never leaves the cave in which he has fallen asleep and remains, therefore, eternally young.[44] When Leopardi speaks of primitivism, he too refers

---

[44] In the most popular version of the myth, Endymion sleeps a dreamless sleep in a cave on Mount Latmus either because he hated the approach of old age or because Zeus suspected him of desiring Hera, perhaps not unsuccessfully; or because Selene, the moon-goddess who had fallen desperately in love with his beauty, found that she preferred kissing him gently every night to being the object of a passion that had already produced fifty daughters.

mainly to books. For the ancient classics constitute for him the glorious example of a pristine and generous nature. But, and it is a significant distinction, Leopardi knows that the opposition to reason which has taken the century by storm, is emotional in nature and nostalgic in spirit. He is certain, furthermore, that the vaunted innocence and spontaneity of children and primitive people is one of the many benevolent illusions modern man fashions for himself in order to survive. What happened in the beginning holds a perennial allure. We pursue an imaginary origin of language, of mankind, of traumas and obsessions, supposedly buried in prior conditions, in primitive myths, in sub-conscious mental structures, in archaeological digs, in root syllables. Vico had *poetically* intuited that the *a priori* of law, language, religion, and society are difficult to discover because they are buried in the remote past and because they remain enigmatic in nature; in his view, however, such a conundrum excites philosophical wonder. And, indeed, the notion of origins has always interested scientists, philosophers, and literary critics who have repeatedly engaged in a substantial reconstruction of beginnings in the pre-history of an individual or of a branch of knowledge. To limit the inquiry to the early monuments of Western tradition, e.g., Homer and the Bible, that is, to stop at the historically documented origins of our civilization, as Vico, Schiller, and the Romantics appear to do, reveals the desire to claim our beginnings in a recognizable, albeit distant, past, instead of probing a frightfully dark hole. Such efforts may not provide real answers but surely calm our anxieties.

It is here that we must locate Pascoli's most original contribution. For Vico, childhood is a possible cyclical return. For the Romantics, and especially for Leopardi, it is a life-long regret, a memory of happiness linked, in an extremely important way, to the blissful ignorance of disillusionment. Leopardi's feelings about *l'età felice (the happy time of life)*, are, indeed, contradictory since he is convinced that the values of that remote past have become inapplicable and extraneous. We have only to read the words of Tristan to his friend to understand the spirit of someone who has resolutely accepted the condition of adulthood: "Amico mio, questo mondo è di fanciulli" ("My dear friend, this is a world of children").[45] With

---

[45] Leopardi, *Operette morali*, "Dialogo di Tristano e un amico." This dialog is a declaration of misanthropic nihilism. In this work "gli antichi," who had always been defined in Vichian terms as the children of mankind, are viewed as the only adults, the models of accomplished virility. Compared to them, modern men are

similar contempt, Pascoli would say the reverse and he implicitly repeats throughout his essay: "*My child, this world is now full of adults... and, therefore, the very substance of poetry is lost.*" This is why Pascoli invents the idea of the simultaneous presence of the real and the abstract child. When the real child is forced out of childhood the "other" must remain inside, just as he is; *he will be the permanent double of the man,* and he will thus safeguard the perennial and exciting source of poetic vision, along with all the beauty and pleasure of things. To find again the grace of the little child spontaneously dancing to his inner tune may require an enormous effort on the part of the adult, but it remains the ideal: if the children were the poets of the world at its beginning, we must learn to become children again, through knowledge and discipline. Pascoli exemplifies this concept with fine clarity. It is Vergil, representing discipline and learning — for the new poet he is *maestro, padre,* and *duca* — who guides Dante through the after-life to Matelda, image of beauty and joyful simplicity:[46]

Vergil, who represents study, leads Dante to Matelda who is art; art in general and in particular. Dante's art is indeed poetry. So, study led Dante to poetry. Well then, Matelda, or poetry, is in the garden of innocence, she gathers flowers while singing. Her eyes are shining, and she purifies [the man] in the rivers of oblivion and of good will. This means that the poet, through study, has succeeded in finding his childhood again, and, pure as he now is, sees clearly and selects without effort, he selects, while singing, the flowers that appear to sprout before his feet. (*L.C., XIII*)

 Matelda is the one who makes Dante "new" and "pure" by immersion in the lustral waters of Lethe and Eunoe. To consider her the incarnation of poetry and eternal youth is part of Pascoli's personal and original reading of Dante and is in perfect agreement with the poetics of *The Little Child* since forgetfulness and new awareness may correspond to the memories of its own divine origin re-found by the individual soul.

---

children prone to fantasy and self-inflicted delusions. It is impossible, it is immoral and irrational for any man to deny the profound unhappiness of life.

[46] Matelda is a most mysterious character in the *Comedia*, the only one who has no precise referent either in mythology or in history. Commentators have identified her as a new Eve, the incarnation of the active versus the contemplative life, the *donna gentile* of *Vita Nuova* and *Convivium;* Matilde di Canossa, or, less likely, as other historical figures bearing the name Matilde, or as a symbol of originary innocence. She appears in *Purgatory XXVIII* and accompanies Dante the Pilgrim through the Terrestrial Paradise.

All the Romantic traits we have outlined — the child of nature; the child as the embodiment of brotherly love; the child-angel, closer to the heavens; and the child as the myth of origins — are traceable in the little children of Pascoli's poetry. Just to cite one example, an angel-child is the protagonist of a beloved poem by Hugo, "Petit Paul," which Pascoli translates as "Pierino":

> [...] Dunque Pierino nacque,
> fu povero orfanello, ebbe gli occhioni
> di cielo col riflesso
> del latte, e poi, bel bello,
> quel solitario balbettìo sommesso
> che par la boschereccia d'un uccello:
> fu l'angelo ch'è l'uomo,
> avanti d'esser uomo; ed il suo nonno
> lo contemplava al mo' che si contempla
> un cielo che si dora:
> e quel tramonto amava quell'aurora.[47]

We know that the intuitive understanding between the child and the old man and their mutual appeal are based on the fact that they are marginally concerned about practical life and detached from good and bad events, though still dependent on others for the satisfaction of their needs. The old man bends to listen to the voice of the young child and he hears the words of the obscure, universal soul, mysteriously present in all things:

But the older and peaceful man loves to talk with him, to listen to his noisy chattering and to answer back in tune with him and gravely; and the harmony of those voices is very sweet to the ear, like the voice of a nightingale trilling near a murmuring brook.   (L.C., I)

But, while Hugo sees the incarnation of the divine in the benevolent, white-bearded old man and in the infant, Pascoli cannot

---

[47] "Little Peter": "[...] So little Peter was born; he was a poor little orphan with big milky sky-blue eyes, and then, little by little, he had that lonely subdued babbling that sounds like the sylvan song of a bird. He was the angel that is man, before he becomes a man; and his grandfather looked at him as one contemplates a golden sky: and that sunset loved that sunrise."

entertain such an illusion.[48] What Pascoli stresses over and over — even through the frequent metonymy cradle/tomb — is the secret affinity between the two extremes. For him the very old and the very young are both closer to death, therefore the antithesis becomes synthesis, proving an important theoretical principle, i.e., the unity of the natural world. The cradle and the coffin resemble one another, they touch each other, life and death are the same thing. The infinite network of all created things offers to the poet's mind memories of visions once seen, of dreams and regrets; a trace of the original mystery is everywhere; time is not lost. Making the past present, however, can be warranted only by the simultaneous presence of child and man. Through such a hypothesis, Pascoli is able to overcome the stultifying effect of a strictly evolutionary theory of development according to which all the arts would be committed to a pre-reflective stage. In Vico's philosophy, the difficult concept of *ricorsi* is usually interpreted as the cyclical recurrence of historical events. With greater accuracy, *ricorso* may be considered as

the act by which the human spirit renders present and contemporaneous to itself the life of all the individual nations in their eternal and ideal principles. This act of "ricorso" is the supreme and constitutive act of humanity in its own ideas and presence. By this act, the human spirit reaches, so to say, back through all time, that is the time of the life of the individual nations, and down into the depths of

---

[48] About Hugo, in particular, Marina Bethlenfalvay writes: "Méditant ces deux gouffres: Dieu et l'enfance, Hugo arrive à la certitude que 'c'est la même chose, au fond.' Ainsi dans ses derniers recueils, il porte à ses conséquences extrêmes la conception de l'innocence angélique des enfants, et aboutit à une véritable apothéose de l'enfant: 'Ce tourbillon de lumière et de joie', 'cet essaim d'âmes que nous envoie l'amour mystérieux', c'est 'l'immense joie éternelle de Dieux', semée en étoiles dans le ciel et enfants sur terre. L'enfant devient pour Hugo la manifestation la plus claire du divin" (Bethlenfalvay 32). ('Meditating upon such depths as God and infancy, Hugo reaches the certainty that 'in the end, they are the same thing.' And in his latest collections he brings to its extreme consequences the notion of the angelic nature of the young, marking the definitive apotheosis of childhood: 'This vortex of light and joy,' 'this swarm of souls that the mysterious love sends us' is 'God's immense and eternal joy' sown in the stars of the sky and in the infants of earth. The child, in Hugo's view, is the clearest manifestation of the divine.") (My trans.)

consciousness to bring the entire content of history before itself in a single and total act of presence.[49]

Pascoli's Child has this very function and embodies the essential point of this "ricorso" process insofar as it affects the continuity of artistic creativity: "In truth, poetry is such a wonder that if you make a true poem now, it will have the same quality of a true poem of four thousand years ago ..." (*L.C.*, XII).

To recapitulate, the Romantic dream of childhood recaptured was a dream of re-found eternity, a dream of fixed and pacified immortality. The Romantic child ignored the fears and the lack of stability which so often threatened its euphoric state, and disregarded its terror before the monsters of the dark and of its own emotions. In essence, then, this child who so fascinated the imagination of nineteenth century artists had no imagination of his own.

On the contrary, far from manifesting a sense of optimism and hope for the future of mankind — as might be argued from certain sections of the *Fanciullino* — the internal vision of the child that inspires Pascoli's poetry focuses not so much on hope as on the need for hope, and not so much on life and joy as on death and sadness. The splendor of the world is constantly at risk. The sense of reverence before the vital energy of nature is also the terror before its inaccessible and disturbing mystery. Pascoli's concept of the poet-child recognizes the fundamental ambiguity of life and nature. In the life of the earth and in the life of the stars, man is but an insignificant tiny point. The child, however, like the tragic poet of times past, sensing confusion rather than asserting clarity, continues to inquire after reality.

---

[49] Caponigri 141; quoted in Herbert Read, "Vico and the Genetic Theory of Poetry," *Giambattista Vico: An International Symposium* (591-97). In agreeing with Caponigri's definition, the critic remarks: "This interpretation would bring Vico's concept into line not only with the familiar Greek association of memory with inspiration (the Muses) but with recent theories of poetry as recollection (not only Wordsworth's general concept, but also Ernest Schachtel's modern theory of inspiration as a momentary lifting of the veil of childhood amnesia, and Jung's hypothesis of the collective unconscious as a depository of archetypal forms available to the creative artist."

The Child & His Poetry

Countless images of young children animate Pascoli's poems.

They may be grouped according to some emblematic characteristics. There are the newborn who dream of golden woods, icons of pure happiness, unaware of the coming of the storm as in "Fides" (*Myricae*):

> Quando brillava il vespero vermiglio
> e il cipresso pareva oro, oro fino,
> la madre disse al piccoletto figlio:
> Così fatto è lassù tutto un giardino.
> Il bimbo dorme, e sogna i rami d'oro,
> gli alberi d'oro, le foreste d'oro;
> mentre il cipresso nella notte nera
> scagliasi al vento, piange alla bufera.[50]

There are the noisy youngsters *romping amidst the cornhusks*, greedy and quarrelsome as birds — how else can they grow? — not only nightingales and sparrows, as in Leopardi's poems, but robins, larks, mockingbirds, wrens, puffins, mourning doves, chickadees, and cuckoos. The birds speak their own ancient language, as fixed and unchangeable as their species, their own Latin, as Pascoli puts it using a medieval metaphor, a language that fascinates the poet who attempts to reproduce it in numerous and not always graceful onomatopoeias. There are the sick children, frail, crying, speaking to one another as if already remembering time past ("I due orfani"); and a great number of dead babies and youth ("Il morticino," "Morto," "Abbandonato," "Sogno d'ombra," "Mamma e bimba," Rosa's baby of the *Primi poemetti*, "La cunella," and others). With them we could group similar figures of old beggars, poor, blind, and alone. The combined themes of the nest, the cradle, and the tombstone evolve

---

[50] "Fides": "When evening shone vermilion and the cypress looked like gold, pure gold, the mother said to her tiny little boy: 'That's the way it is up there.' The infant sleeps and dreams of golden branches, of golden trees, and golden forests; while in the black night the cypress hurls in the wind, cries in the violent storm."

around these representations, and all the poetry of the homecoming, for instance, is orchestrated on the emotions and needs of a young child whose vulnerability must be protected.

But there is also the dead child of "L'aquilone" ("The Kite"), a text that is fundamental for the understanding of the poet's loving familiarity with and intellectual interest for his theme. This dead child is the child belonging to death, but alluding both to the end of life, and to the possibility of timelessness. All that grows and changes will eventually die. What escapes death is only that which has reached an immutable form. Here, death is regarded as a specifically psychic condition, in which nothing remains but spirit. In this perspective, the dead child may offer healing to what the mind tears apart and places in opposition. Only death secures the perennial resurgence of illusions.

If the Child is, indeed, the poetic feeling, the child that appears sick, frail, or ailing signals danger for its primary qualities: hope for the future, vitality, desire for new beginnings. The dead child is the failed spark, the creative failure, the ill-fated dream. Only the Child buried but kept alive within has the power to speak to us and bring us back to life. "L'aquilone" is a moment of pure suspension; a vision of existence as uncorrupted duration. This dead child is still in his joy. Paradoxically, then, his premature death is not a reason for mourning. Rather, it echoes the old belief of death coming early to the beloved of the gods for it is meant to spare the young the cold winter of disenchantment. Pascoli's child who dies before the death of anything (*felice te che al vento non vedesti cader che gli aquiloni!*) is the one who can leave everything behind: the countryside, the playmates, even his mother. But his death is firmly established in the poet's strategy to gain the only possible form of immortality:

> C'è qualcosa di nuovo oggi nel sole,
> anzi d'antico: io vivo altrove, e sento
> che sono intorno nate le viole.

> Son nate nella selva del convento
> dei cappuccini, tra le morte foglie
> che al ceppo delle quercie agita il vento.

> Si respira una dolce aria che scioglie
> le dure zolle, e visita le chiese
> di campagna, ch'erbose hanno le soglie:

un'aria d'altro luogo e d'altro mese
e d'altra vita: un'aria celestina
che regga molte bianche ali sospese...

sì, gli aquiloni! È questa una mattina
che non c'è scuola. Siamo usciti a schiera
tra le siepi di rovo e d'albaspina.

Le siepi erano brulle, irte; ma c'era
d'autunno ancora qualche mazzo rosso
di bacche, e qualche fior di primavera

bianco; e sui rami nudi il pettirosso
saltava, e la lucertola il capino
mostrava tra le foglie aspre del fosso.

Or siamo fermi: abbiamo in faccia Urbino
ventoso: ognuno manda da una balza
la sua cometa per il ciel turchino.

Ed ecco ondeggia, pencola, urta, sbalza,
risale, prende il vento; ecco pian piano
tra un lungo dei fanciulli urlo s'inalza.

S'inalza; e ruba il filo dalla mano,
come un fiore che fugga su lo stelo
esile, e vada a rifiorir lontano.

S'inalza; e i piedi trepidi e l'anelo
petto del bimbo e l'avida pupilla
e il viso e il cuore, porta tutto in cielo.

Più su, più su: già come un punto brilla
lassù lassù... Ma ecco una ventata
di sbieco, ecco uno strillo alto... — Chi strilla?

Sono le voci della camerata
mia: le conosco tutte all'improvviso,
una dolce, una acuta, una velata...

A uno a uno tutti vi ravviso,
o miei compagni! e te, sì, che abbandoni
su l'omero il pallor muto del viso.

Sì: dissi sopra te l'orazioni,
e piansi: eppur, felice te che al vento
non vedesti cader che gli aquiloni!

Tu eri tutto bianco, io mi rammento:
solo avevi del rosso nei ginocchi,
per quel nostro pregar sul pavimento.

Oh! te felice che chiudesti gli occhi
persuaso, stringendoti sul cuore
il più caro dei tuoi cari balocchi!

Oh! dolcemente, so ben io si muore
la sua stringendo fanciullezza al petto,
come i candidi suoi pètali un fiore

ancora in boccia! O morto giovinetto,
anch'io presto verrò sotto le zolle
là dove dormi placido e soletto...

Meglio venirci ansante, roseo, molle
di sudor, come dopo una gioconda
corsa di gara per salire un colle!

Meglio venirci con la testa bionda,
che poi che fredda giacque sul guanciale
ti pettinò co' bei capelli a onda

tua madre... adagio, per non farti male.[51]

---

[51] "The Kite": "There is something new today in the sunlight, or rather something that is very old. I live elsewhere and I sense that violets have sprung up all around. They came up in the woods of the capuchin convent, amidst the dead leaves the wind stirs at the foot of the oak trees. There is the smell of a sweet air now thawing the frozen turf and visiting the country churches with their grassy thresholds; [it is] the air of another place, of another month, and of another life, a light blue air that hovers on many white wings... Of course, the kites! This is a morning when there is no school. We went out together among the hedges of briar and hawthorn. The hedges were barren and erect, but there were still a few bunches of red berries, left from the autumn, and a few white spring flowers; and the robins were hopping along the dry branches, and the lizard poked its little head up from the sharp leaves

This is the Child who does not grow into adulthood, and, therefore, keeps alive for us the serene wonder and the tinkling voice. Only the child-that-does-not-grow-up has the full freedom to pursue fantasy. He does not have to verify his own intuitions, nor does he have to channel his sexual impulses toward any relationships, his unlimited energy toward any productive work. Pinocchio, at the end of his playful adventures, will become a good little boy in order to fulfill the aspirations of a newly constituted *bourgeois* Italy. Peter Pan, on the other hand, will continue forever his narcissistic flight, free of all human worries and attachments. The child of "L'aquilone" who dies full of life and untouched by evil, protected and hopeful: "persuaso" as it were, is the Child of the archetype. He comes to personify a component of our psyche, and therefore he inhabits childhood as a state of being. He is not meant to change but to continue as he is, as child, fixed and intact, an image of certain fundamental realities that require this metaphor and cannot be presented in any other way. "The child is one of the faces of God, one of his ways of being," says

---

of the ditch. And now we stand still. We are facing windy Urbino: and from a cliff each one of us launches his comet into the clear blue sky. And lo! the kite waves, sways, bumps, jolts, soars again, catches the wind. Lo!. gently it rises amid the prolonged shouting of the children. It rises; and it steals the long string from the hand, like a flower fleeing on its slender stem and going off to bloom once more, and far away. It rises; and the restless feet, the panting breast of the child and his keen eyes, and face, and heart, it carries all away up to the sky. Higher and higher; it is already a shining little speck, way, way up high... But suddenly there is a gust of wind, at an angle, suddenly there is a loud shout...— Who is shouting? These are the voices of my schoolmates, all at once I recognize them all — one is sweet, one is sharp, one is muffled... And one by one I recognize you, all of you, my friends! And you, yes, you who let droop on your shoulder the mute pallor of your face. Yes: I prayed over you, and cried. And yet, lucky you are, who saw only the kites struck down by the wind! You were all white; I remember; you only had some redness on your knees from that kneeling in prayer on the floor. Oh, happy you are who closed your eyes still full of certainty, clutching to your heart the dearest of your dear toys. Oh, sweetly, I know well, one dies clasping one's childhood to one's breast, like a budding flower [holds fast] its white petals! Oh dead child, I too, will soon come beneath the sod, there where you sleep peacefully and alone...Better to come there breathless, rosy cheeked, skin soft with sweat, as after a happy race up a hill! Better to come there with a blonde head, like yours, that your mother combed in nice curls, after it lay cold on the pillow ... [ever so] gently, in order not to hurt yourself."

Jung. There cannot be any question of improvement, of increase, or divergence. It is surely not by chance that in this poem the child's favorite toy should be a kite, a beautiful illustration of the archetype. Between sky and earth, miraculously vibrant and balanced, yet so easily crushed by the same strong wind that has encouraged and supported its gliding, the kite stands for ever tenuous life itself. This is how Pascoli sees his Child. And even more momentously, this Child is emblematic of *primeval* reminiscence: *C'è qualcosa di nuovo oggi nel sole, anzi d'antico* ..., and, therefore, once again, he is at the very origin of poetic feeling, as the discovery and the retrieval of what is lost.

After Leopardi, Carducci had also considered childhood as a precious good lost for ever. The poignant regret for early youth is the central theme of some of his best known poems; we readily recall the perfect image of the little boy, ecstatically happy, his hand in the hand of his mother in "Sogno d'estate." Childhood itself, however, is a condition that is firmly rejected: "or non è più quel tempo e quell'età" ("now it is not that time and not that age") in "Davanti San Guido." A fabulous child is certainly Ippolito Nievo's Carlino as he appears in the first three chapters of the *Confessioni di un italiano*. He is candid, and spontaneous. The house of his childhood is the center of his life. And the kitchen is the belly of that house; it is the place of all metamorphoses: from the raw to the cooked, from flatness to volume. It is a warm, fantastic place inhabited by cats and witches; its gigantic hearth is an acherontic depth full of smells, thick smoke, and endless noises. In this house, take place events that will influence the rest of Carlino's life; but the fairy-tale of the little child evolves into a much wider frame, in the solemnity of a political and moral judgement. The intentions of the author are, in fact, openly exemplary and educational, although not overbearingly so. The past must be known in order to prepare the future.

For Pascoli and D'Annunzio, on the other hand, childhood has a distinct mythical quality. The frequent return of the two poets to the place of their birth testifies to this conviction; so does the voyage to Greece, real for the one, imagined for the other. Revisiting the center of their recognized beginning is not a simple act of nostalgic homage; rather, it is the conscious reappropriation of those early experiences and of their purifying effect. The poetic journey of D'Annunzio's Laudi, *Le Laudi del cielo, del mare, della terra e degli eroi*, may very well take its title from a reading of *Il fanciullino*. In evidence of this stands one of the most inspired declarations of the essay's final chapter: "Poets have beautified for the eyes of men, for their memory and their thoughts, *the earth, the sea, the sky, and*

love, and grief, and virtue" (*L.C.*, XX). This statement definitely proposes the same fundamental idea of the rediscovery of originality through culture. To go back to the origins means to become new, innovative, once again original. For Pascoli, the poet who embarks on such a venture seeks not to find models, as was the case throughout the Renaissance, but to present, proudly even, the instance of his own personal and spiritual rebirth. In fact, Pascoli says, the poet is the one who, spontaneously responding to a vital need, creates new myths in order to bear witness to the human condition. He does not, he cannot explain or give answers, he can only reflect life, re-presenting it through a succession of events, of joys and sorrows, and inventing *mythos* and not *logos*, tales and not discursive speech. His is truly the wonder of the human being who begins to question his destiny. To represent the universe, to name things and to recount events are ways of making them personal and universal at the same time. Lessing believed that only the facts that are experienced in this form enter into history; only the events that have been narrated, remembered, re-told by someone are open to our individual interpretation and thus acquire meaning for us again. Here lies the function of the artist of all times. It is through remembering, therefore, that we review and renew the mysterious laws that permit us to understand the world. It is that that prompts Pascoli to re-claim the child; and it is the way in which he goes back to Greece and reinterprets the classics in such a collection of atypically long and ambitious poems as *Poemi conviviali.*[52]

The *religio litterarum*, the eternal appeal of the Graeco-Roman tradition had its own linguistic mechanisms, well known and cultivated by all of Carducci's students. Pascoli was the most rigorous and the most famous of them, winner of many gold medals at the Amsterdam competition for poetry in Latin. In the *Poemi conviviali*, however, the technical virtuosity and the strikingly new formulas of the Parnassian poet, recognized with ambivalent praises by all his critics, conceal a semi-

---

[52] The poetry of *Poemi conviviali* (1895-1904) is based on a most original idea, and it opens, in Italy at least, that process of re-interpretation of myths from an anthropological perspective that was to be so fruitful in our century. The poems form a very unusual book, complex, difficult, surely imperfect, but full of flashes of pure poetry. They represent the stories, symbols, and heroes of the classical world as they appear to the melancholic eyes not of the *puer* but of the *senex*, that is, of a mature man disillusioned and saddened by his own unexpressed and unfulfilled desires.

conscious strategy. Pascoli leaves behind the historical-geographic landscape of his *maestro* and develops a more modern, anthropological perspective. Men are suffering creatures. They interest the poet for their psychological make-up and their existential needs, unique and universal at the same time; and because of all that is not available through the knowledge of laws, norms, institutions, in short, through the historical methods so dear to the positivistic school. History may give a sense of what is authentic; of what is real or true. Yet, for all that, it limits the possible. In contrast, Pascoli intends to make his own life and his own choices exemplary, and he meditates over his past and the past of civilization, finding in both the same illusions, the same anxieties, and the same disappointments. Therefore, he projects the absurdity and confusion of his internal and external reality into the structure of the myth, and re-charges the figures of mythology with their original potential function. All theoretical premises of knowledge and perception have become debatable after the crisis of nineteenth century epistemology; equally uncertain are the criteria of aesthetic communication. The child archetype, because of its a-historical and pre-historical tendencies, allows him to abandon history and empowers him to see everything anew. Following the child, Pascoli never seems to ask: "What happened?" Rather, he looks for an answer to "What happened to the soul?" since he believes that the purpose of all poetry is to bring the reader's soul into contact with the soul of the world. Hence, in the *Conviviali*, the hero himself is not presented as a model of pristine virtue for a now degraded humanity, as Carducci saw him; nor is he only the protagonist of a magnificent adventure. He is, instead, an elusive and always different object of varying interpretation and contrasting considerations. Distances of time and space become irrelevant, and events of the past are filtered through personal experience and perspective. This spontaneous dual modality gains further clarity once we realize that many compositions of *Poemi conviviali* were written at the same time as *Myricae*. Neither *Myricae* nor *Poemi conviviali* are structured in logical continuity; the poet does not follow reason and rationality, rather he juxtaposes images, moments, and events that he considers essential in order to evoke an awareness of the primary events. First, access to knowledge is provided by the decodification of natural signs; hence the unconstrained language of the fragment-like lyrics of *Myricae*. Then comes the world of the poetry already made, already celebrated. We move from the apparently *naïve* to the admittedly *sentimental*; from the simple, common things of everyday life to the heroic protagonists of universal history. But what sustains the poetry of both collections is the same tension created by wonder and freedom: freedom from all stylistic

and linguistic rules, from the torment of life in the fulfillment of a creative vision, from that fear of death that darkens the heart of Cebes, the Theban. This is achieved not in denial, but rather in painstaking acceptance. Achilles sings his last song, knowing it is time to die; old Odysseus finally completes his destiny, not in the punishment of Hell, but shipwrecking upon the rocks that are supposed to symbolize his useless thirst for knowledge; old Solon, who has never loved, listens to the songs of Eros and Death; Alexandros cries at the edge of the world, regretting the end of his dream. Death is the real protagonist of the poems, and death is the answer Pascoli has to offer to the active pursuit of conquest, greatness, and fame. Nevertheless, what is sustained throughout the poems is the renewed responsibility of the poet. The heroes, legends, and deeds of the mythical and historical past of humanity must not fall into oblivion: they are the memories of primordial ideas, the archetypal metaphors of human experience. Life is contradictory and unpredictable, and truth is whatever we can reach: the world of the day to day routine and the world of the unknown are not so far apart, they can be integrated. The crucial principle is that the miracle is part of the ordinary, that beauty is not ineffable or exotic, it is not magisterial and haughty, it is not capital words or abstraction, it is not even a refuge for our weaknesses. Only the Child can guide the poet to an appreciation of the conclusions of Hesiod against the generous dreams of Homer. Beauty is the secret foundation of life. Pain, love, joy, work, mourning, and death are thus viewed from the perspective of the one who sees in a different way and, therefore, anew.

He is the one who cries and laughs without cause, of things that escape our senses and our reason. He is the one who, at the death of a loved one, comes out with that little word which makes us burst into tears and saves us. He is the one who in the wildest excitement utters, without thinking, the grave word which restrains us.

(*L.C.*, III)

The alibi of the child grants Pascoli the chance to find meaning for what has no meaning, either in practice or in theory; to confer on all things the special status granted by the power of imagination. New, before the things he has renewed in his poetry, Pascoli creates a poetry that is vivid, dynamic, and eurhythmic at the same time; a poetry of movement and color, psychological and visual. It is a poetry, furthermore, based on the serene recollection of the detail that keeps its freshness even when filtered through the rich baggage of cultural memory.

For the poet is not a child.

He is cultured and worldly, and he works in full consciousness and with the support of his past. Yet, Pascoli is in a situation where culture does not provide any exits or offer any solutions. He knows he is a separate entity, at odds with the world of objective reality, perpetually dissatisfied, and ever desirous of reconciling oppositions into unity. Thus, beyond its fundamental significance and value, Pascoli's poetry is an act of faith, a form of reassurance, insistently repeated in order to partake of eternity. It is in this sense that it can acquire, once more, the saving function of the myth. In this sense, childhood is the great infinite space into which all things are absorbed: all meanings, all actions, all discoveries. And it is the realm of solid, definitive reality where signifiers and signified coincide. All things have, in childhood, their own recognizable distinctiveness, their shape and color. They are an avowal of eternal existence the child maintains against the world that is teaching him differently. And so, Pascoli's child lives in a reality that is tangible, recognizable, perfectly enclosed. He may con-fuse, or fuse together, reality and imagination, but he tends to give color, weight, and form to his dreams and fantasies, not the other way around. In fact, all of Pascoli's best poetry offers pictures of physical elements, of real objects and actions. It is a universe of simple and natural things focused up close and yet vertiginously remote, since tangible details always converge into transparent, fluid images that would be more proper of fictions and dreams. Obviously, the scientific precision, the inclusion of botanical and utilitarian terms, which were the accomplishment of the positivist, cannot absorb the attention or the interest of the poet, who wants to suggest something else, something beyond. Technical expertise, knowledge and study, strict discipline and a very fine musical ear (if we have to agree with Contini and deny Pascoli any formal knowledge of music)[53] combine to realize the poet's purpose. The partiality the poet shows to the unusual, small, or unimportant things of nature ensures their specificity and, at the same time, their eternal value: "the tree, the spider, the bee, the blade of grass are things old by many centuries, or a year, or only an hour ..." ("L'ora di Barga"). But those things are the ones that have been there since the beginning of time and will be there until the end. Perhaps this is also the reason for the poet's search for the archaic roots of the words he uses and for his decision to restore to the spoken language many old terms connected with the life and work of the land. Agriculture, after all, marks

---

[53] G. Contini, *Pascoli: Poesie*, Milano: Oscar Mondadori, vol. 1, LVIII.

the origin of civilization; it is the revolutionary step forward from the stage of hunters and gatherers. Pascoli's detailed descriptions, his enumerations of the things and aspects of nature mark the realistic approach of someone who, without ever rejecting reality, does not stop at appearances but seeks to evoke a primitive state where all things are accepted and understood in their essential mystery. This is why the discovery of the concrete beauty of the world, along with the religion of love and nature which had been the themes of Horace and Vergil long before Ruskin's and Pater's theoretical statements, appear in Pascoli's poetry as visions amounting to epiphanic moments.

The vision of the child is never total, synthetic. On the contrary, it isolates each distinct part, it enlarges it, and establishes it as the concluding term of the representation. As a result, the poem seems to be made up of unessential fragments, data that appear unrelated to the development of the text and leave a large shadowy area about the center. It is the only way in which the visionary poet can dominate the events: erasing the subjectivity of the point of view in the objectivity of the representation, erasing the objectivity of the representation in the lack of realism of the perspective. An example of this we find in *Arano (Myricae)*, where the robin and the sparrow share the privilege of giving meaning to scenes and actions:

> Al campo, dove roggio nel filare
> qualche pampano brilla, e dalle fratte
> sembra la nebbia mattinal fumare
>
> arano: a lente grida, uno le lente
> vacche spinge; altri semina; un ribatte
> le porche con sua marra paziente;
>
> ché il passero saputo in cor già gode,
> e il tutto spia dai rami irti del moro;
> e il pettirosso: nelle siepi s'ode
> il suo sottil tintinno come d'oro.[54]

---

[54] "They are plowing": "In the field, where some russet vine leaves stand out in rows and the morning fog seems to steam from the thickets, they are plowing. One slowly shouting, the slow cows urges on; others sow; one, with his patient hoe, beats down the biggest clumps of dirt; so that the wise sparrow already delights in its heart, and watches the whole thing from the rough branches of the mulberry-

And we see again the same in "Ceppo" (*Myricae*), where the anecdote narrated dissolves in a series of short, enigmatic signs. It is Christmas night, a time that in the hagiographic tradition is reserved for miracles and, in fact, the Madonna appears with her Child in a hut where a mother is dying. Our eyes stare into the small, enclosed space and focus on the objects: a boiling kettle, a small burning log. Only these objects seem to have life. Everything else is still, waiting for something that does not happen:

> È mezzanotte. Nevica. Alla pieve,
> suonano a doppio; suonano l'entrata.
> Va la Madonna bianca tra la neve:
> spinge una porta; l'apre: era accostata.
> Entra nella capanna: la cucina
> è piena d'un sentor di medicina.
> Un bricco al fuoco s'ode borbottare:
> piccolo il ceppo brucia al focolare.
>
> Un gran silenzio. Sono a Messa? Bene.
> Gesù trema; Maria si accosta al fuoco.
> Ma ecco un suono, un rantolo che viene
> di su, sempre più fievole e più roco.
> Il bricco versa e sfrigge: la campana,
> col vento, or s'avvicina, or s'allontana.
> La Madonna, con una mano al cuore,
> geme: Una mamma, figlio mio, che muore!
>
> E piano piano, col suo bimbo fiso
> nel ceppo, torna all'uscio, apre, s'avvia.
> Il ceppo sbracia e crepita improvviso,
> il bricco versa e sfrigola via via:
> quel rantolo… è finito. O Maria stanca!
> Bianca tu passi tra la neve bianca.
> Suona d'intorno il doppio dell'entrata:
> voce velata, malata, sognata.[55]

---

tree. So does the robin: and among the bushes is heard the thin thrilling of its golden voice."

[55] "The log": "It is midnight. It is snowing. In the parish church they are ringing at full peal; they are playing the entrance hymn. The Madonna walks, white in the snow: she pushes a door; she opens it: it was ajar. She enters the hut: the kitchen is full of the smell of medicines. A small pot is heard bubbling on the fire: a small log

The direct way in which the details are exposed in short, essential sentences eliminates any excessive sentiment, and metaphors turn into images rich in rhetorical pathos. Many of Pascoli's poems are generally pathetic in nature, but, in the best ones the pathos of every detail is diffused through an indirect, allusive tone, or it resides, mysteriously, only in the title as in "Orfano," "Morto," "Abbandonato," "Fanciullo mendico" ("The Orphan," "Dead," "Abandoned," "The Child Beggar."). The witness to the episodes represented does not have the role of organizing the poetic text, of sending messages, or clarifying meanings. In "L'or di notte" *(Canti di Castevecchio),* what counts is the repetition of sounds and images with minimal variations:

> [...] pel camino nero il vento,
> tra lo scoppiettar dei ciocchi,
> porta un suono lungo e lento,
> tre, poi cinque, sette tocchi,
> da un paese assai lontano;
> tre, poi cinque, sette voci,
> lente e languide di gente:
> voci dal borgo alle croci,
> gente che non ha più niente:
> — Fate piano! Piano! Piano! [...][56]

The descriptive details are focused on one at a time and then multiplied: the family, the late hour of the night, the sound of distant bells, the voices of

---

burns in the hearth. A deep silence all around. Are they all at Mass? Good. Jesus trembles; Mary approaches the fire. But there is a sound, a death-rattle that comes from upstairs, ever more feeble and more hoarse. The pot boils over and hisses:, in the wind, the church bell sounds near, now, and now sounds far away. With a hand on her heart, the Madonna cries: my child, It is a mother, who is dying! And very slowly, with her child intent upon the log, she goes to the door, opens it, and goes away. The log suddenly sputters and crackles. The pot boils over and hisses slowly: that rattling sound ... is over. Oh tired Mary! You walk by, white in the white snow. And all around it is the entrance hymn: a voice that's hidden, sick, a longed for voice."

[56] "The Night Hour": "[...] among the crackling of the logs, the wind carries a long and slow sound up through the black chimney. Three, then five, then seven strokes from a village far away; three, then five, then seven voices, slow and weary sounds of people: voices from the village at the crossroads; people who no longer have anything: — Be quiet! Quiet! Quiet! [...]."

the living and the dead, while events never progress beyond a mere suggestiveness.

A good example of the way Pascoli envisions his work is offered, in great earnest and sincerity, by "La poesia" (*Canti di Castelvecchio*). This lyric is a testament to achieved safety and reassurance. Forms, things, images appear to be entirely disconnected: the lamp that burns — and in the Italian *ardere* the denotation of warmth is stronger than that of light — and has eyes to see and ears to listen; the spindles as soft as spun wool; the placid oxen in the distance; the voices of the people, gathered around the table. All these things, however, conjure up a feeling of comfort and solace. And comfort and solace in beauty are the ultimate function of poetry:

> Io sono una lampada ch'arda
> soave!
> la lampada, forse, che guarda,
> pendendo alla fumida trave,
> la veglia che fila;
>
> e ascolta novelle e ragioni
> da bocche
> celate nell'ombra, ai cantoni,
> là dietro le soffici rocche
> che albeggiano in fila:
>
> ragioni, novelle, e saluti
> d'amore, all'orecchio, confusi:
> gli assidui bisbigli perduti
> nel sibilo assiduo dei fusi;
> le vecchie parole sentite
> da presso con palpiti nuovi,
> tra il sordo rimastico mite
>   dei bovi
>
> [...] Io sono la lampada ch'arde
>   soave!
> nell'ore più sole e più tarde,
> nell'ombra più mesta, più grave,
> più buona, o fratello!
>
> Ch'io penda sul capo a fanciulla
> che pensa,
> su madre che prega, su culla

che piange, su garrula mensa,
su tacito avello;

lontano risplende l'ardore
mio casto all'errante che trita
notturno, piangendo nel cuore,
la pallida via della vita:
s'arresta; ma vede il mio raggio,
che gli arde nell'anima blando:
riprende l'oscuro viaggio
cantando.[57]

In willful disagreement with the positions held by his teachers and his friends, Pascoli casts aside the idea — and the illusion — of the poet as interpreter of life and history, inspirer of strong passions and social reforms, which had been the ideal of De Sanctis and was still safeguarded by Croce. He confesses instead, very early on, to an uncertain and elusive world-view, impressionistic and excitable, and proposes a poetics that transgresses the boundaries of historical and social realism to focus on the external and internal space where life and death go on equally unmotivated and unexplainable.

The poet is a poet, not an orator or a preacher, not a philosopher, not a historian, not a teacher, not a tribune or demagogue, not a statesman or courtier. And he is not even, be it by leave of the Teacher, an artisan who fashions swords and shields

---

[57] "Poetry": "I am a lamp that may burn sweetly! Perhaps the lamp that observes, hanging from a smoky beam, women spinning [late at night]; [the lamp] that listens to stories and arguments from tongues hidden in shadows, in corners, there, behind soft, spinning poles looming white in a row; talks, tales, words of love, [that come] to the hear, in confusion; assiduous whisperings lost in the incessant hissing of the spindles; old words heard from up close with new emotion, amidst the muffled mild chewing of a herd of cows. [...] I am the lamp that burns sweetly! In the loneliest, in the latest hours, in the gloomiest, in the most thoughtful, in the best darkness, o my brother! Whether I may hang over the head of a young maiden thinking, over a mother praying, over a cradle crying, over a noisy repast, over a quiet sepulcher; my chaste light shines far for the wanderer who at nightime, weeping in his heart, carries on the insignificant journey of his life; he comes to a halt; but he sees my ray [of light], which gently burns in his soul; so he starts again his obscure journey, singing."

and ploughs;[58] and not even, by leave of many others, an artist who decorates and chisels the gold others may offer him. To make a poet, his feeling and his vision count much more than the way in which he transmits them to others. Moreover, when the poet transmits them, even before an audience, he speaks more to himself, than to it. Of the audience he does not even seem to be aware.

(*L.C.,* XI)

Nor is he interested in tracing variations of aesthetic thought through different traditions and different times. Historians and literary critics may affirm that poetry "progresses, that it decays, that it is born, that it dies, that it rises again, that it dies again." But, for Pascoli, poetry "is such a wonder that if you make a true poem now, it will have the same quality of a true poem of four thousand years ago" (*L.C.,* XII). The laborer and the banker, the farmer and the professor, when they are touched by poetry, leave the small circle of their prosaic existence and become aware of the most powerful and subtle correspondences between the real world and the secret world where dreams and fantasies are born. Poetry, then, may refer to all affects and all circumstances, or appeal to beliefs that are totally unverifiable; it may be useful, delightful, wise but, in the end, it simply exists and it does not mean anything but itself. Its only purpose is to touch the soul of each one of us, and to bring comfort to our lives in ways that are at once unfamiliar and perfectly recognizable, disturbing and soothing. However, the fact that poetry is considered by Pascoli the first form of human intelligence, free from reflection and conceptualizations, does not imply that poetry has no purpose, or that it does not deal with all of our life values and necessities. On the contrary, the systematic defense of the principle of the autonomy of poetry confirms its fundamental influence on life: all things, all events can be poetry and poetry alone can usher us into the abyss of truth.

Such an imperious and explicit declaration of the universal roots of true poetry is set, polemically, against all post-romantic European poetics. Equally polemical is the declaration that every aesthetic judgment should be

---

[58] Here the reference is obviously to the image of the poet created by Carducci who conceived of the poet in the classicist and pagan model of the man of genius bent over his forge, fashioning shields and swords for liberty and fortitude, diadems to beauty and tripods and tabernacles. This was, more or less consciously, the poetic embodiment of Goethe's maxim that every poem 'must be occasioned,' that is to say that the poet must find both impulse and material in reality.

independent of moralistic considerations as well as of the biography of the poet, "since the man could be even a brigand and have within him a Child who sings the delights of peace and innocence, and the house where he must not rest any longer, and the church where he can no longer pray" (*L.C.*, X). We find anticipated, in these pages of the *Fanciullino*, all the final conclusions of Croce's aesthetics: lyricity, morality, autonomy, and totality of the artistic experience.

The Child & His Judge

And so it comes about that, just as we have physicists, philosophers, historians, mathematicians, we have men of letters; which is to say, together with the growers of hemp, and the growers of vines, of wheat, of olives, we also have experts on spades and ploughs who do not deal with anything else, and they believe that one should not be concerned about anything else, and, it is clear to me, they consider theirs to be the noblest of occupations. And if only they were at least the ones to make those instruments! But no, they "judge" them and they "collect" them. We now call such idleness literary criticism and literary history.

(*L.C.,* XII)

Plato had warned against the tendency to pass judgment on others, but, at the beginning of our century, Benedetto Croce was taking upon himself that very role with the precise intent to check and contain every innovative impulse, all in the name of tradition. Pascoli's antipathy for the professional literary critic, whom he considers the impious judge and the cold dissector of the artistic creation, is evident in the pages of the *Fanciullino*, and his target, albeit a general one, is also very specific.

It has been said that Croce's condemnation of Pascoli's poetry is the result of a deep misunderstanding: the poetry is confused with the man, and the aesthetic judgment is based on ethical concerns. Given, as he is, to praising strong, healthy action, the critic cannot approve of mere attempts and indecisions; and he accuses Pascoli of putting together lovely bricks for an improbable edifice he is never able to construct.[59] What Croce fails to see is that Pascoli's passivity and self-denial maintain rather than obliterate the ideal of the irreducible value of the individual; that he intends his poetry

---

[59] Pascoli lived in a time that called for will, for power, and action. He, however, preferred to remain isolated and uncommitted in a nation where dreamy solitude is still considered something suspicious if not downright despicable. Hence, his perpetual sense of a lack of balance between himself and his society. Against the ideal of health, strength, and action, we recognize in him the sufferance of doubt, the less heroic, and truly human quality of a constant perturbation. Cesare Garboli sees in Pascoli's earliest writings the first expression of this enduring struggle, the first manipulation of his dreams that are meant to correct the unpleasant reality of people and things.

to reach not just the heart of a nation but the unity of the cosmos. In *The Little Child* such an objective is clearly indicated in the second song of the Child (*L.C.*, XIX) where we may note the proud, and unusual, insistence on the subject pronoun: *I want, I want, I want....*

Croce will only acknowledge, at best, the perfect beauty of many poetic fragments and he underlines the originality of a rhythm he calls "a-symphonic," the fluidity and evenness of the stanza. But the philosopher of synthesis could not have loved or understood a poet who saw and felt reality as conflict in action, as perpetual crisis, and he repeatedly conveyed a negative, almost malevolent, evaluation based on psychological and moralistic reasons. It is obvious that the critic resents his own inability to establish clear, chronological parameters of aesthetic values for this new poet. Excitedly, he looks for the proper label and finds the one that seems to fit best, almost by default: Pascoli is not an ascetic, because he does not reject worldly ambitions in his search for God; nor is he a convinced epicurean; and he is not a real decadent, since he seems attracted only by the humble and rustic life. Croce speaks, then, of a poetic nature that overindulges its idyllic disposition. According to him, Pascoli would not fight for his own rights and resignedly accepted his duties, reducing risk taking to the least: "his life's ideal is one in which conflicts and movements are minimal, keeping only that little bit that is indispensable to the very essence of life."[60] It is interesting to note that, much more than his faint praises, Croce's disapproving comments, while deciding for a very long time the ill fate of one of the major artists of the century, highlighted the modernity of Pascoli's inspiration. In the critic's evaluation, in fact, Pascoli is not able to look at one single aspect of things. He hovers constantly between reality and dream; his poetry is too difficult and complex, or else too simple. Pascoli is a nature poet but privileges dawns and early evenings, things that are just born or are about to die, or are temporarily galvanized by memory. Even when reality is caught directly, in joyful and fresh sounds and colors, it always lacks definite contours. In sum, Croce considers the poet a strange blend of artifice and spontaneity, entirely unable to dominate and harmonize the rich motifs of his art. The critic rejects in many pages, and often with convincing and acute arguments, the myth of the nest, the sweet ever-so-present sister, completely subjugated; the memories of all past sufferings; the house with its small orchard and, nearby, the graveyard

---

[60] Croce, *Giovanni Pascoli. Studio critico* 48 (my translation).

and the family ghosts; the great many images of beggars, blind men, old men, crying infants, and weak children. And he finally, and explicitly, brands Pascoli as *a minor poet*! The condemnation of Pascoli's poetry is all the more surprising because, whether or not directly indebted to Pascoli's views, Croce's first *Aesthetics* (1902) conceived poetry as the intuition that preceded all categories of space and time, did not conform to logical thinking, and remained primitively naive.[61] Quite naturally, however, the self-appointed guardian of past greatness could not concede that any of his patented revelations of aesthetics might have been anticipated by others, certainly not by Pascoli, a poet of the new "industry of the void." In his negative reading of Pascoli's *Fanciullino*, in particular, Croce astutely deals with the form, not with the essence of Pascoli's concepts. Moreover, he accurately identifies the major components of the mytheme, the *puer* and the *senex*, but he does not seem to know what to do with them. Surprisingly enough, he fails to recognize them as a Schillerian, Romantic construct elaborated by Pascoli with undisputed originality. As always, Croce is too strongly set against the unhealthy blend of the clear and the obscure, the definite and the indefinite; he cannot perceive but as negative the special coexistence of the naïve and the sentimental, which is at the core of my study. Schiller's formula, in fact, provides the scaffolding for two different modes at the basis of the creative process that should not be evaluated against each other. Pascoli is not only the poet of the small things, the spontaneous interpreter of nature; nor is he only the eccentric lover of rhetorical perfection, eternal enigmas, and refined feelings. In perfect consonance with his antipathy for classifications and schools, he cannot be considered a realist, a positivist, an impressionist; nor a mystic, an idealist, or a decadent. He responded to all the challenges active in Europe at the

---

[61] We may remember the basic points of Croce's first *Aesthetics*. Art is pure imagination or pure expression. Given this premise, art will not exclude any content, or any feeling. No other theoretical principle should motivate the critic. Rules about literary genres are arbitrary, so are all schools and artistic and literary laws. An accurate philological and historical investigation has the hermeneutic value of allowing the critic/reader to enter in closest communion with the spirit of the artist and his times. Once this understanding is reached the work of the critic is that of establishing what in the work analyzed is genuine, what is pure poetry from what is intentional, decorative, inflated to receive praise, or left unfinished for lack of inspiration or sheer laziness. The similarities with Pascoli's views in the *Fanciullino* are certainly striking.

end of the nineteenth century. And at the same time, he became the instrument of a [r]evolution, which firmly established the direction Italian poetry was going to take in the years to follow. Hence, the ambiguities, the contradictions, at times the inconsistencies that can be found in his works. Hence, the very different readings and judgments of his work by artists, readers, and critics alike.[62]

As we know, Croce moves in defense of the systematic structure of the human mind. He is often pedantic, biased, hyper-logical, but his discussions on art are based on genuine concerns. Aesthetics is a science. Therefore, modern criticism requires a philosophical dimension, historical background, artistic sensibility, analytical acumen, and synthetic power. It is a difficult discipline of which Croce is as proud as he openly claims to be, and he devotes himself to the task of separating what is poetic, artistic, intuitive from what is not. Ironically, this very distinction between intuition or poetic thought and non-poetic or extra-poetic thought — one of the

---

[62] Between 1919 and 1920 (issues I, n. 7, 8; II, n. 1), *La Ronda*, the most prestigious Roman literary journal, opened a discussion on Pascoli's poetry that confirmed a substantially negative judgment even from the poet's friends and admirers. Basically, we are presented with an interesting phenomenon: the critic wants to seize and dominate in order to understand and the poet slips away, defying logic, coherence and any pre-programmed system of labels. This pattern can be clearly identified in the writings of Benedetto Croce, beginning with his *Giovanni Pascoli: Studio critico*, 1906, and its subsequent editions: 1911, 1915, 1947. At this first stage and for many years to come, the definitive word of the most influential and authoritative arbiter of Italian letters dominates the mind and, more insidiously, the taste of critics and readers. Renato Serra, for instance, who first identifies Pascoli's form in the 'lack of all form' and places his poetry 'in the heart of things,' will comment later, almost with hostility, on how vague, awkward, rhetorical and inconclusive these 'things' are! Analogously, Emilio Cecchi praises the poet's pure, sensual abandonment to reality, but he notes that the initial inspiration is often betrayed and that too many contradictions, too many uncertainties fail to come together, and remain distinct, isolated, 'cloven by the shiver of pain and mystery.' But this very uncertainty, this suspension of sudden premonitions is the original accomplishment of a poet who was much more modern than his critics. Galletti, Turolla, Benedetti, Manara Valgimigli find Pascoli enchanting, his poetry 'authentic poetry of the ineffable,' capable to find echoes of unknown origin. Therefore, they rush with suggestions and labels of mysticism or quasi-mysticism. In times much closer to ours, critics like Anceschi, Contini, or Getto appear satisfied with the identification of Pascoli as a symbolist poet.

most remarkable accomplishments of modern aesthetics — is carefully studied and elaborated by Pascoli who is a critic much more severe than Croce:

We divide [poetry] by centuries and by schools, we call it Arcadian, Romantic, Classic, Realistic, Naturalistic, Idealistic, and so on. We affirm that it progresses, that it decays, that it is born, that it dies, that it rises again, that it dies again. In truth, poetry is such a wonder that if you compose a true poem now, it will have the same quality as a true poem of four thousand years ago. How come? Because [...] the psychic make-up is the same in the children of all peoples. A child is a child in the same way everywhere. Therefore there is no Arcadian, Romantic, or Classic poetry, no Italian, Greek or Sanskrit poetry; but just poetry, only poetry, and ... non-poetry.

(L.C., XII)

By the same token, Pascoli maintains, the only worthy mission of the critic ought to be that of re-creating the visions and dreams of the artist. Beauty is the ultimate mystery of the world in which we live. Every attempt to interpret, explain, and label a work of art is but a useless exercise if it is not meant primarily as a service to beauty. It is not important to identify sources: poems are echoes of one another; as we are the heirs of a millenary past that re-begins with each one of us.[63] Nor are temporal and

---

[63] Pascoli's power of assimilation is extraordinary. Even Croce recognizes, for instance, that in the *Poemi conviviali* Pascoli is able to 'speak Greek.' Everything the poet learns, however, becomes remarkably personal, a fact that makes the study of sources and influences even more dangerous for him than for other artists. Sources have great usefulness in tracing the boundaries of Pascoli's cultural development; they have proven futile, however, in establishing dependencies that are often deceptive. For the same reason it is rather difficult to assign a poet like Pascoli to a movement or school, however loosely determined. There are obvious points of commonality between Pascoli and the decadent and the symbolist poets of his time, but I would tend to agree with what G. Cecchetti states with fine clarity: "in Pascoli decadentism, symbolism, romanticism, mysticism and positivism are internal dispositions which become expressive necessities. The poets of the future will learn from him the best he had to offer: the suggestive fragment; the surprising analogy; the attention to the phonetic make up of words and verse; the irregular or less used syntactical combinations" (*La poesia del Pascoli*; my trans.). And, as Pascoli himself says in the *Fanciullino*, labels and schools can only help the critic to define and to understand poetry. This is their only function.

spatial perspectives useful to distinguish poetry from non-poetry, which is the only thing that matters. Pascoli's anti-historical position, his fragmented approach, his very contradictions are in keeping with his basic convictions and are also the peculiar seal of his art. The poets of the past are occasions for erudite investigation in mythology and rhetoric, in metrical and technical devices; but history, philology, and comparative analysis are only the means for freeing his own intuitions of life and of the human spirit. They have little to do with poetry. Poetry is the splendid revelation of the essence of things, prior and superior to the practical understanding of them, always identical to itself as it flows out from the very center where universal life originates.

Once again, it is obvious that the most significant source of the *Fanciullino* is fundamentally platonic. Even more specifically, I am thinking of the *Phaedo*, to which no explicit reference is made in the course of the essay, other than in the few lines at the opening. Pascoli fully understands and more or less consciously accepts the concept of *nostalgia*, the longing for a life before life, whose memories are spread throughout in the world, haunting forever the receptive soul. For Pascoli, however, much more tragically than for the Romantics, things can no longer be images of the essence; *they are the only essence* and they flow out in the poetry as a testimonial to man's desperate need for that Absolute which reason and mature intelligence deny. Pascoli's Child pushes his questions into the inmost nature of things all the way back to their beginnings. He thus becomes a betrayed echo of the biblical injunction: happy because he is before knowledge and before evil; bent to acquire, through his senses only, the understanding of his surroundings in order to satisfy, like every other living creature, his primary needs.

The sense of kinship to a past he has not lived, the communion with things he cannot remember — *the child is the one who in the daylight dreams, or appears to dream, remembering things he has never seen* — the perplexity and the mystery of contradiction have not been perceived and understood with such clarity before.

The Child & His Mother

Very early on, every human being learns to be condemned to solitude and to an everlasting feeling of regret. A series of escapes and returns, conditioned by the ties with father-mother-family-home-of-birth, recapitulates the fundamental itinerary of his life, and a sense of absence comes to seal every new-found form of autonomy. In the midst of all the visions and passions of a multiform reality that disoriented him, Pascoli faced, at all times, the nostalgic longing for the strength and warmth of a maternal world, an order of things chaste, tender, compassionate, and in tune with nature like that typical of the little child belonging to the essence out of which it was born. The maternal womb is the threshold from which life labors to achieve new essential form. In the eyes of the mother, as in the eyes of the young child, small things grow important while large and serious things become simple and natural.[64]

Pascoli's mother, sublimated by her premature death, stands, forever, as a symbol of complete acceptance, as guardian of the home, and as the dialectical other of Pascoli's actions. She is present as love and serenity as well as duty and remorse. The adult man's experiences, his work, his travels have one declared aim: the return home and the surrender of every conscious or semi-conscious desire. For Pascoli's central abstraction remains that of man naked and alone, without social defenses and overwhelmed by evil. Only the ideal of spontaneity and naturalness, which he believed peculiar to childhood, can counteract such a desperate notion.

Therefore, the poet remembers his now idealized childhood and voices his melancholy for a time when he lived closer to the purity of his being, and to the origins of life. Therefore, his real home becomes the secure harbor for his vulnerability; what is rejected everywhere else must be allowed at home. Therefore, in his case, being at home or returning home

---

[64] According to archetypal psychology, all the sudden spontaneous affects of the heart: weakness and longing, egocentric demands and complaints, playfulness, fantasies of conquest and specialness connect us to the archetype of the Mother. The mother makes things great, exaggerates, infuses the power of life and death into each detail. The growth she furthers is absolute and passionate, the death overwhelming.

does not suggest moving back to prior and inferior patterns. On the contrary, the poet's homecomings are pilgrimages of discovery; a repeated striving to recapture a blessed state; and the features of his birthplace find the most vivid expression in images that are tangible and perfectly charming:

> Sempre un villaggio, sempre una campagna
> mi ride al cuore (o piange), Severino:
> il paese ove, andando, ci accompagna
> l'azzurra vision di San Marino.[65]

"Romagna" (*Myricae*) is a rare example of a condition of exhilaration, resulting from the poet's certainty to be communicating his own internal emotion. In all the poems of the homecoming, however, Pascoli reveals an extraordinary ability to capture the first impressions of the world and evokes a reassuring intimacy, never completely free of pain and melancholy. In order to discover and to possess this world, the poet has embarked on a long and difficult search that is innovative, original, and severely disciplined. He has learned to subtract, not to add; to simplify not to exaggerate; to interpret not to embellish; and he has received, in return, the intuitive vision that belongs to the Child:

For the art of the poet is always a sacrifice. I have said he has to take away not add: and this is renunciation. He must do without many arabesques, so easy to make, without many embellishments, so pleasing to the eye, without much gilding, which gives such an idea of one's own wealth; and this is renunciation. He must leave much that is rough and unfinished. Oh, how necessary imperfection is, in order to be perfect.

(L.C., XIV)

Thus, the work of the poet appears first as an unmaking, in order to restore the mind to its original condition, then as a making anew of a condition when the things of the mind could truly be related to the things of nature. We may remember that in *The New Science* this process of unmaking had already taken the form of an appeal to humility, a solicitation that we rid ourselves of all beliefs in the magnificent origins of our social world, and

---

[65] "Romagna": "Always that village, always that countryside, laughs in my heart (or cries) o Severino: the town where, as we go on, we follow the blue vision of San Marino."

thus go back to "the wild and savage natures" of the first men, which we recognize within ourselves, in order to experience again the process by which our history and all our institutions were created. In Pascoli's poetic version of the concept, the grown man returning home recognizes every flower, every insect of the land of his childhhod, and he can now name them as he identifies the emotions of his youth. In that enclosed space, where everything is known and loved, the poet can return to reflect upon his estranged existence. The hours of the day, the foliage of the trees, the light, the birds, the sounds constitute the concrete, immediately identifiable landscape of his homecomings. And the mother is the forceful instrument and symbol of such repossession. She is the one who gives life and nourishes, suffers and participates, hopes and fears for her children, loves them and protects them long after her death. Even though only a few poems are addressed to her directly, the mother is the dominating figure in *Myricae*, both real and angel-like. Her image is sung in simple, linear stanzas that have the fullness and poignancy of reality. Nothing is excessive or unnecessary in *Colloquio* or in the lyrics of *Ritorno a San Mauro*. Every word contributes to recapture the vision:

> Brulli i pioppi nell'aria di viola
> sorgono sopra i lecci, sfavillando
> come oro: sopra il tetto della scuola
> si sfrangia un orlo a fiocchi rosei; quando
> lieve come un sospiro, entra; poi sola,
> bianca, le mani al cuore, ristà, ansando [...]
>
> ("Colloquio I")[66]

> Non piangere... Sarebbe così bello
> questo mondo odorato di mistero!
> Sarebbe la tua via come un sentiero
> con l'erba intatta, all'ombra dell'ornello [...]
>
> ("Colloquio III")[67]

---

[66] "The barren poplars rise above the oak, sparkling like gold in the violet air: over the school-house roof a border ends in roseate knots; when, gentle like a sigh, she enters; then alone, white, her hands on her heart, she stops, breathing."

[67] "Do not cry.... This world would be so beautiful, scented with mystery! Your road would be like a grassy path, intact, under the shadow of the flowering ash...."

Me la miravo accanto
esile sì, ma bella:
pallida sì, ma tanto
giovane! Una sorella!
Bionda così com'era
　quando da noi partì.[...]

("Mia madre")[68]

Mia madre era al cancello.
Che pianto fu! Quante ore!
Lì sotto il verde ombrello
della mimosa in fiore!
M'era la casa avanti,
tacita al vespro puro,
tutta fiorita al muro
di rose rampicanti. [...]

("Casa mia")[69]

The mother represents also the most unbreakable chain: the womb is the cradle, is the prison, is the coffin, is the death;[70] and to the figure of the mother, obsessive and returning presence, is connected a strong feeling of annihilation, a desire of self-annullment, often explicitly and a bit theatrically professed: "Io devo dirti cosa da molti anni / chiusa dentro. E non piangere. La vita / che tu mi desti – o madre, tu! – non l'amo" ("Colloquio, I") ("I must tell you something / hidden within me for a long, long time. And do not weep. I do not love / the life you gave me – o mother, you!"). Accordingly, the return home is an accepted metaphor for the desire to be reabsorbed in the most distant past:

---

[68] "My Mother": "I looked at her beside me, delicate, yes, but beautiful: pale yes, but so very young! A sister! Blonde as she was when she departed from us."

[69] "Home": "My mother was at the gate. Oh how she cried! For how many hours! There, under the green umbrella of the mimosa in bloom! The house was before me, quiet in the pure light of vesper, its walls covered with blossoms of climbing roses."

[70] It is Bachelard who remarks, in his now classic study, that the mother's womb and the tomb are two phases of the same image (162).

"La mia sera" *(Canti di Castelvecchio)*

Il giorno fu pieno di lampi;
ma ora verranno le stelle,
le tacite stelle. Nei campi
c'è un breve gre gre di ranelle.
Le tremule foglie dei pioppi
trascorre una gioia leggiera.
Nel giorno, che lampi! che scoppi!
Che pace, la sera!
[…]
Don… Don… E mi dicono, Dormi!
mi cantano, Dormi! Sussurrano,
Dormi! bisbigliano, Dormi!
là, voci di tenebra azzurra …
Mi sembrano canti di culla,
che fanno ch'io torni com'era …
sentivo mia madre … poi nulla …
sul far della sera.[71]

The day is troubled by pain and uncertainties; on the contrary, it is the evening, sterile of action, that promotes beauty and grants the retreat of the soul within itself, in the dark security known only before life began. In view of the poet's predilection for the condition of early youth, it is curious that a series of neutral or negative attributes should accompany the lexemes morning or day, the child's ideal time of freedom and joy, of activity and movement. For the child, darkness and shadows correspond to a fearsome state of loneliness and abandonment. The adult poet, contemplating in memory, maintains the same spirit but inverts the causes of anxiety. The day is often *dark, black, muggy, short*, while the evening is presented as *festive, golden, sweet, glass-like, limpid*; it is a magical element that surrounds and covers what is real but allows a better perception of the essence of things.

---

[71] "My Evening": 'The day was full of lightning; but now the stars will come out, the silent stars. In the fields there is the staccato croaking of little frogs. A touch of joy runs through the fluttering leaves of the poplars. During the day what flashes, what bursts of thunder! What peace in the evening! [...] Ding... Dong... And they tell me, Sleep! They sing to me, Sleep! They murmur, Sleep! There, sounds of blue darkness... They seem to be lullabies, that make me return as I was... I heard my mother... then nothing... as evening fell."

Only the dark fosters reminiscence and comes to hide the poet's quiet ecstasies and his defeats.

As in the poem just quoted, the wish to go back, as often as possible, in reality and in memory, to the intimacy of the family home, soon becomes the desire to remain there forever, to die there. Pascoli's longing is, in fact, at once regret for all-embracing, protective maternal love, and for a time of complete trust and innocence in accord with everything around. The fact that such a time, such a harmony, perhaps even such a love never truly existed is totally irrelevant. Life after childhood is but a long exile. The poet's sad soul, forever wandering, tends towards his home, surrounded by the vineyard, by the orderly orchard; the door protected by the two trees. This is the other home-nest in Pascoli's life, the archetype of refuge for the new little family Pascoli has rebuilt with his two younger sisters. All the images connected with this place reinforce ideas of warmth and security. What he smells and touches there, what he hears and sees in his favorite time of day, between light and shadows of dawns and twilights, invites him to a dream of what was before, to a quasi-archaic dimension, radically new in Italian poetry. The severe, rugged beauty of the Barga landscape suggests to him a sense of mystery together with a feeling of eerie permanence. Even today, walking untrodden paths off the few main roads that surround the hills, still miraculously spared from modern progress, one is overcome by the emotional certainty that this is how it must have *always* been, since the beginning.

It is evident that for our poet family ties acquire a certain ideological overtone; blood relations seem to have a mystical value; and so does the ethos of land-ownership which translates into having roots and therefore legitimizes one's own existence. We are reminded of the sharp, resolute question in the letter dated May 11 of Foscolo's *Ortis*, that '*Have you any possessions?*' which brands young Jacopo as a *déraciné*. For Pascoli, owning one's land responds to the same divine law which firmly attaches the tree to the soil. Quite naturally then, the concept of compassionate motherhood that permeates his poetry is transposed into the image of earth as mother of men. To the mother and to the earth is connected that translucent beauty of childhood, that radiance of the first awareness of life that never seem to fade in the mature poet. When most men become prisoners of routines and obsessions, he preferred to remain the child *trembling* — it is one of Pascoli's key words — with awe in the midst of existence. And throughout his life he endeavored to recapture the primal splendor in which once appeared flower and bird, wind and sea, closeness and distance, for he strongly believed in the power of reverence and

wonderment as the source of all spiritual activity. His joy is the rapture of the child who listens to the birds singing of solitude and mystery, reposing and trusting in the unknowable. His sorrows are the inexplicable tears the child sheds in the dark, in a crowd, or before the ocean.

The Child & Nature

In the beginning there is a garden... a real garden, not a theological symbol, or an analogical formula. A garden of vegetables, flowers, trees, and medicinal herbs, each with its specific name; a garden filled with birds and insects that make their particular sounds and follow their characteristic habits.

The poet's ideal is that little old man Cilicius, transplanted from his own birthplace in the vicinity of Taranto. He had obtained a few jugers of land not good for wheat or meadowland or vineyard: a barren spot, a sterile moor. Well, the fine old fellow had turned it into a garden, and not only with cabbage but also lilies and roses, and fruit trees, and beehives, and greenhouses.

(*L.C.*, IX)

Like little old Cilicius, Pascoli is the lord of his own piece of land, in the high hills above Lucca. This is the place he loved in real life, and this is the place for his poet-child, since the child is the privileged creature to whom the garden belongs. In the garden, in nature that is, everything is charged with sensory awareness, and the child reacts to it with fervent alertness. He is never passive, bored, or indifferent. Rather, he seems to be immersed in the milk sea of organic, vegetative life. He lives through his senses and in the flow of pre-conscious impulses and premonitions that are strong and vital, before education and social sophistication intervene to push them to the side. With the same wonderment of his Eternal Child, Pascoli accepts in himself the metamorphoses of places and things, of scents and tastes, making worthy of his art everything that arrests his attention in the incessant and ordinary succession of events. Under his careful watch, every detail of the landscape is recomposed in a new order, which is the ancient, eternal order: the snow, the mare, the water, the earth, the lightning in the sky... And his poetry, which recovers the spontaneous and innocent disposition of the very young with respect to nature, becomes the poetry of things, moving the Romantics' theory of knowledge back to an earlier stage: perceptions, sensations are *before* sentiments.

The title of our essay confirms here one of its meanings. If the Child is poetry, the Little Child, the *Fanciullino*, is the very beginning of the knowledge that leads to poetry and is intimately connected with it: the

knowledge of sensory recognitions. For the human baby everything else is confused and unexplainable. Its laughter and its crying have no reason; they are the outward signs of the inner vibrations of the human soul, the same vibrations in all places and all times. Pascoli's appeal to the priority of immediate feelings discloses an intuitive persuasion that life and truth transcend knowledge and relate to fantasy and imagination as well as to other forms of spiritual activity. The reality we need is that one created by the soul in the beginning. It is that of myth and legend and of all those benevolent illusions children always accept as truths, since "even after thirty centuries men are not born at age thirty, and even after they are thirty, they remain, in part, childlike (*L.C.,* II). Notwithstanding their full commitment to the here and now, children firmly believe, in fact, in the existence of an invisible world. When they play, they are able to leave reality and transfer themselves onto another plane where everything is more true than real and makes much more sense. The child's day-dreams, his solitary wandering while murmuring to himself, his invention of fictitious persons and imaginary surroundings imply a spontaneous detachment from tangible facts. The perception of the external world is incomplete and, therefore, it excites surprise, curiosity, and a desire to fill in the gaps with at least the semblance of knowledge. The distant chain of hills faintly visible, the clouds beyond reach, the sea, the changeful moon occupy every child's mind, as do also dark woods and caves. Common is the idea of a totally new world beyond the horizon, beyond lakes and woods and hills, as all writers of fairy tales know so well.[72] The clever filling up of the remote and the hidden is charged with emotion; the unseen contains unknown possibilities, something fearful and horrid, or something wondrously and positively beautiful. This child's attitude, happily combining fancy with inadequate understanding is considered extremely poetic; it certainly resembles the myth-making impulse of the world at its beginnings when the scarcity of knowledge was hidden behind an excess of fantasy. All things were possible then and all things are possible for the very young who have not tried anything yet. Nothing will ever be more beautiful than what does not yet exist. What strength comes from this very fact!

Armed only with his youth, the child is in a state of constant discovery, and he conquers the world, attracted by its mystery; play is his primary and most intense activity; it is the visible expression of his

[74] I am thinking in particular of L. Tieck's *The Elfs,* which is among the most explicit declarations of romantic poetics I have read.

imagination, and can tell us the story of the ideas and needs of our common past; it is the mirror where we should look to find what has been lost or neglected, what troubles and what consoles humanity, what we can do to help it. Here, the link with the creative effort of the artist appears natural since both acts are born of the desire to give form to emotions and ideas, forgetting the surrounding reality and the real self. Children at play and artists at work enjoy giving body to mental images, mimicking, copying, and inventing:

Ainsi l'enfant passe-t-il par une phase où il est castor, passionné de faire des barrages dans chaque filet d'eau; puis il est jardinier, puis constructeur, réinventant avec ses cubes l'architecture celtique et pélasgique. Et ce n'est pas seulement le développement culturel de l'homme que l'enfant retrace. Geoffroy de Saint-Hilaire, le zoologue, a cru reconnaître dans chaque stade de l'embryon humain "la fidèle reproduction des métamorphoses animales", depuis l'amibe jusqu'au singe, découvrant ainsi, au sein de la femme "le mystère de la fraternité universelle."[73]

For the child the most negligible event is a call, is permission, is joy. Being so full of life, so close to life, he can enliven everything around him. Pascoli is impressed with the child's interest, with the solemnity and complete absorption that characterize all his actions. He wants to recapture the same intensity before a world that has become, instead, too old and too well known, and he wants to express it with the same immediacy.

The world is born to everyone who is born to the world. And herein is the mystery of your essence and of your function. You are most ancient, Child! And very old is the world which you see ever new*!*

(L.C., V)

It is clear that, for Pascoli, the work of art resides in the effort of giving form to our psychic reality rather than in the production of meaning;

---

[75] ("And so the child moves on through a phase where he is a beaver, eager to construct dams in every little stream of water; then he is gardener; then builder, and he reinvents with his blocks Celtic and Pelasgic architecture. And the child does not retrace only the cultural development of mankind. The zoologist Geoffroy de Saint-Hilaire claims to recognize in each stage of the human embryo 'the faithful reproductions of animal changes' from the ameba to the monkey, discovering thus, in the female womb 'the mystery of universal brotherhood'"; my trans.). See Bethlenfalvay 65.

that the only function as well as the long lasting charm of poetry is the capacity to cause a "commotion," that is to say to set into action our feelings in order to create new relations and new affects. As a result, or as a premise, we succeed in communicating with the artist when we are capable of communicating with the world of images we keep locked up in ourselves. The underlying belief of this approach is that affects and phenomena are eternal and take on an ever new perspective which goes back to that primum that is the first awareness of mankind. If most of the data important for survival and understanding are channeled to the little child through his senses, it follows that a complete openness to the natural environment as well as a continual interchange of bodily impressions and responses is the proper requirement for physical and mental growth. But sense and imagination do not stand neatly apart, and children appear to be the most direct observers of reality and the most fanciful dreamers, passing from one state to the other as the mood takes them and with a flair grown people may well envy. They spontaneously picture out what they want to say and believe that everything that moves — thunder and lightning, engines and falling leaves — is endowed with emotions. All things are tangible and substantial, and all things make sense. Nothing ever begins and ends in an absolute. Things become larger, and then smaller, and then larger again: Gulliver goes from the land of the Giants to the town of the Lilliputians; Alice is so small that she falls down the rabbit-hole and so big that when she looked down at her feet, they seemed to be almost out of sight; Pinocchio's nose grows and shrinks back to size according to his behavior and his feelings; people become old and old people turn back into babies.

Childhood and nature are the first, universal, and eternal reality of humanity, pharmacon for the suffering of adult life. And as Nature is the foundation of our experience it is to Nature that the poet-child turns first. However, the natural world of Pascoli's poetry is not only the countryside of his childhood, and indeed of his mature years — though memories of it recur in profusion. Nor is it exclusively the special locus of childhood, although the life of the little child, outwardly and visibly based on instincts and appetites, is immersed in and saturated with nature. It is clear that Pascoli's nature is predominantly a symbolic condition under the sign of the child, where the child comes to coincide with the unconscious, and with a state of happiness and simplicity. Nature is the poet's safeguard, and Pascoli goes back to nature, anthropologically, in order to re-establish the deep kinship between man and his world.

Schiller's essay *Über naive und sentimentalische Dichtung* begins:

There are moments in our life when we accord to nature in plants, minerals, animals, landscapes, as well as to human nature in children, in the customs of country people and of the primitive worlds, a sort of love and touching respect, not because it pleases our senses nor because it satisfies our intellect or taste (the opposite of both can often be the case), but merely because it is nature. [...] In this way of looking at things, nature for us is nothing other than voluntary existence, the continuation of things through themselves, existence according to its own uncheangeable laws. [...] What could a modest flower, a spring, a mossy stone, the twittering of the birds, the humming of the bees, etc. have in themselves that would be so pleasing to us? What could give them a claim on our love, even? It is not these objects, it is an idea represented by them which we love in them. In them we love the calm, creative life, the quiet functioning from within themselves, the existence according to their own laws, the inner necessity, the eternal unity with themselves. They are what we were; they are what we should become again. We were natural like them and our culture should lead us back to nature along the path of reason and freedom." [74]

This is probably the page that fascinated and inspired the great nature poetry of the century from Novalis to Nerval, to Whitman, and Baudelaire. Right from the start, for instance, Whitman conceives of poetry as green grass sprouting ever anew, endlessly. This beautiful image of the grass forcing its way out of the graves (an image that returns in Pascoli's poetry) reflects the understanding of the intimate connection between life and death; instinct and growth are the same everywhere! Like the leaves of grass, the symbolic self is part of all things. Consequently, as each single consciousness can subsume the context of total existence, every single poet can produce and force new growth, sowing over everything, harvesting everywhere. Poetry is boundless and always the same; each verse is one and new, while yet echoing the voices of all poets.[75]

---

[74] Schiller, "Über naïve und sentimentalische Dichtung" (706-08); trans. Helen Watanabe-O'Kelly, *On the Naïve and Sentimental in Literature*, Manchester: Carcanet New Press, 1981, 22.

[75] In the Preface to the 1855 edition of *Leaves of Grass*, Whitman states emphatically: "The great man of letters deciphers nature — the only complete, actual poem — careless of the criticism of the day, of the endless and wordy chatterers, conscious only of the soul, the permanent identity, the something that fully satisfies." The poet is essentially a seer, a prophet, a visionary, and his purpose is to bring the reader's soul into contact with the soul of the world. The poet is the one "who sees the farthest and has the most faith." Walt Whitman is the great primitive, the last

We find similar ideas in all of Pascoli's theoretical writings where he openly professes to eliminate the "I" as the subject/object of poetry. Yet, he says, poetry is bent on speaking only of the self, illuminating one's own interiority and maturation. But from within the heart of objects, of physical events; seeing, hearing, sensing; never standing above things, never selecting, judging, and operating syntheses. Pascoli's mourning for the death of his dear ones is felt as universal mourning in which earth and sky share. The destroyed nest ("La quercia caduta"), the crying horse ("Cavallina storna"), the dead bird and the falling stars ("X Agosto") are all signs of Nature's sympathizing grief. So are the songs of the mocking-bird, the wood-lark, and the owl; they are the innermost voices of Nature herself, the bountiful joy of Life, the ghostly voice of Death.

And the favor of Nature is also what links the naïve poet and the child to the object; it is what grants them the simplicity necessary to create symbols.[76] Children's feelings for likeness are sharp and subtle; knowledge of the real relation among things has not yet intervened to control and direct their free far-ranging impulse, and before the qualities and the

---

'naïve' poet who knows how to use literature spontaneously. His 'barbaric and thoughtful land' (as Cesare Pavese calls it), burdened with the world's past and yet young and innocent, happy and aggressive, crossed by the open roads where everything is possible, captures the imagination of all European artists who, toward the end of the century, witness the last transformation of Romantic ideology. Whitman's powerful vision of an unformed and unencumbered nature is almost 'excessive' for a poet like Pascoli who is, however, extremely responsive to the imagery of the American poet (the 'blade of grass' returns with insistence in his own poetry) and to the general theory that the poetic calling is founded in the power of sympathy with the crying and laughing voices of the world.

[76] Schiller's words again (718-19): "The naïve is a *childlike quality where it is no longer expected* and cannot therefore be attributed in the strictest sense to real childhood" (24). And further on: "Every true genius, in order to be one, must be naïve. It is his naiveté alone which makes him a genius and what he is in the intellectual and aesthetic field he cannot avoid being in the moral field. Unacquainted with the rules, the crutches of weakness and the taskmasters of affection, guided only by nature or instinct, his guardian angel, he moves calmly and surely through all the snares of false taste in which he who is not a genius, if he is not clever enough to avoid them from afar, remains inevitably entangled. [...] . The most complex tasks must be solved by the genius with undemanding simplicity and ease..." (28); trans. Helen Watanabe-O'Kelly, *On the Naïve and Sentimental in Literature*. Manchester: Carcanet New Press, 1981).

connections between objects become interesting in themselves, they intrigue the inexhaustible art of childish imagination for their colors, shapes, and sounds.

Pascoli who tries to see as the child sees, contemplates and dissects the simple and the complex, showing them at the same time. A simultaneity of sensory responses shapes his fantasy. He watches every change in the seasons, every minute existence, and seems to hear all the cries — the cries of children, of birds, of stones, of trees. Among them is the voice of the mother, her calling, her tears, her songs. In the poetry, this anxious, aimless, and at times unpredictably happy rapport with nature is transposed into images that are very distinct and yet appear suspended in a void like isolated points of light.[77] Reality is a living fact. Things are part of it without connections with other things, and so they lose, paradoxically, their concrete configuration and appear as the product of strange and unexpected analogies, if not of spontaneous anaphonies.

However, nature is observed primarily by the lucid eyes of the philologist and student of nature. Species and specimens of plants and trees, birds, animals, and insects, up to then ignored or considered lowly, find their place in Pascoli's poetry. So do the tools, crafts, and toil of the simple farming life with which he is familiar; the domestic chores determined by seasonal changes and daylight patterns; the proverbs and refrains of popular wisdom; the expressions of the speech, still alive after many centuries, among the mountain people and the farmers of his Garfagnana: "i miei contadini e montanini usano parole ancora vive dopo tanti secoli, parole più corte e con l'accento sulla radicale, che rendono più perfettamente e più velocemente."[78] Such refined semantic expertise is not

---

[77] Pascoli's revelations focus on the things and creatures of ordinary life and find an echo in the vastness of the world and in the soul of man. Such 'magical accord' between the internal and external reality so characteristic of *Myricae* has been considered the first stage of Pascoli's inspiration. On the contrary, I believe that it is the trademark of all his poetry: of the epigrammatic flashes of *Myricae*, where the discovery is synchronic; of the more articulate tales and personal memories in *Primi poemetti*, *Nuovi poemetti*, and *Canti di Castelvecchio*; as well as of the cultural memories of the species in *Poemi conviviali*. Nor is the spontaneity of *Myricae* any less carefully constructed than the later collections in all their complexity. What changes occur are simply in technique and intent.

[78] ("My farmers and my mountain people use words that are still alive after many centuries, shorter words, stressed on the root syllable, words that transmit meaning

proper to the language of the child, of course, but it responds to Pascoli's program; it is the only way for the poet to give old things new sounds and new signs, so that they may be found by the poets of the future and bring him recognition and renown.[79]

Something else motivates the choice of the poet and aligns him with the innovators of twentieth-century aesthetics: the domestic and simple objects presented in clear details, seem different from those we ordinarily see, hear, and touch. Pascoli has intervened on the objects, interpreting them, in order to reveal them to us.[80] In fact, the objects he presents us move our imagination toward an existential awareness, in a direction contrary to realism and incompatible with the poetics of the little things of nature. Once again, the contradiction is resolved once we recognize that what Pascoli wants to find in the objects is their symbolic, mythical essence, that inmost necessity of which Schiller speaks. To this effect, even the rhetorical devices the poet prefers are chosen to cast a fabulous and indistinct light on the representation of the verisimilar. For example, we can easily notice that most of Pascoli's poems are built on paratactic relations where the connective, if any, is the simple conjunction

---

faster and more fully.") The newest and the oldest words, the most common and the unfamiliar become, then, Pascoli's own terms, both in practice and in theory. Writing about Catullus' language, for instance, he finds that its eloquence is a combination of lively provincialisms and elegant Graecisms; and he praises the logical links of the prose, the expressions of ordinary conversation, and the 'precious' diminutives: *solaciolum, misellus, turgiduli, versiculi, munuscula*, and so on, used without a trace of pretense, pity, or derision.

[79] Horace states in his *Ars Poetica:* "It has been held permissible and always will be to introduce a word marked with a contemporary stamp. Just as woods change their leaves with the onward movement of the years, the first leaves falling: even so when words advance in age, they pass away and others born but lately, like the young, flourish and thrive. [...] Many words which have disappeared will be reborn, many which now enjoy prestige will disappear, at the dictate of usage, in whose power lies the judgment of speech and the right to judge it and the standard by which to judge it" (*Ars Poetica*, 58-62; 70-72; trans. James Hynd, SUNY Albany Press (1974): 45-46.

[80] In only a few years a new aesthetics championed by the avant-garde poet Guillaume Apollinaire will open the artistic world to the familiar everyday objects of the bistro table: packets of tobacco, bottles of Pernod, dice, glasses and pipes; flowers and trees, lamps and candlestcks in front of windows, all signs of a reality decipherable through logic and reason and yet meant to represent the puzzling and enigmatic territory of the pre-conscious.

"and." But such a choice is purposely paradoxical, because the statements made are contradictory. Correspondingly, while the message of a poem may claim to be unequivocal, the figures of speech Pascoli favors are oxymorons, synesthesias, chiasms, richly devious tropes that convey a high degree of poetic ambiguity. The celebrated precision of Pascoli's language is then illusory; it is a constant insinuation, built on a reality that is undetermined, enigmatic, indecisive:

Quando si usa un linguaggio normale, vuol dire che dell'universo si ha un'idea sicura e precisa, che si crede in un mondo certo, ontologicamente molto ben determinato, in un mondo gerarchizzato dove i rapporti stessi tra l'io e il non-io, tra l'uomo e il cosmo sono determinati, hanno dei limiti esatti, delle frontiere precognite. Le eccezioni alla norma significheranno allora che il rapporto fra l'io e il mondo in Pascoli è un rapporto critico, non è più un rapporto tradizionale.[81]

Furthermore, the poet reaches his own greatness when he is capable of confusing the boundary between the connotative and denotative value of the word, when the word itself becomes part of an intricate system of relations with other words and other sounds. Rather than translating in familiar terms what is unfamiliar, Pascoli, we shall see, bestows "strangeness" upon the ordinary, and exploits the acoustic elements of the line, or all those semantic values that derive from the contextual position of the words, or, conversely, from their de-contextualization. So that birds and bells, cherry and medlar trees elude a clear perception and escape full mental comprehension; they become musical and psychological effusions.

Certainly, a renovation of language is the preoccupation of every poet. Pascoli finds it more or less unchanged from Horace to the poets of his own day. Working within an established thrust toward a "purism" which rejected the new or unusual word in matters of style, Horace had exhorted the artist "to be spare and cautious in the sowing of words," but promised that the poetic speech would be exceptional if "cleverness of

---

[83] "When one uses a normal language, it means that one has a clear and precise idea of the universe, that one believes in a world that is certain, ontologically well determined, in a hierarchical world where relationships between the I and the non-I, between man and the cosmos are fixed, have exact limits, recognized boundaries. Exceptions to the norm will thus mean that the relationship between the I and the world in Pascoli is a critical relationship, it is no longer a traditional relationship." (My translation of Contini, "Il linguaggio di Pascoli," *Varianti e altra linguistica* 224.)

order and connection render a known word novel." New signs are then permissible to indicate "things unseen before"; while novel and recently fashioned words "will carry conviction if their fountainhead is Greek and they have been drawn off sparingly." (*Ars Poetica*, 46-53). Evidently, the language of everyday and everyone was never considered appropriate to poetic creation. At the end of the nineteenth century, all forms of discretion and prudence are entirely outmoded. As we all know, Vérlaine discards the precision, eloquence, and coherence of literary form as a pedantic prejudice, and Rimbaud repeats that all formal orders, such as the paragraph, the strophe, the measure of the line, the logical sense of the expression must be overturned. In Italy, the values of classical tradition are more deeply ingrained, but Pascoli also maintains that new ways must be found to build new rhyme patterns and to create words on the most diverse roots, both elegant and popular, capable of representing the elusive responses of the poet's soul. In order to find freedom and lightness, and to express this regained virginity, poetry must reject rhetoric, eloquence, history, and science. It must overcome rules of syntax and literary models, and attempt to restore language, style, and versification to the simplicity of the origins.

Thus, for Pascoli, the vision of the child becomes an aesthetic and psychological credo, a program. That vision is the fundamental means to create poetry, since it is the poet-child who observes and seizes the most imponderable aspects of nature and proceeds to combine all that he sees in order to create a new haven for the self. Only the poet-child can take the reader to the special place where blossom the flowers of the night; and by virtue of a mysterious complicity, the reader too enters the territory of the creative mind. Such a re-found ability to see everything as if for the first time, along with feelings of happiness and sadness that overcome the heart, without logical reasons but in tune with the comedy and tragedy of life, is the crucial point of Pascoli's poetics. It also sanctions the illusion of forgetting all that is feigned and spurious in order to consider oneself, indeed one's very existence, as part of universal life. As Pascoli says repeatedly, the poet must learn from the Child to perceive the world in its symbolic aspect; he has to resort, that is, to the irrational faculties of the mind which help the child to capture reality through the senses. Only in this way, will the concrete generate the abstract, the imaginary become real and vice-versa. The visible and the invisible can then be integrated in a reciprocal transfusion of strength, as they influence and modify one another, and thus helping each one of us to organize and represent our inner world correlating in a coherent fashion the various systems of

knowledge. Vico had called this process *il figurare fantastico*, imaginative representation, and had established the images and rhythms of our first language in a pre-knowledge which went beyond the intent to signify.

The first men knew nothing; they knew what you know, Child. Surely they resembled you, because in them the inner child blended, so to speak, with the whole man. They marveled, with all their indistinct being, at everything; because, at that time, everything was really new, and not only for the child, but for the man. They stood in wonder with mixed feelings of joy and sadness, of hope and fear.

(L.C., V)

The aesthetic experience, Cassirer says (*Philosophy of Symbolic Forms*, 1923), is primary insofar as it is tied to sensory perceptions present in the young human baby from the moment of birth. Rudimentary as it may be, and undoubtedly is, it cannot be considered any longer the result of psychic development, but rather, as the condition for such development. From a very early age, and before they acquire the words to express them, children endow external objects with forms that become internalized. Such forms allow the child to organize its imaginative life and condition its ability to create symbols; they constitute an unconscious structure that remains the prototype of all creative endeavors for it prepares the ability to see and to appreciate beauty.[82]

It is not difficult to catch some of the characteristics of the child's quasi-aesthetic responses, the direction of its observation. In the first few years of life, all children seem to be fascinated by the same things and by particular natural events. They are not attuned to the sense of expansion connected with the sublime; on the contrary, the immensity of the sea, the height and distance of the mountains provoke a deep-set anxiety in them, while they react with pleasure to all those less overwhelming natural forms,

---

[82] Here finds its origin the enormous importance of the maternal archetype. The relationship with the mother represents, in the words of the psychologists, the first transformational object. The mother is an object that possesses its form and therefore has its own aesthetic value. The child nursing at his mother's breast, enjoys the sound of her voice, explores the contours of her face, meets her loving glance. The mother is beautiful, available, and gentle. She remains, however, enigmatic and fundamentally unknown. Most importantly, she disappears for long stretches of time, forcing the child to represent her in his imagination. See Melzer and Harris (1988) for their findings on child observation and clinical elaboration.

like flowers and little animals, birds, shells, insects, which share their own fragility and tenderness:

Look at children when they are so deeply engrossed at play. You can see that in their hands they always have little things they have found on the ground, in their path. Things that are of interest only to them and so they alone seem to see them: little snails, little bones, pebbles. The poet does the same.

(*L.C.*, XIV)

Wanting "to do the same," and keeping in mind Horace's ideal of *mediocritas*, Pascoli rejects the hierarchical value system established by the adults and chooses to focus on the smallest and simplest details, repeating them, enriching them, "making things small in order to see them, making them big in order to admire them" (L.C., *III*). What is represented in poetry is great, beautiful, and important not objectively in itself, but because the poet-child thinks it is so, as he goes on re-discovering the world. This is the reason why he tells us his truths, choosing things that are common either in the domesticated nature of rural fields or in the home:

will you say that there is more poetic feeling in the one who, turning or lifting his eyes from the surrounding reality, finds beautiful and worthy of his song only the flowers of the American agave, or in the one who admires and causes others to admire even the tiny red blossoms of the pimpernel on the grassy slope where he sits?

(*L.C.*, VIII)

In an essay by Robert de la Sizeranne widely read and known at the time, we find the very same sentiment:

Ces caractères de Beauté que Dieu a mis dans notre nature d'aimer, il les a imprimés sur les formes qui, dans le monde de chaque jour, sont les plus familières aux yeux des hommes... Oui, seulement un coteau et un enfoncement d'eau calme et une exhalaison de brume et un rayon de soleil. Les plus simple des choses, les plus banales, les plus chères que vous pouvez voir chaque soir d'été le long de mille milliers de cours d'eau parmi les collines basses de vos vieilles contrées familiales. Aimez-les et voyez-les avec droiture! L'Amazone et l'Indus, les Andes et le Caucase ne peuvent nous en donner de plus.[83]

---

[83] ("The traits of Beauty that God has predisposed us to love, He has imprinted in the shapes that are most familiar to our eyes, in our ordinary world... Yes, only a

And in a similar mood, though in order to sustain the decision to abandon his vocation as a writer, since words cannot ever fully express the reality of things, Hofmannsthal speaks of the many and simultaneous voices imprisoned in the most ordinary things and of their secret, intangible life:

A watering can, a plough abandoned in a country field, a dog stretched in the sun, a poor cemetery, a crippled, a small farm house, in all these things I may recognize an epiphany. Each one of these things, and a thousand similar others, on which the eye is used to moving over with natural indifference, suddenly, in any moment that in any way I may be able to recall, may take on a noble and touching color, that no word could aptly render. Yes, it may happen that even the precise evocation of something that is not there be destined to be filled with that sweet and impetuously growing energy of a divine sentiment.[84]

Pascoli too, is certain that all things hide, behind their surface, a second and richer quality, difficult to capture, resisting all efforts of schematization; he senses the world as disorderly and fragmented. But he is not at all ready to consent to ineffability. On the contrary, his poetry finds its reason and its essence in the special intensity of each word, in the relations between words, and between each word and the thing it represents. In his poems, the life of nature and the life of objects is neither still nor silent, but well articulated and even dramatic. Under each tree, each pot, each utensil, each cloud, there seems to lie in wait a secret, a whole story. In truth, nothing is what it appears to be. It is therefore possible to live in the imagination a succession of perfectly ordinary incidents, since to be a poet means to find the beauty of all things and to let all natural sights, sounds, and events penetrate the soul and awaken the imagination. This process reflects the way in which the reality of the world appears to the

---

small slope, and a pond of still water, and the lifting of fog, and a beam of sunlight. The simplest things, the most irrelevant, the dearest ones, the ones that you can see every summer evening along thousands of streams of water, among the low hills of your old familiar regions. Love them, and look at them in the proper way! The Amazon and the Indus, the Andes and the Caucasus could never give us more beauty." My trans.) See Robert de la Sizeranne, *Ruskin et la religion de la beauté*, Paris, 1897, 216-17, as quoted in G. Leonelli, "Pascoli esteta," *Itinerari del Fanciullino*, 77-78.

[84] My trans. of the quotation from the German-Italian edition of Hugo von Hofmannsthal, *Ein Brief* (1902), Milano: BUR, 1985.

eyes of the young child who resorts to his expectations of order and
regularity to bring meaning, a consistent meaning, into the multitude of
information he receives.[85] By following this pattern, the poet restores close
contact with all things, reclaiming the relationship of things to life and
seeing the objects as metaphors. Pascoli is, in this, clear and coherent: the
poet contemplates facts and events, finding the unusual in the most
ordinary things, eliciting a different reaction to them, rejecting the habitual
(nothing hinders the poetic feeling more than the sense of habituation!).
The poet must strive to see with the fresh eyes of spring the most ancient
of things; he must recapture the fullness of meaning, outside of time, the
self-enclosed certainty, the capacity to conceive things in their totality and
in their parts that very capacity attributable to our early years. But the effort
is great. The adult has learned to divide, analyze, classify, and instead, in
making poetry, he wants to see unity and uniqueness at the same time. The
eyes of the child have to provide him with the abundance of means that he
needs.

We said that Pascoli's poetry strives to awaken a sense of proximity
and attentive immediacy. This was the result of his personal background
and cultural preparation. It was also a way to provide him with the only
certainty and the only joy: the un-mediated authenticity of the objects. Only
what is there to be heard and seen, touched and smelled can declare at once
the reality of the world, that of the self, and their reciprocal adaptation. It is
from the primordial experience of this common resonance that a sense of
peace and well being can be gained. For Pascoli, there is truly nothing else.
His "passion for the objects" reveals, then, a much deeper philosophical
conviction. It asserts the objective truth of human mortality, and proudly
overcomes, in himself first of all, the controlling force of the old wish for
eternity. It is a return to the self, to the real limits that have been violated
by the imaginative invention of the afterlife. In his view, the new "man of
genius" must find, once again, the simplicity of the poor, of woman, and of
child, in short, of all those who are believed to be linked in intuitive
sympathy to the things of our physical world. From the child, as from the

---

[85] Croce called this final stage in the process of perception the 'intuition' of form.
But the word is not essential. And Pascoli would disagree with it. It is also not
essential that the 'meaning' have logical sense; it is sufficient if a reliable coherence
is 'manifested' (in Wittgenstein's sense), that is to say, if it is present in the
consciousness as significant form.

man of genius [86] in whom the functions of the heart overpower reason, the people can expect once more the regeneration of society. Obviously, Pascoli believes that the artist, like society itself, must make infinite voyages of discovery into the realm of childhood, into that precocious stream of "nonsense," shaped by accident, inner vitality, and freshness of vision that is peculiar to that age. The adult world is stable, fixed in its habits, ruled by legitimacy, analysis, and classification of all phenomena, preoccupied with

---

[88] Baudelaire likens childhood to the state of renewed attachment to life proper of convalescence and to the vibrant curiosity of the man of genius in a well-known passage of "Le Peintre de la vie moderne" (*Oeuvres complètes*, Paris:Laffont,1980:794-95): "Now, convalescence is like a return towards childhood.. The convalescent, like the child, is possessed in the highest degree of the faculty of keenly interesting himself in things, be they apparently of the most trivial. Let us go back, if we can, by a retrospective effort of the imagination, towards our most youthful, our earliest, impressions, and we will recognize that they had a strange kinship with those brightly coloured impressions which we were later to receive in the aftermath of a physical illness, always provided that that illness had left our spiritual capacities pure and unharmed. The child sees everything in a state of newness; he is always *drunk*. Nothing more resembles what we call inspiration than the delight with which a child absorbs form and colour. [...] The man of genius has sound nerves; while those of the child are weak. With the one, Reason has taken up a considerable position; with the other, Sensibility is almost the whole being. But genius is nothing more nor less than *childhood recovered* at will, childhood now equipped for self-expression with manhood's capacities, and a power of analysis which enables it to order the mass of raw material which it involuntarily accumulated. It is by this deep and joyful curiosity that we may explain the fixed and animally ecstatic gaze of a child confronted with something new, whatever it be, whether a face, a landscape, gilding, colorus, shimmering stuff, or the magic of physical beauty assisted by the cosmetic art" (*The Painter of Modern Life and Other Essays*, trans. Jonathan Mayne, London, Phaidon, 1965: 7-8). The same fundamental concept is presented also in *Les Paradis artificiels* ("Le Génie Enfant"). And to the same effect Ruskin will reiterate: "They look back to the days of childhood as of greatest happiness, because those were the days of greatest wonder, greatest simplicity, and most vigorous imagination. And the whole difference between a man of genius and other men, it has been said a thousand times, and most truly, is that the first *remains in great part a child, seeing with the large eyes of children, in perpetual wonder, not conscious of much knowledge,* — conscious, rather of infinite ignorance, and yet infinite power; a fountain of eternal admiration, delight and creative force within him, meeting the ocean of visible and governable things around him" (*The Stones of Venice*, London, 1905, 3:52-53).

profit and mechanization. "The grown man," Horace says "seeks wealth and connections, is a slave to prestige, and anxious not to do anything that will shortly take effort to alter." (*Ars Poetica*, 166-8). The child, on the other hand, personifies and manifests flexibility, experimentation, naturalness. These are, indeed, the characteristics of childhood Pascoli chooses to underline in his essay. What he carefully *studies*, in order to become a naïve poet, is the child's state of pure receptivity. Therefore, the improbability and proven disinterest of a direct observation of young children's life and behavior are remedied by the books. Recent research has amended considerably the image of Pascoli as the little professor who read only his classics, as the provincial poet, lagging behind or ignoring the newest theoretical and critical trends. The opposite is true and Pascoli appears to be committed and very informed, well aware of the newest developments in the visual arts, and extremely interested in the methodical investigation on the nature of childhood conducted by men trained in scientific observation. Particularly interesting, among the 35.000 volumes of the Castelvecchio library, is James Sully's *Studies of Childhood*, a book that Pascoli read in the French translation as early as 1897. Sully's precisely articulated accounts of the characteristics of the child's imagination, the development of its intelligence, the beginning of reasoning and thinking, corroborate the poet's intuitions and contribute to Pascoli's *fanciullino* the features of a carefully drawn theoretical paradigm, studied in precise details; a model that is far from being over-emotional and abstract, and is responsible also for the occasional failings in poetic inspiration.[87] Even the excesses in language, the concession to morbidity and tears, the occasional slipping into cuteness, and the indulgence toward data of his own personal biography — rather annoying at times — may be viewed as part of a deliberate plan: the small world of the little child represents the natural and instinctual sensoriality at the foundation of the cognitive process.

---

[87] See James Sully, *Studies of Childhood*, New York: D. Appleton, 1896. Equally valuable is Eduard von Hartmann's *Philosophy of the Unconscious*, a work, also present in the Castelvecchio library, that began to map the imaginary territory of the mind in order to understand its functioning. According to Fulvio Cantoni (*Il Resto del Carlino*, 7 Aprile 1912), the works of Michelet and Hartmann's *Philosophy of the Unconscious* were *livres de chevet* for the young Pascoli when he was a student in Bologna. I am indebted to the work done by some of Pascoli's more recent scholars: Furio Felcini, Giuseppe Leonelli, Giuseppe Nava, and Maurizio Perugi are among the most sensitive of them.

Words & Things

You must only judge (if you have this mania of judging) if those were eyes that did indeed see.

(L.C., XII)

Gifted with a peculiar instinct to understand the most remote relationships among things, the child prefers to relate and connect, rather than separate and analyze, and he responds to the natural world with intuitive immediacy. He sees the various elements of the landscape one by one, and returns them to the poet in separate fragments of vision — the plough abandoned in the middle of the field of "Lavandare" ("The Washer-women"), the apple tree in the moonlit evening of "L'assiuolo" ("The Night Owl"), the green eyes of "Un gatto nero" ("A Black Cat").

These fragments are presented in sequences that are somewhat capricious, ostensibly without any reason that could justify the choice.[88] But we know that, in Pascoli's view, logic should not matter since what makes a poet is his feeling and his vision, more than the way in which he may express them. Poetry is not the expression of adult emotions and ideas, it does not ask for passions, complex experiences, and plans of action. Rather, pure poetry is to be found in all that stops the continuous flow of consciousness — without decorative intents — and in the internal responses to the things of life — without literary models. The poet speaks to himself or to others like him; he does not intend to dominate and convince, he only accepts and repeats the echoes that things leave in his spirit.[89] Therefore, poetic language is a challenge to the normal ways of

---

[88] Debenedetti analyzes as emblematic the images that take shape in the eyes and ears of the wayfarer in "Nella macchia." Here, the details follow one another without a particular logic, or consequentiality; they could be tied to the walking of the man, but we are told that he has no aim; they are more closely connected by the quality of the ascending rhythm: an iambic anapestic nine syllables verse which imitates the walking of the pilgrim.

[89] Leonelli quotes (79) a page from Ruskin's *Stones of Venice* that appears remarkably similar to Pascoli's observations: "The whole function of the artist in the world is to be a seeing and feeling creature; it is to be an instrument of such tenderness and

communication; it specifically differs from the speech of scientists and orators, politicians or business men: "the poet is a poet, not an orator or a preacher, not a philosopher, not a historian, not a teacher, not a tribune or demagogue, not a statesman or courtier" (L.C., XI). Most importantly, poetry is a way to see and to hear differently; and it is mythopoesis, founded on language and founding language, repeating Adam's first act of making all things created exist by giving them names:

And he chatters in the meantime, without ever stopping; and without him, not only would we not see many things to which we ordinarily do not pay attention, but we could not even think them or say them, because the Child is the Adam who gives the name to all that he sees and hears.

(L.C., III)

Thus, the poet, if he wants to make poetry, must every so often allow himself to say: "And this, what is it? What does it mean?" Oh, pedantic, annoying poet! And yet, this is what the poet should do, and let himself say, in the hope that, if nothing else, his effort will be to the benefit of future poets, who will find many names in wide use that before were not known and, for this reason, were termed obscure. In truth, is he not the Adam who first gives names to things?

(L.C., XIV)

Poetry, therefore, need only provide the certainty that all the things to which a name is given become alive, are comprehensible to all, and enter, as through some kind of sorcery, into a state of harmony with each other. As such, Heidegger contends, poetry is an establishment of being by means of the word: "The poet names the gods and names all things as what they are. The naming does not consist merely in something already known being

---

sensitiveness that no shadow, no hue, no line, no instantaneous and evanescent expression of the visible things around him, nor any of the emotions, which they are capable of conveying to the spirit which has been given him, shall either be left unrecorded, or fade from the book of record. It is not his business either to think, to judge, to argue, or to know. His place is neither in the closet, nor on the bench, nor at the bar, nor in the library. They are for other men, and other work. He may think, in a by-way; reason, now and then, when he has nothing better to do; know such fragments of knowledge as he can gather without stooping, or reach without pains; but none of these are to be his care. The work of his life is to be twofold only: to see, to feel" (J. Ruskin, *The stones of Venice* 37). Research, however, has not ascertained that Ruskin had read or known the Italian poet

supplied with a name, it is rather that, when the poet speaks the essential word, the existent is by this naming nominated as what it is. So it becomes known as existent."[90] Naming is, indeed, the first act of taking possession of the world.

In the mind of the young child words do have the mysterious power of maintaining, at least in part, the objective and immediate reality of the things they represent. Through the language of the poet, things must regain that same status; they must be recaptured beyond their conventional meanings. *Things* exist, then, in the *Words* the poet is able to find, according to the ambition of the *artifex additus artifici* that Pascoli shares with the artists of his time, indeed of all times.

> *Poiesis*, in fact, is a play-function. [...] It lies beyond seriousness, on the more primitive and original level where the child, the animal, the savage, and the seer belong, in the region of dream, enchantment, ecstasy, laughter. To understand poetry we must be capable of donning the child's soul like a magic cloak and of forsaking man's wisdom for the child's.[91]

Everyone knows that young children enjoy playing with words. They hear the sounds they produce and fall in love with them. Very early on, they learn to prolong their babbling in endless iterations, and accompany it with simple rhythms for the mere pleasure this brings. It is an instinctive and universal phenomenon that seems connected to the biological organization of the nervous system and associated with the first rudiment of song and music:[92]

---

[90] *Existence and Being*, trans. Douglas Scott, London, Vision Press, 1949: 304.

[91] Johan Huizinga defines play in general as a free activity "standing quite consciously outside ordinary life, as being not serious, but, at the same time, absorbing the player intensely and completely. Play is an activity unconnected with material interest, and no profit can be gained by it. It proceeds within its own proper boundaries of time and space, in an orderly manner and according to fixed rules. It promotes the formation of social groupings which tend to surround themselves with secrecy and to stress their difference from the common world by disguise or other means" (141).

[92] This primordial "babbling" which appears in periods of happy contentment, is wonderfully rich and varied: "Thus the child will bring out a string of a's and other vowel sounds. In this baby-twittering the several vowel sounds of our tongue become better distinguishable, and are strung together in queer ways" (Sully 135). According to Preyer, also quoted in Sully's work, this infant's babbling contains

You sing, like all children who jump and play at some well timed sing-song of theirs, not only when they are somewhat grown, but even when they are still nursing and making wild woodland sounds, and babble to themselves in measured rhythm their long strings of *pa pa* and *ma ma.*

(L.C., V)

In language, the imaginative play of the child becomes freer and, at the same time, more complex, more intensely creative. And the link between language and play is revealed by the presence of the obvious sign of joy: laughter. Laughter is the unexpected gift, the sign of a liberation and of an absolute value that pacifies and unites the soul of the one to the souls of the many. Through laughter and through language, the young child becomes aware of being connected to others, in sympathy and solidarity. Imitating the speech of the adults who surround them, children reduce it to shorter sounds that seem to privilege the first or the last syllable, the stressed syllable and the vowel sounds. What is always striking is the care for metrical qualities and the disregard for articulatory characteristics. In his poetry, Pascoli tries to break down traditional rhyming patterns in order to create a different kind of musicality, based on repetitions and correspondences. He literally interrupts the long, flowing rhythm of the verse, at times with the use of *enjambements*, still a rather traditional method, even when used in the middle of a word: "io mi ritrovo a piangere infinita- / mente con te: morire così presto!" (I find myself again crying endless- / ly with you: to die so young!"). More often with fragmenting punctuation: "Dormono. L'uomo parte. Il cipresso / freme di nuovi brevi bisbigli" ("Passeri a sera"). ("They are asleep. The man leaves. The cypress / shivers with new short murmurs" ("Sparrows in the Evening"). Even more anomalously with the usage of parentheses and incidental expressions: "Ecco l'alba (tra selve aride i fossi / vanno col fumo di vaporiere), piena

---

most if not all the sounds which are afterwards used in speaking, and, among these, some which cause much difficulty later on. The number of syllabic sounds, the distribution of stress, as well as the rise and fall of vocal pitch, are the first things to be attended to, and these are on the whole, carefully replicated when the constituent sounds are changed into other and often very unlike ones. It is thus an ingenious plan of nature by which the child is made to rehearse months beforehand for the difficult performances of articulate speech. (To speak is to use a sound intentionally as the sign of an idea. On the contrary, the only signification of primitive articulation, was and is emotional; it grows out of expressive cries, as Vico had so clearly stated.)

d'un tintinnio di pettirossi, / cui risponde un tac tac di capinere...." ("The hammerless gun") or with the ways of direct discourse: apostrophes, questions and answers, often monosyllabic: "Chi è?" "Non so" "Chi sei? Che fai?" Più nulla. / "Dorme?" " Non so." ("Il Naufrago") ("Who is he?" "I do not know." " Who are you? What do you do?" Nothing more, / "Is he asleep?" "I do not know." ("The shipwreck"); or "Chi?" disse, "Il Papa" "Il Papa, che?" "Sta male!" ("La morte del Papa") ('Who?' he said, "The Pope" "The Pope, what?" "He is sick!") ("Death of the Pope"). The line is then reconstructed on a low-toned musicality, believed to be more instinctive and child-like, committed to alliterations, assonances and consonances, which repeat the sounds present in key words and, at the same time, succeed in enlarging the meaning of the poetic message: "Io sì: ci ritornai; / e le rividi le mie bianche suore, / e li rivissi i dolci anni che sai; / quei piccoli anni così dolci al cuore..." ("Digitale purpurea"). ("Instead I did, I went back there, and I again saw my white Sisters, / and I relived the sweet years that you remember. Those early years so dear to everyone's heart..." ("The purple foxglove"). The poet, who has elected the little child as model, shares with him a half-playful, half-serious scrutiny of the words. He seeks to simplify forms, to get rid of irregularities, and to discover unusual affinities in verbal sounds and their occasional punning effect. Accordingly, he catches the intrinsic sensory qualities of a word or a group of words, and tries to find new names and new rhythms, or to express old ones in new ways. The most widely recognized and lauded trait of Pascoli's style is this heightened sensitivity for the value of the signifier, for the phonic element of each line. We hear, for example, the train and the thunder, the singing voices of birds, the galloping of horses. But the mimetic intent is neutralized to evoke not clear but rather confused emotions; adjectives and nouns are cleverly equivocal, as they stop before being fully discernible, and transmit, instead, a presentiment of a hidden reality. An often quoted example is that of the cry of the *chiù* ('L'assiuolo"), a nocturnal bird, perhaps the mourning dove, whose lamenting voice, full of mystery and pain, returns to obsess the poet:

"L'assiuolo" (*Myricae*)

Dov'era la luna? ché il cielo
notava in un'alba di perla,
ed ergersi il mandorlo e il melo
parevano a meglio vederla.
Venivano soffi di lampi

da un nero di nubi laggiù;
veniva una voce dai campi
chiù...
Le stelle lucevano rare
tra mezzo alla nebbia di latte:
sentivo il cullare del mare
sentivo un fru fru tra le fratte;
sentivo nel cuore un sussulto,
com'eco d'un grido che fu.
Sonava lontano il singulto:
chiù...
Su tutte le lucide vette
tremava un sospiro di vento
squassavano le cavallette
finissimi sistri d'argento
(tintinni a invisibili porte
che forse non s'aprono più? ...);
e c'era quel pianto di morte...
chiù...[93]

In this poem, the thematic word *chiù* ties the adjoining words to its sound, communicating to them and receiving from them something of its own verbal nature and reinforcing the meaning of the words through insistent repercussion. The external, natural detail changes into its psychic, spiritual counterpart; the end of each stanza presents images of decreasing clarity, and the singing of the *chiù* is first a voice, then a sob, then a cry; it is a sudden apperception, from the heart, of the reality of death. The unusual combinations of the nouns used to describe natural incidents — *soffi di vento, nero di nubi, nebbia di latte, cullare del mare, sospiro di vento (breath of wind, blackness of clouds, mist of milk, lulling of the sea, sigh of wind)* — generate a series of analogies with internal states and visions. Each particular word is an

---

[93] "The night owl": "Where was the moon? For the sky was swimming in a pearly dawn, and the apple and the almond trees seemed to rise to see it better. From a blackness of clouds, over there, came flashes of lightning; from the field came a call: *chiù* ... The stars shone sparingly through the milky clouds: I heard the lulling of the sea, I heard a rustling in the bushes, I felt a leap in my heart like an echo of an erstwhile scream. Far away sounded that sob: *chiù*.... Over all the shining peaks trembled a breath of wind. The locusts were shaking tiny silver rattles (tinkling sounds at invisible doors that perhaps will no longer open?...) and there was that cry of death... *chiù*...."

element in a system of relationships not only with other words, but with other sounds, so that the sound of a word more than its meaning appears to determine the choice of the following one. On the multiple or ambiguous meanings which connect the literal to the symbolic, Lévinas writes:

Le mot n'est pas séparable du sens. Mais il y a d'abord la matérialité du son qu'il remplit et qui permet de le ramener à la sensation et à la musicalité telle que nous venons de la définir: il est susceptible de rythme, de rimes, de mètres, d'allitérations, etc. Mais le mot se détache de son sens objectif et retourne à l'élément du sensible encore d'une autre manière: en tant qu'il s'attache à une multiplicité de sens, en tant d'ambiguïté qu'il peut tenir de son voisinage avec d'autres mots.[94]

At any rate, Pascoli's objective is not only that of a mechanical and, in the case of language, utterly problematic reproduction of "things" no matter how phonic the singing of birds, the rustling of leaves, the sounds of water or storm may be. Rather, he wants to discover again that feeling for quality of sound and tone, that instinctive pleasure in simple tunes, in well-marked and easily recognizable time divisions that are so quieting and so exciting for the human baby. Pascoli's combinatory ability and his skillful imitation of the real sounds of rain, trains, frogs, crickets, and birds manifest the intention to go beyond the denotative power of the words and to experiment with their timbre, pitch, and vibrations, more like the English and American poets he knew and loved (he translated Poe, Shelley, Tennyson, and Byron) than his tradition-laden compatriots. The non-semantic elements of his language, such as alliterations, assonances, repetitions, catch our attention as if to command the renewal of the meaning. Such devices may very well be the product of technical virtuosity, but they are also the poet's way to play, to have fun.[95] And the words are

---

[96] "The word cannot be separated from the meaning. But, first, there is the material substance of the sound that allows us to link it to sensation and musicality the way we have defined them: it is susceptible of rhythm, rime, meter, alliterations, etc. However, the word detaches itself from its objective meaning and goes back to sensation in yet another way: because it attaches itself to a multiplicity of meanings, because it keeps the ambiguity of its closeness with other words." (My trans.) See Lévinas 86-87.

[95] The Italian Futurists, Palazzeschi in particular, all the poets of the *Crepuscolarismo*, the *neo-avant-garde* of the '60s will rediscover the ludic dimension of the creative imagination and the possibility of absorbing the metrical structure in mental

studied with the same rapt attention Pascoli supposes to have been proper of the earliest attempts at communication:

They, the first men, pronounced with uniform slowness, with measured gravity, that difficult word which they marveled could fly and shine and sound, could belong to them and could belong to others and carry the soul of the one who emitted it after long, silent meditation. Oh! they did not throw them around, as vile things in excess, those words just born, bound with the slightest of knots, stamped with the sharpest markings, wrought in the most ingenious niello designs! They recognized all their qualities, and the weight and the tone of their metal and the sound with which they first broke forth from their parted lips, and the sound which finally resounded in their open ears. Now, you, Child, do as they did because you are like them.

(*L.C.*, V)

Often such earnest enrichment of the sounds counts more than the enrichment of the sense. As when two distinct meanings are expressed with signifiers that closely resemble each other: "*moviamo, moriamo*," for instance, or "*ora si dora*"; or when the words are chosen in order to produce sound contrasts, or are bent to find the strange and the dissonant in what appears concordant.[96] Equally significant and enjoyable are the frequent inversions of the usual order in grammatical structure, the apparent incongruities, the use of antithesis, the economy of expression, so typical of children's language, where words stand for a variety of meanings and prepositions are not always necessary to indicate exact relationships. Not unlike the listener of the child, the reader of Pascoli's poetry must enter

---

discourse. The new poets will learn to eliminate, as much as possible, logical and syntactic connections in favor of the essential value of the words. These are among the gifts of innovation Pascoli contributed to the world of poetry. Equally important are the ways in which he was able to create mental associations guided only by a process of stream of consciousness *avant la lettre* in the meanderings of the unconscious and the oneiric.

[96] "L'uccellino del freddo" is the often cited example of a lyric where the dissonant expressionism — built on an accumulation of deformations, verbal inventions, and dialectal acquisitions — is not at all bent on resolving words into music but rather on creating a degree of diminished significance, a slowing down of communication. In other words, the sounds are meant to attract attention to the rarity of the language, to the difficulty of comprehension of the single elements making up the discourse. See Barberi Squarotti, *Simboli e strutture della poesia del Pascoli* 368-69.

into the play and confer meaning to the form through the process of interpretation for the best of Pascoli's poetry springs from the fragments of a reality constantly in motion and remains purposely equivocal built as it is on the regular interplay of realism and surrealism. In fact, the poet moves continuously from a position of clear consciousness in which things have distinct outlines, to a somewhat oneiric state where all images are only vaguely recognized. He reasons by way of images not concepts. Thus, immense metaphors of subconscious motifs are transformed into things, objects, and people belonging to a familiar, physical reality. Conversely, his language of symbols is concrete and universally intelligible, rigorous and accurate, but behind the structure of classical invention the representations reveal the ambiguous and chaotic connotations of contradiction. As in De Chirico's metaphysical paintings, the objective things Pascoli presents us become part of a very subjective story. To this effect, Pascoli consistently chooses semantemes that attract and diffuse different sensations, since, in his view, poetry is also the exploration of the formless and the unknown, that is to say, of all that has not been organized by the rational mind. In other words, the poet wants to paint, but he avoids the clean lines of the foreground and proposes suggestively fluid settings of obscurity, haze, or mist, which, in turn, become very real. The poet wants to compose and, indeed, a solid pattern of lines ties together his lyrics which he prefers to make rather short. Yet the compact vocal orchestration does not strengthen a specific suggestion; on the contrary, it alludes to a pattern of evasion built on a number of imprecise qualifiers, or combinations of noun and adjective, that do not define the object, but rather seem to move around it, widening it, eliminating the individual, and bringing everything back to a primordial essence.

Alfonso Traina (*Il latino del Pascoli*) called Pascoli's distinctive circumlocutions *onomatopoeic cells*. Gianluigi Beccaria ("Polivalenza e dissolvenza nel linguaggio poetico pascoliano") calls them *phonic periphrases* and gives us numerous examples of them, taken mostly from *Myricae*. He lists privileged words that are applicable, analogically, to more than one sensory field — light, sound, movement.[97] Often these adjectives and

---

[97] Of the two major sensory perceptions employed in Pascoli's synesthesias the auditory often appears more suggestive. In the sound, in fact, resides the infinite power of the word, and the sound can more easily allude to arcane, spiritual spheres. For example, *tremulo* or *stridulo* are very frequent adjectives chosen because they are movement and sound at the same time (Cecchetti).

nouns suggest a reduced, diminished, or frail vitality, that of the newborn or the little child that is supposed to live in fervor and vivacity but is constantly threatened by intimations of the unknown: *tremulous, querulous, pearlescent, opalescent, translucent, ashen, waifish, fragile; tacit, flat, muffled, veiled; breath, tension, shiver, shake, wave, tremor, throbbing, quiver.* Things are therefore only pretexts, occasions. Pascoli faces them in his own special way; nature, for him, is everything we see, hear, and understand confusedly, as small children do, because we are part of it. And only as such can nature be transmitted. The keenest perceptions are useless, in fact, if they do not appear as premonitions of something else. For the poet is the metaphorical, not the literal man, and he gives light to things, bringing them to the foreground, concentrating on them a constantly renewed attention.

Untroubled by the complexity of things, the child is occupied only with what is valuable and fastens his attention on features that he deems attractive, creating extravagant similarities. Pascoli seems to construct his own knowledge of the world the way the child does, overlaying changeable analogies on every concrete object, privileging expansiveness and unconventionality over clear data and abstract conceptions:

He discovers the most ingenious resemblances and relations among things. He adapts the name of the bigger thing to the smaller and vice versa. And he is moved to do this by wonder, rather than by ignorance, and by curiosity, rather than mere loquacity: he makes things small in order to see them, he makes things big in order to admire them.

(*L.C.*, III)

Children describe what they see or hear by analogy with something they know already, assimilating the new and strange to the familiar, lending not only body but also soul to the wind that howls at night, to the stars of the sky:

Augusto Conti tells of one of his little girls: "When she looked at the moon or the stars, she screamed with joy and pointed them out to me, and called to them as living things, offering them whatever she had in her hands, even her clothes." In my mind I go over all the poems I have read. I do not find one that is more poetry than this!

(*L.C.*, footnote 7)

"To give names to nameless things by transference [metaphora] from things kindred or similar in appearance" is how Aristotle describes the function of metaphor (*Rh.* III.II. 1405a34). But metaphors are not just an

embellishment of poetic discourse or a means of enriching language; metaphors are authentic epistemological factors. "To know how to invent fine metaphors means to know how to grasp the resemblances that objects bear to one another" (*Poetics* 1459a); and furthermore: "in philosophy, too, the ability to perceive similarities between objects which are far apart is evidence of an acute mind" (*Rh.* III II. 1414a. 9). Studying the mental development of the child, James Sully observes: "The transference of qualities from object to object through the apprehension of a likeness or assimilation constitutes one of the most interesting manifestations of children's originality. Words lodge like flying seedlings in the fertile brain, and shoot up into strange imaginative growths" (148). The particular line of analogical extension seems to depend on the nature of the first impressions or experiences recognized by the individual child. One may prefer sounds, another is stimulated by movement, or color, by soft touching, or smells. All the senses are involved, however, as all the senses and bodily responses shape the structures of the spontaneous imagination and become part of language in similes, analogies, synergies, and metaphors the way Vico had intuited: "It is noteworthy that in all languages the greater part of the expressions relating to inanimate things are formed by metaphors from the human body and its parts" (*N .S.*, 405).[98] Both the ordinary, descriptive reference and a new reference are held in tension by the metaphorical mode of looking at the world.[99] Metaphorical sense is truly a verbal action;

---

[98] Bachelard has shown that all our dreams and daydreams are determined by our relationships with the physical world, and clustered around the elements of pre-socratic philosophy, the basic elements of life. Images of the house of birth, of valleys and caves, of small enclosures in the earth, of anything reminiscent of the cradle or better yet, of the maternal womb, appear, with great frequency and poignancy, around the theme of the child. Equally important are the returning images of water, small brooks, rivers, the sea, always shining from afar — in which modern psychoanalysis identifies a symbol of the soul in touch with its origins, close to the great prenatal lake.

[99] Today's linguists tend to confer on the metaphorical element a value that is much less universal. They also hypothesize different developments of discourse in the two operations: metaphoric and metonymic. For Jakobson (*Essais de linguistique générale*, 1963), the metaphorical process (a process based on similarity) will have priority over the metonymic process (a process based on contiguity) in poetic creations that have a symbolic tendency, whereas the metonymic process will prevail in 'realistic' literary trends. For Pascoli, as for Vico, such distinctions are much more blurred. What is of relevance is the belief that in the metaphor there

moreover, it is an action that disturbs and/or amuses us every time we encounter it, because it violates the code of congruity and appropriateness that determines ordinary communication. By its power, a shift of distance from far to near, from large to small, catches the mind in a play of apparent discrepancy and brings together two heterogeneous things. Talking about Homer, the first poet-child, Pascoli remarks:

Most of all, in order to have his thoughts fully understood, when talking about a fact or an event that was newer and different, he tried to work with similes that were very familiar to him and to his listeners. And, in so doing, he followed two opposite ways: at times he remembered a small fact to make a big one understood; at others he used the greater one to set off the lesser. And so, he represented a rough sea casting itself against the shore with big foamy waves, roaring and thundering, in order to indicate a multitude of men arriving in one place; and he described a swarm of flies around a pail filled to the brim with milk, in order to express the vast and confused massing of an army of warriors.

(*L.C.*, II)

This is the way in which the eyes of the little child catch the splendor of literal truth and guide us to see better:

You say, in your own way open and simple things that you see and feel in your own way clear and immediate, and you are satisfied with what you say, when whoever listens to you exclaims: "I also see *now*. *Now* I hear what you are saying and what was, certainly, outside and inside of me, even previously, even though I was not at all aware of it or not as well as I am now!"

(*L.C.*, IV)

The mind projects sameness upon difference; it pulls things together in relationships, but it maintains the difference between them because it reaches out to conceive images that cannot be combined since they do not derive from the same level of reality: one is actual, one is possible. Reaching out for that difference, shifting the mind from the particulars of sensory experience to something other than the facts, engaging the mind in a story that constantly re-begins, is what Pascoli's idea of poetry is all about, and what his best poetry is. The coexistence of

---

remains some residue of the ancient faculty of linking up, by sudden illumination, the rational and irrational, the conceptual and imaginative, the emotional and referential aspects of reality.

opposites — the very large and the very small, the visible and the invisible, dreams and visions, hopes and fears — forms the intriguing map of the imagination and lends infinite motifs to the poetic feeling of the adult man. But, once again, Plato and the neo-platonists had already been champions of ideal realism, and, as Pascoli himself remembers, Plato was the first to create *mythos and logos*.

In Pascoli's poetry the rhetorical figures of metaphor and synesthesia seem to correspond to a mechanism of expansion, while the density or concentration of the message is attained through metonymies and oxymorons. The intellectual paradox of the oxymoron appears to reflect the particular disposition of the poet in affirming *and* denying his own existential condition, often articulated in the contrast between the feeling of a basic entitlement to life and to joy, and the resigned submission to a reality of duties and problems that have to be solved, or limits that have been reached. The oxymoron is, indeed, a trademark of Pascoli's poetry and certainly could be interpreted as the revelatory sign of his own instability as well as the conscious determination to underscore the basic ambiguity of existence.

The expansion of the semantic sphere is much simpler. It is obtained often with the fusion of two different sensorial impressions, as in the *tenebra sonora* of *Notte* — that *resounding darkness* where the adjective widens its own semantic sphere (the sense of sound) as well as that of the noun it qualifies (the sense of sight). Nothing could explain this practice better than an analysis of one of Pascoli's favorite devices, the *endiadi simulata* (the metaphor of the genitive), wherein two nouns are connected by the preposition "of": *sospiro di vento; nero di pece; alba di perla; nebbia di latte; frulli d'uccelli; pianto di morte (breath of wind; blackness of tar; dawn of pearl; fog of milk; flutter of birds; cry of death)*.[100] As we have noted already, one of the two nouns is concrete and definable but its sensoriality melts into the figurative halo of the other noun which is supposed to qualify it.

Admittedly, the power of the metaphor derives from its promise to grant us a better, truer, more complete understanding than is available

---

[100] See the fine, precise analysis by Teresa Ferri, *Pascoli: Il labirinto del segno*. The critic observes that, however renewed, the model is Homeric in origin. So is the repetition of the meaning in the negation of its contrary: *to live, not at all to die*; the ellipsis of some parts of grammar; the suspended periods; the *yesses* and *nos*; the *maybes*; the '*I don't know what*'; the alliterative onomatopeias, the phonosymbolic figures which have unnerved — or delighted — critics and readers.

through the meaning of each individual word. A metaphor is a kind of symbol, just like the lover of the *Symposium*: "Each one of us is but the *symbolon* of a human being" says Aristophanes "sliced in half like a flatfish, two instead of one, and each pursues a never ending search for the symbolon of himself."[101] This image of lovers as people cut in half is comical and impeccable. All desire seems to be for the part of oneself that has been lost, or so it painfully feels to the person in love. It is the same with creativity. All of a sudden, something tremendously powerful passes through the poet's mind and for an instant a great many things look knowable, reachable, and pleasant. Then the barrier re-asserts itself. The fleeting glimpse of that enhanced meaning is a saddening thing, because it is inseparable from the conviction of its impossibility. The strange power of writing poetry is then delusory, as Plato maintains in the *Phaedrus* (275d).[102] It is the absurd conviction of making things knowable and clear for all times while emotional ambivalence splits the soul. The shift was only momentary; still, it was enough to give us the sense of being very close to the place where feelings and ideas form. Moreover, neither the writer nor

---

[101] Plato, *Symposium* (91d). We may remember that in the ancient Greek *symbolon* referred to one half of a knucklebone carried as a token of identity, and therefore recognition, to someone who has the other half. Together the two halves constitute one meaning.

[102] In the *Phaedrus*, Eros and Logos fit tightly together. Phaedrus is in love with a written text, an erotic logos composed by Lysias. It is a subversive theory of non-love based on the invariably transient nature of erotic desire, beautifully manipulated by Socrates to prove the opposite point: the action of eros does harm to the beloved since the lover takes a controlling attitude that wants to freeze the beloved in time. A similar damage occurs to the process of wisdom when the reader or writer expects words to be permanently fixed in their meaning. Wisdom is something alive that happens between two people when they talk. The written logos fixes living things in time and space giving them the appearance of animation although they are abstracted from life and incapable of change. It is of interest to note that also in the *Phaedrus* (276b-d), Pascoli found that rich analogy between writers and gardeners that returns so convincingly in his *Little Child*. Gardens of letters, like gardens of Adonis are sown for fun, they are a denial of commitment and cannot be taken seriously. The plants that bloom in eight days for the festivals have no roots; they are an image of quickly accessible wisdom. Serious thoughts need different cultivation and time to grow. Planted as seeds of living speech in the ground of an appropriate soul, they will take root and, as in the parable of the Gospel, they will ripen and bear fruit.

the reader of poetry, would ever willingly give up the game; illusion and delusion must coexist. To the poet, the joy of inspiration, the pain of expression are all an integral part of the creative endeavor. Such a necessity comes to differentiate the creative activity of the poet from that of the child at play. Asking the Child to define the purpose of his activity, Pascoli cannot overlook the torment and hardship of severe discipline:

To please yourself? Well, if this were your goal, you would enclose your vision within yourself, and you would enjoy it solely with me, without all that anguish that comes from trying to communicate the vision to others.

(*L.C.,* XV)

Notwithstanding what he musingly and half-ironically maintains in some passages of *Il fanciullino*:

Today's readers are so used to the mysteries and tricks of authors who, all too conveniently, are forever wanting others to understand beyond what they say, that, when you say in your simple way your simple things, lo! they do not understand you any more. They look in your work for what is not there, and since they do not find it, they are left disappointed. And if they do understand you, which is to say if they understand that you mean to say only what you are saying, and do not imply anything more, and do not expect, as is commonly and absurdly done, that the readers be the ones to lend meaning to what you write, then the majority do not appreciate you.

(*L.C.,* XVI)

Pascoli conceives the act of communication as a close collaboration between writer and reader. Generally, the poet insists on distracting attention from analysis, while the mind of the reader, drawn into conflicting emotional responses, keeps shifting from the level of images and sensory clues to the level of constructs and analysis. Thus, writer and reader create another triangular structure in trying to compose a meaning that is not accessible to others and that seems to make permanent, perfect sense. In fact, neither writer nor reader ever achieves such completeness. Poetry may well be the means to express what is within, above, or beyond human consciousness; a way to touch the mystery of life; the arbitrary and charming play through which reality acquires a more vibrant dimension. The fact remains that the birth of authentic poetry is a curious and unpredictable event, quite independent of the poet's aesthetic views, his intentions, and even the chosen mode and genre of expression. The poet,

just like the reader, may recognize when the special moment of grace comes, but he is unable to explain fully the nature of his inspiration or the meaning of his work.

The debate is an ancient one: to what degree is the poet conscious or aware of his own creative process? On this subject, Horace quotes one of Democritus' most famous fragments: "what the poet writes comes to him from divine possession, from sacred inspiration." And Democritus is not the only one, nor the most prestigious interpreter of such a theory, though he may well be the first. We know that, in his systematic search for people wiser than himself, Socrates goes to the poets, only to realize that "they do not compose their poems with knowledge..." (*Apology* 22, b-c). Their inspiration is attributed to the mysterious will and thought of a god. The possessed is the modest spokesman, the accidental transmitter of a message that he does not comprehend: "a melody runs through him, like air in the bag pipes." In *The Little Child*, Pascoli firmly sustains this fundamental concept of the immediacy and spontaneity of poetry. Poetry, he implies, is born of a sudden connection established between an image and the soul of the poet, in a moment in which the spirit rests upon the objects of reality. True creativity does not happen except in that unanticipated contact when the poet penetrates to the existence of a thing, understands the relation among things, and isolates in them the detail that has universal meaning. The poetic state is, then, irregular, unstable, fragile. The poet attains it, and loses it, almost by accident: "Frulla un tratto l'idea nell'aria immota; / canta nel cielo. Il cacciator la vede, / l'ode; la segue: il cuor dentro gli nuota" ("Il cacciatore" *Myricae*) ("Suddenly the idea whirls in the still air; / sings in the sky. The hunter sees it,/ hears it; follows it: his heart leaps within him"; "The hunter"). Much more often, however, and with much greater clarity and pride, Pascoli disavows such a mystical conception of creativity and insists on the patience, drudgery, and humility of writing good verse. The poet does not compose out of excitement or pure inspiration alone. Rather, the initial suggestion, the joyous accident is followed by a long, frustrating, and painstaking weighing of expressive possibilities, by a constant act of choice and attention, for poets are mostly *finders, inventors, and systematic organizers of words*. Like Horace who never tires of asserting that he is a simple "versifier," Pascoli appears to indulge in an ironic self-glorifying appraisal, as if he were saying, not only am I a very good poet; I am probably the best shaper of verses of my time!

Obviously the debate of inspiration versus craftsmanship cannot ever be resolved. The contradictions we find in Pascoli's poetics are present, and with the same incongruity, in Plato himself who, in the *Ion,*

talking about the artistic endeavor, sees inspiration in direct contrast with technique and discipline for all the arts, but not for poetry. At the end of the nineteenth century, the new poets accept with enthusiasm this idea of an "intellectual" poetry. The creative process appears, thus, as the integration of two mental activities, as D'Annunzio maintains in these lines of his "Fanciullo" in *Alcyone*:

> Natura ed Arte sono un dio bifronte
> che conduce il tuo passo armonioso
> per tutti i campi della Terra pura.
> Tu non distingui l'un dall'altro volto
> ma pulsar odi il cuor che si nasconde
> unico della duplice figura.[103]

Similarly, the immediacy of Pascoli's little child does not stand alone. Rather, it must enter into a dialectical relation with the concept of culture as learning and as technical know-how, as a deep and constantly renewed knowledge of the classics but also, and more originally, as an activity of the mind willfully bent on recovering innocence, spontaneity, and ethical virtue:

The poet, if and when he is truly a poet, that is, such a one that signifies only what the Child dictates within, is therefore an inspirer of good and civil customs, of love of country, family and mankind.

(L.C., XI)

Traditionally, the voice that dictates within is of course also *Amor*, and the obvious referent this time is Dante: "I' mi son un che, quando/ Amor mi spira, noto, e a quel modo/ ch'e' ditta dentro vo significando" (*Purgatory* 24:52-54). The poetic feeling speaks in the heart of the poet and gives wings of strength and harmony to his words. *Eros* has wings also, and with his wings he moves love in and out of all creatures. The ancient analogy between language and love could not be more persuasive.[104] *Eros* is

---

[103] Nature and Art are a two-faced god who guides your harmonious passage through all the fields of the innocent Earth. You cannot distinguish one face from the other, but you hear only the beating of one heart hidden in the double figure.

[104] In ancient Greek myth, the same goddess, Peitho, presides over seduction and rhetorical persuasion. On the topic of love and language see the persuasive study by Carson, *Eros the Bittersweet*. I am indebted to the author for a number of classical references.

located in the process of knowing or thinking as Socrates asserts that his knowledge is nothing but a knowledge of erotic things (*ta erotika: Symp.* 177d; *Theag.* 128b); it is central to two principles of reasoning operating simultaneously and bent on understanding all things that pertain to life. In the same way, Pascoli, completing yet another triangle, links the Child, that is the beginning of life, and *Eros*, that is life itself, to what he calls the poetic feeling of mankind. All these triangular designs imply a reaching for the unknown. But the unknown must remain unknown, so that we can keep on writing and reading and falling in love. What is called forth between the self and the object of knowledge is a space where reality and imagination are paradoxically together. Once again, this is the space of Pascoli's poet-child, a very excitable realist in a sentimental domain, acting out of love of paradox, folding all objects out of sight and into a blind point where known and unknown, near and far, now and then can coincide:

"Allora" (*Myricae*)

Allora... in un tempo assai lunge
felice fui molto; non ora:
ma quanta dolcezza mi giunge
da tanta dolcezza d'allora!

Quell'anno! per anni che poi
fuggirono, che fuggiranno,
non puoi, mio pensiero, non puoi,
portare con te, che quell'anno!

Un giorno fu quello, ch'è senza
compagno, ch'è senza ritorno;
la vita fu vana parvenza
sì prima sì dopo quel giorno!

Un punto!... così passeggero,
che in vero passò non raggiunto,
ma bello così, che molto ero
felice, felice, quel punto!

"One Day"

One day, long ago! ... Oh, one day,
I was more than happy; not now.

But oh, the delight that still comes
from all the delight of that day!

That year! Through the years that have fled,
and ever are fleeing from here,
my thoughts, you can rob me of all
but certainly not of that year!

It was an unparalleled day
that will nevermore come your way;
my life was an empty appearance
before and then after that day!

One moment! ... so fleeting, that truly,
before it was mine, it was flown;
 so lovely, that I was so happy,
so happy that moment alone!

(J. Tusiani's translation)

Remembrance alone may provide joy without the anxiety over its passing, giving it an otherwise impossible duration.

We have said that the intent of Pascoli's search for expression and, consequently, of his poetics — not the other way around — is to represent the deepest sensations of the human heart. The poet wants to transform what exists in reality into elements of the soul. For this metamorphosis to occur he has to discover secret analogies and unforeseen connections. The words chosen to qualify the concrete detail must be dressed up with special meanings and empowered to evoke older sensations stored in memory, or deeper yet, in a subconscious or collective memory. We find a good example in the first stanza of "The Kite": "There is something new today in the sunlight, or rather something that is very old. I live elsewhere and I sense that violets have sprung up all around."

In this sort of evocative process, every word calls forth a specific and clear sensory perception, which, in turn, suggests more words and newer sensations generally organized around one idea, or, better, one image: the flower, for instance; or around one central sound: the galloping horse of death, the lamenting bird, the thunder, the mother's voice; or around a vision: the lightning, the tree, the cloud. The poet's metric and philological expertise elaborates and enriches the words so that they prolong their intensity beyond their denotative meaning in a multiplication

of analogies and anaphonies that tend to create musical waves of charm and wonder.[105]

Objects, animals, plants lose their materiality and become the signifiers of a mysterious writing which intends to pose, not answer, questions, to instill, not resolve, doubts. And often the short questioning sentences of the poems are followed by enigmatic suspended periods. There is only one explicit solution, that Death, Death, Death of "Scalpitio":

Si sente un galoppo lontano
(è la...?),
che viene, che corre nel piano
con tremula rapidità.

Un piano deserto, infinito;
tutto ampio, tutt'arido, eguale:
qualche ombra d'uccello smarrito,
che scivola simile a strale:

non altro. Essi fuggono via
da qualche remoto sfacelo;
ma quale, ma dove egli sia,
non sa né la terra, né il cielo.

Si sente un galoppo lontano
più forte,
che viene, che corre nel piano:
la Morte, la Morte, la Morte!

"The Gallop"
A far-away gallop I hear
(is it ...?)
devouring the plainland more near
and ever more trembling and fleet.

---

[105] "Arano," "Lavandare," "La via ferrata" are poems built on visual and auditory impressions; hearing is even more ambiguous and vague than sight. The same complex ambiguity characterizes "Temporale:" in the whole poem there is no verb so that the few verses become pure representation entrusted solely to colors: black, red, white. Along these lines, Anthony Oldcorn offers an incisive reading of "Novembre" as a modern pastoral in *Giovanni Pascoli: poesia e poetica* (347-59).

A plainland, oh, endless and hollow,
and ample and even and dry,
with only the ghost of a swallow
that slides like a dart in the sky:

but this. Far away they all flee
from ruins of long, long ago;
but which and, oh where they may be
both heaven and earth do not know.

A far-away gallop I hear
(hold your breath!),
devouring the plain loud and near:
it is Death! it is Death! it is Death! *(J. Tusiani's translation)*

In modern aesthetics, poetry is the sharp and musical feeling of reality, and music possesses to the highest degree what Diderot called "son propre hiérogliphe," its own way to act upon the sensibility; it is the unknown which appeals to us, it is what moves and arouses our emotions:

Son hiérogliphe est si léger et si furtif, il est si facile de le perdre ou de le mésinterpréter que le plus beau morceau de symphonie ne ferait pas de grand effet si le plaisir infaillible de la sensation pure et simple n'était infiniment au dessus d'une expression souvent équivoque. [...] Comment se fait-il donc que de trois arts imitateurs de la nature celui dont l'expression est la plus arbitraire et la moins précise parle le plus fortement à l'âme? Serait-ce qu'en montrant moins fortement les objets il laisse plus de carrière à notre imagination? [106]

---

[110] "Its hieroglyph is so light and elusive, it is so easy to lose it or to mistake its meaning that the most beautiful symphonic passage would not be of great consequence if the infallible pleasure of sensation – pure and simple–were not infinitely above an expression that is often ambiguous. [...] How is it, then, that of the three arts which imitate nature the one that speaks most powerfully to the soul is the one whose expression is most arbitrary and least precise? Could it be that, since it shows all objects less clearly it gives more room to our imagination?" (my trans.; from the Lettre à Mlle de La chaux, quoted in the Introduction to *Diderot: Ecrits sur la musique*, Paris: Lattès, 1987: 20).

Compared to alphabetical writing, hieroglyphic writing was directly connected to the real entity of the objects and offered an image of them without resorting to the convention of arbitrary signs. The thing was present in the sign which represented it. The sign itself was motivated by the concrete representation which it carried. Originally, hieroglyphs were thought to have an occult and sacred power; hieroglyphic writing was the natural endowment of the priests in their commerce with the divine and appeared to carry with it part of the mystery. The religious and philosophical avatars of such a notion allow us to understand better Pascoli's conception of poetry, as well as his inability, or reluctance, to define his thoughts and to establish logical connections among them. For all late Romantic and Symbolist artists, the logical form of musical structures is a privileged medium of expression and offers a heightened resemblance to our emotional life. More specifically, only music can be captured intuitively, for it is a language of extraordinary metaphorical power that goes directly from the mind to the body, in pre-verbal, pre-symbolic forms. Pascoli's constant strive for musicality and his astute technical command aspire to generate a wealth of internal vibrations. For instance, "Bellis perennis" (*Nuovi pemetti*) begins with the marvelous spontaneity Pascoli is often able to achieve: "Chi vede mai le pratelline in boccia?" ("Who ever sees the little daisies blooming?"); and with it is the allusion to the coming to life and the dying of all things, always sudden, unexpected, and unexplainable. "Temporale" (*Myricae*) communicates a special warning. Something sinister and obscure, something of a destructive force is threatening life and nature; the poet's spirit is beguiled; his conscience is assailed by vague memories and fears:

> Un bubbolio lontano...
> Rosseggia l'orizzonte,
> come affocato, a mare:
> nero di pece, a monte,
> stracci di nubi chiare:
> tra il nero un casolare:
> un'ala di gabbiano.[107]

---

[107] "Thunderstorm ": "A far off rumbling.... The horizon glows red, as if on fire, over the sea; [it is] black as pitch over the mountains; shreds of pale clouds: in the blackness a lone cottage: a gull's wing."

All the adjectives and nouns echo the far-sounding storm; the one verb, *rosseggia* (reddens, glows red), emphasizes a color that is in motion against the pervasive rumbling sound of the thunder. A final ruin threatens all things and a sense of anxiety accentuates feelings of fragility and defenselessness: the clouds in shreds, the solitary cottage, the white wing of the seagull. The poet sees, and listens; he does not search for the cause and the reason of things. Nothing is ever definable. Nature is the subject and object of all transformations, the giver of all sustenance as well of death. In "Temporale," as in "Il lampo," "Il tuono" ("Thunderstorm", "The Lighning" "The Thunder") — not surprisingly the natural events that frighten all small children — death is, indeed, the preeminent symbolic presence. It is what looms behind all things; it is the very meaning of all fears and all evil, horrible and never rationally controllable, foreign only to the new mother and her sleeping infant.

"Il tuono" *(Myricae)*

E nella notte nera come il nulla,
a un tratto, col fragor d'arduo dirupo
che frana, il tuono rimbombò di schianto:
rimbombò, rimbalzò, rotolò cupo,
e tacque, e poi rimareggiò rinfranto,
e poi vanì. Soave allora un canto
s'udì di madre, e il moto di una culla.[108]

"Novembre" *(Myricae)* is another example of Pascoli's symbolic technique. The poet underscores the opposition between appearances: the reality of the season so close to the dead of winter appears not like spring, but like the remembrance of spring. The ideographic process is built on direct physical sensations; but each word is suggestive of a symbolical analogue:

---

[108] "The Thunder": "And in the night as black as nothingness, suddenly, with the roar of a rocky crag crushing down, the thunder resounded violently. It roared, re-echoed back, rolled on darkly, and was still, and then again it surged, breaking up like waves on the shore, and then vanished. Sweetly thereupon, a mother-song was heard, and the rocking of a cradle."

Novembre

Gèmmea l'aria, il sole così chiaro
che tu ricerchi gli albicocchi in fiore,
e del prunalbo l'odorino amaro
    senti nel cuore...

Ma secco è il pruno e le stecchite
piante
di nere trame segnano il sereno,
e vuoto il cielo, e cavo al piè sonante
    sembra il terreno..

Silenzio, intorno; solo, alle ventate,
odi lontano, da giardini ed orti,
di foglie un cader fragile. E' l'estate
    fredda, dei morti.

November

The air is perlaceous, and the sun so bright,
you look for blooming apricot-trees;
the thorn-bush sends a whiff of bitter fragrance
    into your heart...

And yet the bush is dry, and the stark plants
mark all this brightness with their black designs;
the sky is empty, and you hear from the ground
    a hollow sound.

Silence all over: only, in the wind,
from fields and gardens far away you hear
leaves frailly falling: it's the dread,
    cold summer of the dead.

                                        (J.Tusiani's translation)

Particularly representative in this regard, are the brief descriptions of *L'ultima passeggiata* and *Finestra illuminata*, two of the most celebrated sections of *Myricae*. Here, every descriptive element rises to lyrical intensity; the visible world is the reflection of an invisible one, but not in some kind of forced layering, rather, in a reciprocal transfusion of strength. Words and things are mutually supportive elements, constantly changing state, taking

on the qualifying traits of one another. The sensory and the mental realm, the precise and the vague, the definite and the indefinite touch each other and mesh. What ensues is a deep-seated sense of ambiguity that must be accepted in its own right, yet is never fully understood. As an example we offer two lyrics which must be read together since they follow one another in an unusual, extended *enjambement*:

> "Mezzanotte"
> Otto... nove... anche un tocco: e lenta scorre
> l'ora; ed un tratto... un altro. Uggiola un cane.
> Un chiù singhiozza da non so qual torre.
> E' mezzanotte. Un doppio suon di pesta
> s'ode, che passa. C'è per vie lontane
> un rotolio di carri che s'arresta
> di colpo. Tutto è chiuso, senza forme,
> senza colori, senza vita. Brilla,
> sola nel mezzo alla città che dorme,
> una finestra, come una pupilla

> "Un gatto nero"
> aperta. Uomo che vegli nella stanza
> illuminata, chi ti fa vegliare?
> dolore antico o giovine speranza?
> Tu cerchi un Vero. Il tuo pensier somiglia
> un mare immenso: nell'immenso mare,
> una conchiglia; dentro la conchiglia,
> una perla: la vuoi. Vecchio, un gran bosco
> nevato, ai primi languidi scirocchi,
> par la tua faccia. Un gatto nero, un
> fosco viso di sfinge, t'apre i suoi verdi occhi.[109]

---

[109] "Midnight": "Eight ... Nine ... Another stroke and slowly the hour passes; and, after a while, another... A dog howls. A screech owl sobs from I know not what tower. It is midnight. A loud sound of footsteps is heard, passing. Through distant streets there is the sound of carriage wheels that suddenly stops. Everything is closed up, formless, colorless, lifeless. Alone, in the middle of the sleeping city, a window shines, like the pupil of an eye."
"A black cat": "open. O man, awake in the lighted room, what keeps you awake? An old sorrow or a novel hope? You are looking for a Truth. Your thoughts resemble an immense ocean: in the immense ocean [there is] a shell; inside that shell, a pearl: you want it. Old man, your face at the first sultry winds, is like a

In these lyrics, a real masterpiece of visual and musical representation,[110] the unassuming poet of the rustic life succeeds in renewing the old meters of the classical tradition, combining a variety of harmonies and reaching a rare clarity of sounds. Without any ostentation or fanfare, Pascoli comes to represent best, in Italy at least, the artistic ideal theorized by Wagner, Ruskin, and Pater, where the word truly becomes the *total work of art*.[111]

Pascoli never establishes a theory of interferences among the different levels of consciousness, but in his poetry, the repressed, or unexpressed, contents of the psychic life are connected to the mind by the powerful lines of symbolic association.[112] The poet revisits the elements of the external world and proceeds to twist and disjoint the objects of his representation so that the concreteness fostered by his uncanny semantic precision — to know the names of things is to be part of them — gives way to suggestive, obscure meanings. Here is the root of Pascoli's art of allusion. His world has lost order and organization. And he has never been able to find any for himself. Thus, his poems are metaphors of the

---

snow-capped wood. A black cat, a dark sphinx-like face, opens its green eyes to you."

[110] The equivalence of poetry and painting goes back, of course, to Horace's *ut pictura poesis*. The mysterious power of language, along with its affinity with music, has origins that could be tied to Vergil's *Eclogae*, but they are probably older. Orpheus with his mystical command over nature in music, and Amphion who raised the walls of Thebes with his lyre are among the oldest mythical references, and Pascoli remembers both in *The Little Child*: "Hence, the belief and the fact that it was the sound of the lyre that gathered the stones to build the walls of the city, and gave life to the plants and tamed the wild animals of the primordial forest; and that the singers guided and educated the people" (*L.C.*, XI).

[111] Certainly it is not by chance that the three 'great men' who dominate the intellectual climate of European *fin de siècle* culture were very well known in the circle of the *Marzocco*, the Florentine literary journal where Pascoli was publishing extensively.

[112] Very often, a detailed analysis shows that each word includes a double meaning: that of the objective image and that of the symbol. The identification is perfect. To such a degree that the image of the mistletoe ("Il vischio"), for instance, loses its reality and becomes an abstract universal idea that embraces the real and the spiritual. Consistently, however, the imaginative content controls the 'metaphysical' statements.

immobility of existence; they are intimations of passions and eternal meanings. They are meant to free what resides at the bottom of the soul: the poetic feeling of mankind. Images, thoughts, syntax, and metrical structures must respond only to the laws imposed by poetic feeling.[113]

Pascoli's major ambition remains, in fact, the orchestration of a special, new language in which technical and scientific designations and unusual phonetic sequences combine to express the most abstract ideas. Contini's formula of "lofty imprecision conditioned by lofty precision" aptly synthesizes the poet's efforts. The tension is between submission to a collective linguistic system, to definite rules and established techniques, and a joyful display of personal energy and sensitivity. Such a way of thinking and constructing poetry — free, fragmented, and open to continuous and sudden changes in the development of every line — is very close to an impressionistic, Proustian, or neo-emotional poetics, filled with all the restlessness of the new century.

A realistic conception of art, and of life, is based not on the belief that the world is perfectly definable but on the premise that it must be so. From what we have said up to now, it is clear that Pascoli could not be further from such a position. He can only test, experiment with reality. To his child-eyes things are bright little spots in the dark, like stars in the late summer sky. The poet only wants to re-present them, re-awakening visual and auditory sensations, showing again the wonder they evoke in those who can see them, the pleasure and the pain the world metes out, without reason and without explanation. In "Le rane" (*Canti di Castelvecchio*), the poet-child combines, with impressionistic immediacy, colors and sounds, tastes and smells. And he repeats "ho visto, ho visto" (I saw, I saw) before the opulence of nature with its red and green, white and brown; poplars and thistle bushes, birds and bells. Then come the questions to the large

---

[113] Coleridge had spoken in similar terms of poetic passion. Poetic passion alone is at the origin of the symbolic system and organizes instinct and reason, matter and spirit, subjective and objective, tradition and innovation. The poetic passion, Coleridge says, manifests itself in sudden flashes of the imagination and reconciles simultaneity and succession. The poet recurs then to the image of the undulating movement of the snake to distinguish poetry from ordinary communication. Poetry must harmonize the discontinuity of the sudden flash with the continuity of reason and the depth of thought. Will, reason, and imagination contribute to the creation of poetry, but the imagination is the very soul of the poetic genius.

and small things displayed before him; and these questions are as genuine as those of every four-year-old, and must remain equally unanswered:

> [...] Qual è questa via senza fine
> che all'alba è sì tremula d'ali?
> Chi chiamano le canapine
> coi lunghi lor gemiti uguali?
> Tra i rami giallicci del moro
> chi squilla il suo tinnulo invito?
> chi svolge dal cielo i gomitoli
> d'oro?[114]

No matter how clear and well defined, images like these are part of a world that is formless, weightless, beautiful, and incoherent. The poet is the disenchanted witness of its beauty and its consternation; he is the receptive voice of humanity, aware only of the limits and fatality of all things. He must keep on singing of this world, however, outlining every object; he has to go on presenting the fundamental aspects of life wherever he sees them and hears them — within the walls of the beloved family home, or in nature at large; amid the toils and the days of the simple people around him, or in the magnificent actions of the memorable past. The adult may be the privileged interpreter of reality and history; he may sing of passions, politics, and ideas and elaborate reasons for social action. But Pascoli's child looks at the world in an alternative, genetically different way, always half-dreaming, always ready to laugh and cry. Once such a concept of poetry is understood it is easy to establish the division between poetry and everything else which becomes, therefore, *non-poetry*.

---

[114] "Frogs": "[...] What is this road without end that at dawn is so lively with wings? Whom are the warblers calling with their long, constant moanings? In the yellowish branches of the mulberry, who is sounding out its jingling invitation? Who is unraveling golden skeins from above?"

Pleasure & Pain

He is the one who cries and laughs without cause, at things that escape our senses and our reason. [...] He makes bearable both happiness and misfortune, tempering them with bitterness and sweetness, and making of them things equally sweet to memory.

(*L.C.,* III)

Happiness and misfortune, bitterness and sweetness. Poetry, then, like life itself, is bittersweet. Life's joy is inseparable from its grief and each shares in the act of loving and in the will to knowledge. The components of the contradiction are evident. The pleasures of love and life are inviting, while every ending, every death saddens the heart with feelings of disillusionment and betrayal. What is of interest, however, is the fact that Pascoli consistently presents the two emotions not in contrast, or in succession, but together.[115] Obviously, in his view, life is not concerned with the happiness and the security of the living. From the start, it forces itself upon every newborn who obediently begins its journey of tears and smiles in frequent and incomprehensible combination.

The warnings of pleasure and pain are the methods used by nature to educate her children; they are considered the only effective ways to guide the young towards those ends they ought to seek and away from those they ought to avoid. "Les premières sensations des enfants" — writes Rousseau echoing Plato and Aristotle – "sont purement affectives; ils n'apperçoivent que le plaisir et la douleur" (Book 1, 419) (The first sensations of all

---

[115] In the first few pages of the *Phaedo* Pascoli finds many references to the 'double feeling' of pleasure and pain. After Xanthippe is led away crying out and beating herself, Socrates, musingly observes: "How singular is the thing called pleasure, and how curiously related to pain, which might be thought to be the opposite of it; for they are never present to a man at the same instant, and yet he who pursues either is generally compelled to take the other; their bodies are two but they are joined by a single head. And I cannot help thinking that if Aesop had remembered them, he would have made a fable about God trying to reconcile their strife, and how, when he could not, he fastened their heads together."

children are purely affective, they feel nothing but pleasure and pain.).[116] According to such theory, genuine and universal moral values characterize the deep heart of the child. Only a few wise words — Pascoli repeats in his *Discourses* — are necessary to awaken the child's feelings of love, piety, and compassion; to brighten his mind, and make him gentler. It is often suggested that the world is made for the joy of children, who, like birds, run, laugh, and cry out their pleasure to be alive. The child's goodness and sympathy for others, on the other hand, are cultivated effectively through the awareness of suffering and grief. Hence, the appeal to the tears that, in Pascoli's poetry, trace a most troublesome itinerary among cripples, beggars, little corpses, blind people of all ages, orphans, and abandoned children. Pascoli's position could easily slip into sentimentalism — indeed, at times it does – but more often his Child is meant to represent a universal ethic. He awakens our sense of the laughter in things, while the thought of the approaching storm, of which he is much more acutely aware than the Romantic child or the child of contemporary pedagogical and psychological studies, adds the special poignancy of mystery and eventual disillusion. In the adaptability of the child, Pascoli sees, in fact, a most painful state of fragility. The poet does not deny the reality of a happy childhood. But he experience of ecstatic unity with things, which is the ideal of the reasoning theoretician in the *Fanciullino*, is overshadowed by the awareness of pain in the poetry, where the child is under the constant threat of solitude and fear. Thus, pleasure and pain must be viewed as the two emotions to which all representations of life and character relate; they call for the comic and the tragic side of things. Pleasure and pain are indeed symptoms of life; and

---

[116] In the *Laws* (653A-B) children are spoken of as creatures whose first sensations are pleasure and pain. In this form virtue and vice enter their soul, but, according to Plato, children are incapable of reasoning (*Laws* 760A) and great emphasis is placed on education for the development of a child into a wise and good human being. In Aristotle's *Nicomachean Ethics* (1174 a2) we read: "No one would choose to live with the intellect of a child throughout his life, however much he were to be pleased at the things that children are pleased at, not to get enjoyment by doing some disgraceful deed, though he were never to feel any pain in consequence." (Translated by W. D. Ross, Oxford, 1924 and quoted by George Boas in *The Cult of Childhood* 13).

movement and change, as the recurrent tensions of all desires, constitute its drama.[117]

Pascoli knows that, together with the instinct for play and creativity, desire is the magnetic force behind all the innovations of physical existence. Eros is the sustaining power of the cosmos; it penetrates everywhere and culminates in the birth of every new thing. In Pascoli's poetry, a pervading sexual energy is connected to the life of plants and animals, of which the child who lives in contact with nature acquires an easy fore-knowledge. All creatures living and dead labor in the desire to find each other, to change and transfer themselves into each other and constantly recreate life. Grass, flowers, plants, and trees germinate and grow. The forces of earth toil on in eternal movement, fomenting life and death. From this perspective as well, the child is of the earth, in contact with all natural elements; he keeps within him something of the animal; and is connected with the Great Mother, feeling her shivers, her grumbles, her secret power. Often the poet alludes to the rapture of the first sensual awakening in the very young;[118] but he speaks openly of love only as the natural reproductive instinct. The propagation of life is the sweet and rich recompense which follows the sexual act. The theme of conception would not find the powerful images of "Il sogno della vergine" or "Il gelsomino notturno" (both in *Canti di Castelvecchio*) if it were not very familiar to the poet. In "Il sogno della vergine," a young girl dreams of the mystery of life beginning in her womb: "la vergine sogna: ed un rivo / di sangue stupisce le intatte / sue vene, d'un sangue più vivo, più tiepido, come di latte..."

---

[117] Change is what involves every human being, every lover, and every poet in an activity of the imagination. It is not a new idea that the imagination has a powerful role to play in human desire. Aristotle defines the dynamic and imaginative delight of desire in his *Rhetoric*: "Desire is a reaching out for the sweet, and the man who is reaching for some delight, whether in the future as hope or in the past as memory, does so by means of an act of imagination" (which he calls *phantasia* in *Rh.* 1.1370a6). Andreas Capellanus will insist that love, *passio*, is a thoroughly mental event: "The suffering of love does not arise out of any action.... but only from the cogitation of the mind upon what it sees does that suffering issue"(*De Amore* XIV; qtd. Carson, *Eros the Bittersweet* 63).

[118] With notable effectiveness, Pascoli analyzes in *Narciso*, for instance, the special time "of hidden sensations and feelings [which mark] that condition of crisis at the end of childhood in which appear for the first time, however hidden within, the fantasies and excitements of the senses" (Barberi Squarotti 61; my translation).

("The young maiden dreams: and a stream / of blood startles her intact / veins, a blood that is brighter, warmer, like milk ...). Every detail is defined in the dream: the baby that is blossoming is "the child of her soul's most intimate smile." As always, the precise terms of the representation allude to what is elusive and inscrutable in life; reality is undetermined and laden with oneiric meanings. It cannot be conquered, controlled, or understood:

> [...] Stupisce le placide vene
> quel flutto soave e straniero,
> quel rivolo, labile, lene,
> d'ignota sorgente, che sembra
> che inondi di blando mistero
> le pie sigillate sue membra.
>
> Le gracili membra non sanno
> lo schianto, non sanno l'amplesso:
> nel cuore sì, forse un affanno
> c'è, l'ombra di un palpito, l'orma
> d'un grido: il respiro sommesso
> d'un vago ricordo che dorma;
>
> che dorma nel cuore ed esali
> nel cuore il suo sonno romito.
> La vergine sogna: ecco un alito
> piccolo, accanto... un vagito... [119]

With the same acute and unsuspected sensuality, lilies and jasmines, asphodels, narcissi, hemlock, or red digitalis are chosen to suggest a morbid yet delicate contemplation of untouched femininity. Images and rhythm converge in moments of grace; they are visions of wonder, shadowy and imprecise, that help to reveal the secret *correspondances* among the things of

---

[119] "The young maiden's dream": "[...] That stream sweet and strange, that rivulet, frail, delicate, of unknown source, which seems to well up in her pious, untouched limbs with delicate mystery, startles her placid veins. Her slender limbs have never known violence, have not known [physical] love. In her heart, perhaps, there is indeed a yearning, the merest stir of a heartbeat, the vestige of a cry. It is the subdued breathing of a dormant memory; dormant in her heart and breathing in her heart its lonely sleep. The young maiden dreams and there is a slight exhalation, nearby ... [followed by] a whimper...."

the world. *Il gelsomino notturno* focuses on the continuity of purpose between light and dark, night and day. In the depth of night a new life begins in the humid womb of a bride. And, in the morning, it is an accomplished mystery over the necessary sacrifice of the victim, *i petali un poco gualciti*:

Il gelsomino notturno

E s'aprono i fiori notturni,
nell'ora che penso ai miei cari.
Sono apparse in mezzo ai viburni
le farfalle crepuscolari.

Da un pezzo si tacquero i gridi:
là sola una casa bisbiglia.
Sotto l'ali dormono i nidi,
come gli occhi sotto le ciglia.
Dai calici aperti si esala
l'odore di fragole rosse.
Splende un lume là nella sala.
Nasce l'erba sopra le fosse.

Un'ape tardiva sussurra
trovando già prese le celle.
La Chioccetta per l'aia azzurra
va col suo pigolio di stelle.

Per tutta la notte s'esala
l'odore che passa col vento.
Passa il lume su per la scala;
brilla al primo piano: s'è spento...

E' l'alba: si chiudono i petali
un poco gualciti; si cova,
dentro l'urna molle e segreta,
non so che felicità nuova.[120]

---

[120] "The Jasmine of the Night": "And the flowers of the night open up in the hour when I think of my dear ones. The butterflies of the twilight have appeared among the viburnums. It is some time since the cries have grown silent: there, only one house is whispering. Under their wings sleep nests of birds, like eyes under their lids. From the open chalices rises the scent of red strawberries. There, in the room,

Jasmine in the Night

And the buds of the night are in bloom
when I think of my family, dead.
Crepuscular butterflies flutter,
among the guelder-roses spread.

All cries have been still for a while;
but there in that house there is still some unrest.
Like eyes beneath the lashes,
beneath the wings now sleeps each nest.

A scent of red strawberries travels
from open calyxes in waves.
There in that room the light is bright.
The grass is born on the graves.

A tardy bee is humming,
finding its hive already taken.
Through the blue barn the Hen
goes with a chirping of stars.

Throughout the night now fares
the fragrance that comes with the wind.
That light is now climbing the stairs,
shins on the second floor: is dead...

---

a light shines. Grass grows on the graves. A late bee is buzzing, finding the cells already taken. The Little Mother Hen, followed by the chirping of her stars moves along her blue courtyard. Throughout the night rises an odour carried on by the wind. The light passes up through the stairway, shines on the first floor, it is shut off. It is dawn: the somewhat wrinkled petals are now closed. Inside the damp and secret urn nestles I know not what new happiness." Pascoli certainly had a rather unique way of naming flowers and stars, perhaps a different way of looking at them. "Chioccetta" (Little Mother Hen), however, is the name commonly given to the Pleaides by the farmers of his region. As such it could be found in the Forcellni's *Onomasticon*: "Pleiades ... a Latinis dictae Vergiliae et ab Italis Gallinelle" (i.e., little chickens) and in the Tommaseo-Bellini dictionary which identifies the same constellation with the names *Pleiades, Vergilie, Iadi, Gallinelle, Chioccetta, Carretto*.

O dawn! A bit crumpled, the petals
now close; in an urn, wet with dew,
and mysterious, is being born
I know not what happiness new.

(J. Tusiani's translation)

The same double attraction towards what is beautiful, promising, and vital, and toward its very opposite, is at the core of many poems. "Digitale purpurea" (*Primi poemetti*), although overly quoted, is a good example:

Siedono. L'una guarda l'altra. L'una
esile e bionda, semplice di vesti
e di sguardi; ma l'altra, esile e bruna,
l'altra... I due occhi semplici e modesti
fissano gli altri due ch'ardono. "E mai
non ci tornasti?" "Mai!" "Non le vedesti

più?" "Non più, cara." "Io sì, ci ritornai;
e le rividi le mie bianche suore,
e li rivissi i dolci anni che sai;

quei piccoli anni così dolci al cuore..."
L'altra sorrise. "E di': non lo ricordi
quell'orto chiuso, i rovi con le more?

i ginepri tra cui zirlano i tordi?
i bussi amari? quel segreto canto
misterioso, con quel fiore, fior di...?"

"morte: sì, cara." "Ed era vero? Tanto
io ci credeva che non mai, Rachele,
sarei passata al triste fiore accanto.

Chè si diceva: il fiore ha come un miele
che inebria l'aria; un suo vapor che bagna
l'anima d'un oblio dolce e crudele.

[...]"Maria!" "Rachele!" Questa piange, "Addio!"
dice tra sé, poi volta la parola
grave a Maria, ma i neri occhi no: "Io,"

mormora, "sì: sentii quel fiore. Sola
ero con le cetonie verdi. Il vento
portava odor di rose e di viole a

ciocche. Nel cuore, il languido fermento
d'un sogno che notturno arse e che s'era
all'alba, nell'ignara anima, spento.

Maria, ricordo quella grave sera.
L'aria soffiava luce di baleni
silenziosi. M'inoltrai leggiera,

cauta, su per i molli terrapieni
erbosi. I piedi mi tenea la folta
erba. Sorridi? E dirmi sentia: Vieni!

Vieni! E fu molta la dolcezza! molta!
tanta, che, vedi... (l'altra lo stupore
alza degli occhi, e vede ora, ed ascolta

con un suo lungo brivido...) si muore!"[121]

---

[121] "The Purple Foxglove": "[...] They are sitting. They look at each other. One slender and blonde, of simple dress and looks, but the other, slender and dark, the other... The two simple and modest eyes are fixed upon the other two that burn. 'And you never went back there?' 'Never!' 'You never saw them again?' 'Never again, my dear.' 'Instead I did, I went back there, and I again saw my white Sisters, and I relived the sweet years that you remember. Those early years so dear to everyone's heart....' The other smiled. 'And tell me, do you not remember that closed garden, the blackberry bushes with their berries? The junipers where the thrushes whistle? The bitter boxwoods? That secret and mysterious song, with that flower, flower of....' 'Death, yes, dear.' 'And was it true? So much did I believe it was, that never, Rachele, would I have gone near that flower. /For it was said: the flower exudes a honey-like substance that intoxicates the air; a vapor that bathes the soul with a forgetfulness sweet and cruel.'"
"[...] 'Maria!' 'Rachele!' The latter weeps, 'Good bye' she says to herself, then she turns her grave words to Maria, but not her dark eyes: 'I' she murmurs 'yes, I smelled that flower. Alone I was with the green beetles. The wind bore the smell of roses and wallflowers. In my heart was the languid turmoil of a dream that burned at night and had died off at dawn, in my unexpecting soul. Maria, I remember that

Maria does not pick the dangerous flower, the sinuous and sensual foxglove — much more Art Nouveau than the biblical apple, or the romantic red rose.[122] She is the adorable child, before knowledge of evil, before life, but also before death. A sweet and acrid taste marks, in fact, the acceptance of the choice. There is no dialectic mediation between the two points. Maria and Rachele, like Viola and Rosa *(Primi poemetti)*, like Maria and Ida, the two sisters in Pascoli's real life, cannot ever meet. The innocence and purity of childhood cannot be but a memory deep in the soul of the one who chooses to grow up.

Pascoli himself, we know, does not make such a choice. For whatever reason, he never marries; never fathers his own little child; and, as far as we know, never knows mature sexuality. Hypotheses of impotence, of child-like incestuosity, of psycho-sexual immaturity are, of course, possible. Equally valid are the correlated speculations that psychoanalytic theories may offer: inhibitions and censorship from an overpowering super-ego; emotional atrophy due to unused sexuality; virginity complex combined with morbid *erotica* as typical of the bachelor/spinster condition. We can also speculate on the centrality of the mother and on the deep emotional link to her and the loving cult of her memory, and sketch the lines of an unresolved Oedipal complex, which all these elements suggest well beyond the familial and social practices of a time already so distant from our own.[123] The fact remains that Pascoli is among the least erotic of Italian poets; that his women are powerfully idealized, dominated by the

---

grave evening. The air emitted a light of soundless lightning. I went forward, lightly, cautiously, over the soft, grassy terrassing. The thick grass grasped at my feet. You are smiling? And I heard something calling me: 'Come! Come!' And the sweetness was great. Great! So much that, you see ...(the other looks up with amazement in her eyes and now she sees, and listens now with a long shiver ...) one can die!'"

[122] Obviously what is here at work is also the desire to experiment with sounds and images that have not been worn out by poetic usage; objects full of angles, somewhat de-centered or eccentric. Among the flowers we find cyclamens, foxglove, the blossom of the pomegranate, of the apricot and the medlar tree. They are images of an organic nature which energetically gives birth to continually fluid lines. C .F. Goffis analyzes this tendency of Pascoli's aestheticism in "Un capolavoro dello stile Liberty: *I poemi conviviali.*" *Studi per il Centenario della nascita di Giovanni Pascoli*, vol.3, Bologna, 1962.

[123] See the interesting analysis of the role of Pascoli's mother and sisters in the essay by Nadia Ebani which prefaces the publication of one of Pascoli's bizarre fairy-tales: "La Befana" (Verona, 1989).

traits of mother and sister; that his life is closed up in a bachelorhood that could be significant and in a misanthropic solitude often given to excessive drinking and sudden bursts of anger. These traits might allow us to determine a fundamental *aperçu* of the psychic dynamics of the man and, more importantly, of his creativity and imagination. Uncertain are the roots of such possible neuroses, and they ought to be left unresolved. What is important is to identify the undeniable impact such inferences may have had on Pascoli's art to the point of being strongly combined with the elements of his poetics. In fact, it is also this immature eroticism, or, better, this vision of eros, that decides the choice of the central anthropomorphic model to whom Pascoli commits the splendid onus of creativity. For, as we have maintained, the *fanciullino* is not the child, but the *little child*, the human being at the pre-adolescent stage. "For him, women and love have no form and no interest: it is not love nor is it women, however beautiful and goddess-like they might be, that matters to children; but bronze lances and war chariots and long journeys and great adventures" (*L.C.*, II).[124] Love is frightening, and it does not happen without loss of the vital self. This attitude towards eros is grounded in the oldest mythical tradition where the metaphors for the erotic experience are metaphors of war, disease, and bodily dissolution and express an unmistakable concern for the integrity of one's own body. We know the hidden power of Eros/Cupid, the sweet angel whose arrows always prove deadly. In literature and in the visual arts, Eros employs nets, fire, fevers, bridles, and hurricanes to make his assaults; it moves on by melting and icing, stinging and biting, piercing and poisoning. In all cases, its intentions are hostile and its effects harmful:

---

[124] The fear of precise physical and natural responsibilities, much more than the shunning of commitments and adult duties, seem, in fact, to characterize Pascoli's life as evidenced in his massive correspondence, still partially unpublished, and in the detailed biography written by Pascoli's sister (Maria Pascoli, *Lungo la vita di Giovanni Pascoli*. Mondadori). The poet proudly and willingly took upon himself the care of his brothers and sisters. With the two youngest ones, Ida and Maria, he actually created that family nest, whose image obsessively recurs in so many poems.

'Il chiù" (*Nuovi poemetti*)

[...] Splendea lassù la gran luce di Sirio.
Recava odor di fiori pésti il vento.
— Ell'era andata a chissà qual martirio!
Ora, dov'era? A lume acceso o spento?
Buon che le mise al collo, nell'aspetto,
quella sua croce piccola d'argento!

Ella doveva ora vegliar nel letto
sola con lui! senza sperare aiuto! —
Viola i panni si stringea sul petto.

— Che cosa avrebbe egli da lei voluto?
Qual piaga dare tenera e mortale
a quelle carni bianche, di velluto? [...][125]

For the most part, in his poetry and in real life, Pascoli defends himself through denial and moves in a vague, exciting borderland between purity and sensuality. We have noted that a veiled lasciviousness pervades some of his most beautiful and original poems, but, whenever passion seems within reach, a curious feeling of shame or chastity prevails and prevents its expression. Against the desire to experience and appropriate, the poet prefers to anchor his roots among people and things that are known already, people and things that remain unchangeable. But this state without want and without tension is not entirely a desirable condition. To some extent, it solicits a sense of surrender, of submission, a general acquiescence to death.

And certainly the thought of death, ever near and powerful in all natural phenomena, obsesses Pascoli and dominates his poetry.[126] When

---

[125] 'The Little Owl'': 'The great light of Sirius was shining up above. The wind carried a scent of spent flowers.... She had gone off, to who knows what torment! Where was she now? With the lights on or off? Good thing she had put around her [sister's] neck that small silver cross of hers! Surely, she must now be lying awake in bed, alone, with him, without any hope for help! — Viola clutched the sheets to her breast. — What would he have wanted from her? What tender and deadly wound would he want to inflict on that white, velvet flesh? "

[126] Research has shown that in the beginning of his poetic career Pascoli does not indulge in the remembrance of his own family deaths. There is, in fact, nothing epic

expressed in reference to the real death of his family members, it is often excessively sentimental. It is much more interesting when it is presented either as nothingness, or as an obscure reality that asks to be touched, felt, understood — a largely ambiguous abstraction: frightening death, redeeming death, Universal Mother who frees us all. Nobody knows what death is, how it is, but it continually hangs over life, disturbs and caresses every living thing, as in "Scalpitio," "I due cugini," "Il morticino," "Il brivido." At times Death is capitalized, gaining physicality, a real threatening power. At other times it comes in an unusual universe of symbols. It is *magical, feminine, ghost-like, monstrous, winged, bird-like*, and is represented, phonically, as a *stridulous, witch-like laughter* ("La civetta"), or as a *cry* ("L'assiuolo"); visually, as the *eyes of fate* ("Povero dono"), in the *white forehead of the Sphinx* ("Paese notturno"), as soft like the *whispering of wings* ("La civetta")*;* as an *eagle* or *a black cat*; as *black crows* and *infinite shadow*; *ghosts*, and *astral constellations*; as *a dark, hazy cloud*, menacing and fast moving; as *a veiled woman*, or *a baleful wind*.... Death is viewed, also, and more confidently, as the mere interruption of a cycle. The dead form the ultimate nest and the ultimate expression of our unity with *this* world, firmly enduring beyond time. This thought is the most salient characteristic of Pascoli's imagination, part of his very nature; it is what bonds him to all living things and to the stars of the universe. When he places together elements that are clearly opposites, the poet intensifies the idea that a common destiny governs the existence of man and nature; that everything is equally alive, the rock as well as the plant; that all things, in short, are part of the natural, material world, and therefore are all condemned to death. Pascoli is aware of creating in this respect a new poetry, a poetry of the fragility and bewilderment of man who, like the smallest child, cannot have the answers. The deliberate, serious pensiveness that often overcomes the child, making him look lost and worried, is the result of a *natural* menacing force that comes to weaken his *natural* vital instincts.

However happy he might have been as a child and as an adolescent, the young Pascoli develops a world-view that is progressively more restless and apprehensive. He suffers the world, is almost oppressed by it, is filled with discontentment and anger. What is evidenced in all he writes is the tremor and dread he feels before pleasure and pain, before life

---

or unusual in them. Death, and the death of infants, was in his time a matter of daily occurrence. This fact, which can be easily verified, lends a certain objectivity to all those graves and coffins that crowd Pascoli's writing from the very beginning.

and death. *Allecto*, a poem that was published posthumously (*Nuova Antologia* 12, 1927) but dates back to the first months of 1897, the year of the first publication of *Il fanciullino*, reveals all of Pascoli's anxiety before a world that is in the process of organizing imperialistic wars, is in the grips of growing class struggles, and is philosophically beset by the failures of scientific positivism.

The Romantic poets had already, repeatedly affirmed that science had destroyed the miracle of the world and broken the wings of the imagination. The same disappointed appraisal returns in Pascoli who writes to reverse the enthusiasm of the positivist. Science should have conquered pain and death and, instead, has destroyed the few illusions that allowed the tolerance of both. It has expelled all innocence and cast the soul into the depths of darkness. It has poisoned and frightened the heart of man, once the purest of lakes that reflected the stars. Now man is left powerless, stricken with the pain of lost serenity. This is the embittered sense of "L'era nuova" (1899),[127] a brief discourse that outlines Pascoli's spiritual and intellectual contradictions, his inner nature full of unresolved doubts:

Il morire doveva essere tolto dalla scienza; ed ella non l'ha tolto. A morte dunque la scienza! Noi torniamo alla fede che (è verità? E' solo illusione? ma illusione, a ogni modo che ci vale per verità) che non solo ha abolita la morte, ma nella morte ha collocata la vita e la felicità indistruttibile.

("L'era nuova" 112)

(Science was to have eliminated death and it did not do so. Death to science, then! And we will go back to faith that (is it truth? Is it only illusion? Illusion, nonetheless, that could work for us as truth) that not only has abolished death, but has placed in death life, and indestructible happiness.)

("The New Age")

The question marks and exclamation points, that are peculiar to Pascoli's prose, underline the poet's doubts and woes. He himself feels betrayed and seems to weep over the precariousness of life, thus taking a step back from the clear acceptance of life without hope that Leopardi had manifested in his more mature poetry. Modern man cannot be at peace like the birds and the animals any longer; he knows that the loss is irrevocable and he is destined to live in the painful awareness of his nostalgia:

---

[127] Pascoli, *Prose.* Mondadori, 1946, 1: 107-23.

La scienza ha ricondotto le nostre menti alla tristezza del momento tragico dell'uomo; del momento in cui, acquistando la coscienza d'essere mortale, differì istantaneamente dalla sua muta greggia che non sapeva di dover morire e restò più felice di lui. Il bruto diventò uomo quel giorno. E l'uomo differì dal bruto per l'ineffabile tristezza della sua scoperta. Ma non ebbe il coraggio di continuare ad ascendere, di guardare in faccia il suo destino, di essere veramente superiore alla greggia che aveva accanto. Cercò le illusioni e le trovò. Il bruto non sa di dover morire; l'uomo disse a sé di sapere di non dover morire. Tornarono ad assomigliarsi. E penetrò nella sua coscienza qualche cosa di analogo al lento passeggiare per il cielo dei leoni, dei plaustri, dei cacciatori, composti di stelle. E d'allora in poi la morte, una volta negata, non ebbe più dall'animo dell'uomo il suo mesto e totale assentimento. L'uomo non temè di contristare il suo simile, non temè di ucciderlo, non temè di uccidersi, perché non sentì più l'irreparabile.

("L'era nuova" 120)

(Science has brought our minds back to the sadness of man's tragic moment; of the moment when, becoming conscious of his mortality, man immediately differed from his silent flock which, unaware of death, continued to be much happier than he. The brute became man that day. And man differed from the brute because of the ineffable sadness of his discovery. But he lacked the courage of rising further, to face his destiny, to be truly superior to the herd he had beside him. He looked for illusions and he found them. The brute does not know he must die; man told himself he knew he would not have to die. Once again they were alike. And something resembling the slow celestial movement of lions, bears, and hunters made up of stars penetrated his consciousness. And, once it was denied, death never found again its sad and total acceptance in the spirit of man. Man did not fear to hurt his neighbor, to kill him, to kill himself, because he had lost his sense of the irreparable.)

("The New Age")

All Evil is, then, the perverse and disquieting attempt of humanity to stave off death and nothingness, and the madness of the blood of all the victims is the absolute negative sign of a world that cannot progress. Against the presence of death, against the resentment it produces, stunting his own vital instincts, Pascoli cannot feel but horror and pity. According to him, after the failure of science, humanity finds its true definition in its essential suffering. Thus, the only possible hope is not for the optimist, not for the aggressive, not even for the solitary. It is for the charitable. Pascoli's focus remains the individual man, tormented by contradictions, full of darkness and light — for human intelligence is dominated by obscure powers and history is the battlefield of disorders. The universe is magnificent and terrifying; everything in it is bound to self-destruct, in

deathly silence. The sky and all the planets share in such immense sorrow ("L'aurora boreale," "Della cometa di Halley," "Il ciocco," "Il bolide"). Paradoxically enough, only the little, ever-surviving things of the earth can provide solace. Once again, it is the image of a child, dolefully lost in space, that best exemplifies this feeling. "La vertigine" ("Vertigo") is a lyric pervaded by a strong sense of mystery, starting with its subtitle: Si racconta di un fanciullo / che aveva perduto il senso della gravità... (A story tells of a child / who had lost the sense of gravity...):

"La vertigine"

[...] Allora io, sempre, io l'una e l'altra mano
getto a una rupe, a un albero, a uno stelo,
a un filo d'erba, per l'orror del vano?
a un nulla, qui, per non cader in cielo!
[...] sprofondar d'un millennio ogni momento!
di là da ciò che vedo e ciò che penso,
non trovar fondo, non trovar mai posa,
da spazio immenso ad altro spazio immenso;
forse, giù giù, via via, sperar... che cosa?
La sosta! Il fine! Il termine ultimo! Io
io te, di nebulosa in nebulosa, di cielo
in cielo, in vano e sempre Dio! [128]

But God, for the atheist poet, is only the source of all the worldly reality to which our mortal destinies are bound. The poem acts out the very experience of life and creativity as a love experience, both painful and happy. The reach of desire is defined in the desperate action of the child, floating weightless in space; it is beautiful in its object, useless and endless. The earnest action of the preposition "a," expressing motion to, toward, for, in quest of, or reaching after, shapes the poem on every level: in its sounds, rhythmic effects, process of thought, and narrative content. But the

---

[128] "Vertigo": "Then I, always, I the one hand and the other, I thrust towards a rock, a shoot, a blade of grass... [out of the] Terror of emptiness? towards anything, here, in order not to fall into the sky! [...] To sink by a thousand years each moment! beyond all that I see and all that I think, not to find bottom, never to find rest, from one immensity to another immensity of space; perhaps, down down, on on, ever hoping... for what? Respite! The end! The final term! I, I you, from nebula to nebula, from sky to sky, vainly and always God!"

concluding line, the goal that every wandering creature tries so hard to reach is not the divine completeness of Dante, nor the peaceful eternal sleep of Foscolo; it is a frightening void. The hazards of this nothingness forbid any hope of a truly mystical nature; on the contrary, such a discovery helps the poet to accept in full his own mortality. The "return to nothingness" that seals the last lines of "L'ultimo viaggio di Ulisse" (*Poemi conviviali*) is epigrammatic and total: "Non esser mai, non esser mai! Più nulla ma meno morte che non esser più!" ("Never to be born, never to be born! More nothingness but less death than not to be any longer!"). The shipwreck of Ulysses swallows all human ambitions. Death is at the end of all things, and Nothingness prevails. Pascoli does not consider death one of his poetic themes, no matter how important; he does not make it his topic of choice. Nevertheless, Death is at the very foundation of his poetry; it conditions and guides his inspiration; it is omnipresent and intimately connected with the experiences of everyday life. It is, in truth, life's mirror image. It resembles and compliments it. Talking constantly about it, animating it with extraordinary images, making it poetically alive, Pascoli tries to sweeten it, to make it less radically other.

But where does the child belong in such a lucid and disheartened conviction?

We remember the child of the platonic *Phaedo* that Pascoli mentions at the beginning of his essay, the little child that lives deep in Cebes' heart and is hardly assuaged or blandished by philosophical arguments. In order to keep him quiet — to persuade him — Socrates advises his followers to use the language of incantations and enchantments. Immediately after, Cebes is brought to agree with his master that philosophy is indeed the study of death. Pascoli ingeniously combines these elements. Death remains the only cure for the pervasive illness of existence. But the child who is so afraid of it turns into the Child capable of conquering all the anguish and all the obscure menaces the thought of death produces. Since his language is the language of the "charmers," that is, of course, the imaginative medium of myth and poetry. Therefore, poetry acquires the same function as philosophy and comes to occupy the space between life and death. Life is sweet, a sacred and dreadful event. It frightens, like a fire suddenly raging, in the dark of night, for a brief time. Only what is never born does not die, while all that has or gives life is doomed to extinction. At the same time, no one is more unhappy than the one who dies unaware of the finality of death:

La scienza in ciò è benefica, in cui si proclama fallita. Essa ha confermata la sanzione della morte. Ha risuggellate le tombe. Ha trovato, credo, che non si può libare il nettare della vita con Giove in cielo. Il rimprovero che le si fa è il suo vanto. O meglio sarà, quando da questa negazione il poeta sacerdote avrà tratta l'affermazione morale: il poeta, cioè il fanciullo, che d'or innanzi veda, con la sua profonda stupefazione, non più la parvenza, ma l'essenza. Chi sa immaginare le parole per le quali noi sentiremo di girare nello spazio? Per le quali noi sentiremo d'essere mortali? Perché noi sappiamo e questo e quello; non lo sentiamo.

("L'era nuova" 122)

(Science is beneficial for the very reasons for which we proclaim it has failed. For it has confirmed the sanction of death. It has re-sealed the graves. It has found out, I think, that it is not possible for us to partake of the nectar of life with Jupiter in the sky. What we blame in science is really its merit. Or better it will be, when the poet-priest will have transformed such negation into a moral affirmation: the poet, that is the child, who from now on may see in deep awe, not the appearance but the essence. Who can imagine the words that will make us feel we are moving around in space? The words that will make us feel mortal? Because we know these things; we do not feel them.)

("The New Age")

Thus, Pascoli tells us, the poet-child, the new poet-priest is the one who will find the words to make us *feel and accept* the reality of our dying. He will revive moral values beyond any particular creed; reinstate the reality of sense and emotion versus that of logic and reason. He will renew a keener appreciation of beauty and a kind of intuitive wisdom to be contrasted with learning. He will keep his gaze on the phenomena of life and death, at once attracted and cast out, never looking for solutions, but rather bent on catching the essence of things in their colors and sounds. The logic of the reasoning adult commands resignation and acceptance of the inevitability of death; the confidence of the Eternal Child suggests as an antidote an abiding trust in the only life we have.

As we said, Pascoli strongly rejects the illusion of any afterlife — which is the theme of the *Phaedo* — even while talking to his *fanciullino*: "I do not want to tell you (I cherish your illusions), I do not want to tell you that, after death, we shall not hear a thing of what is said about us" (*L.C.*, XVIII). However reluctantly, he appears to substitute for it, if not the wish for glory, the illusion of what Feuerbach had called the good of "recollection":

[...] your individual being, the being that is free of the burden of actuality and the limit of your individuality, is your being as represented, as object of recollection.

[...] The extent and significance of the place that the individual maintains in recollection depend upon the content and extent of the determination of the individual. If the determination of the individual was limited, if the extent of the activities that realized the determination was confined, then the compass of recollection is also small and disappearing. But if the determination was universal, if it contained infinite content, and if the activities that realized this determination were therefore of universal content and extent, then the recollection is also a universal recollection. [...][129]

To center one's own work around the perception of its universal value may be only a fallacy; it seems to be also its essential condition. The strength which saves Pascoli from despair is the need to express the indistinct light that is in all of us. If poetry is the exploration of the formless and the unknown, the cultivation, entirely innate, of the primordial and eternal psyche, he will write about all that finds solution neither in life nor in thought. Ordinary things and hermetic references, moral tales and pathetic appeals, natural representations and existential statements will appear in his poetry in an original crossing of *sermo humilis* and sublime vision.

At times the poetry seems disconnected and too diffused. Often the poet is paralyzed in a painful state of impotence; at other times he gives in to the temptations of the schools — the Parnassian, the Symbolist, the Positivist ... But then, as he so clearly recognizes in the *Fanciullino*, he is not a poet: "No: the schools of poetry are all bad and we must not commit ourselves to any of them. There is no poetry but poetry" (*L.C.*, XII). To find his Muse again, he has to remember his childhood and re-begin his adventure, much more noetic than sentimental or mystic as some critics have stated. In fact, his going back is a strategy; memory and autobiography are functions that allow the poet to redirect the biological-biographical flow of time along the path of ideology, turning events into portents, as in *Myricae, Primi poemetti, Canti di Castelvecchio;* and portents back into events, as in *Poemi conviviali*, or *Odi e Inni.*

The world view of the child is always in opposition to the apparent duties, the fabricated seriousness, and the ceremonies of an adult society that restrains pleasure, controls play, and ultimately decrees a state of loss. Yet, paradoxically, only as an adult will the poet be able to reconstruct and enjoy the emotions and imaginative states of life's first discoveries. Pascoli's *Eternal Child* is given the gift of such a vision, which is the metaphorical

---

[129] Feuerbach, *Thoughts on Death and Immortality* 134.

perspective on the world. But unlike idealistic philosophies of feeling that deny value to knowledge, this child is not intended to be the innocent heart, the primary anti-intellectual "who knows without learning things which are hidden from the learned but revealed unto babes." (Luke 10:21-22). Only superficially, if at all, does his voice speak to the primitive or the uncultured who could not hear it or understand it. Notwithstanding the proclaimed democratization of the poetic feeling — courageous and significant in times of aesthetic elitism, but defensible only as moral disposition — poets are the special ones who have seriously pursued the task and the discipline that make it possible to recapture natural spontaneity. The eyes of the child see the poetry hidden in all simple things; but, we are told, those eyes remain young, fresh, and inquisitive only for the few who do not cloud them with the aspirations of adults. The poet-child enjoys, then, eternal youth; his body may get older but the passing of the years will leave his innocence untouched; he may gain more and more erudition, but his poetic feeling will not change. From this perspective Pascoli's *Fanciullino* becomes the poet's obsessive metaphor and his personal myth.[130] He is, indeed, the disturbing element that intervenes to unmask false appearances, behavioral clichés and hypocrisies: "He is the one who cries and laughs, without cause, over things that escape our senses and our reason. He is the one who, at the death of a loved one, comes out with that little word which makes us burst into tears and saves us" (*L.C.*, III). His spontaneous surprise and frank wonder, his loneliness and vulnerability sustain different modes of experience and perception.

The philosophical theories of a number of thinkers meet and crystallize around the notion of infancy and childhood that seizes Pascoli's imagination. Both Bergson and Freud will guide speculative research into the deep layers of awareness, and into the understanding of the emotional

---

[130] Mauron accepts in theory and practice the applicability of psychoanalysis to literary criticism. In his most famous work, *Des métaphores obsédantes au mythe personnel*, he attempts a coherent methodology bent on finding not only motifs and themes but unconscious structures hidden behind networks of images or situations. In his view, the personal myth of a writer is not the privileged mythical figure that keeps recurring in his work (in our case: the Child); rather, it is the special dynamics of this figure, its history, and dramatic metamorphoses. It is then that the discovery of all obsessive metaphors, facts, and relations present in the artistic work purposely enriches our knowledge of it and contributes to its life.

sources of the individual psyche as well as of the universal *anima mundi*.[131] If artistic composition takes place in the soul, the core of every object that can be seen, or heard, or thought of, has its relation to the soul, and is significant of something there. The poet transmits the oldest truths through primordial images. In each one of them are fragments of the human psyche and of the human destiny, the pleasures and pains man has experienced numberless times in his ancestral history. The little children who recognize each other in the churches and in the theaters — and, therefore, in the sacred domains of religion and art — rich and poor, laborers and bankers, farmers and professors, are linked by their archetypal substratum, by the very fact of being human.

Consistently, the child is glorified in times of transition, when old values are questioned and the new generations claim the right to re-create the world. The literary child at the end of the century stands secure in its identification with the uncorrupted nature of man, whatever this may be. As a polivalent symbol, then, it can embody the exiled soul of the poet, encompassing all suffering and all goodness; or the optimist's faith in a better future; or the victorious will of the man of genius. The differences reflect conscious preoccupations, biases, and obscure regrets. The growing sense of despair that marks our century also finds its beginning in the eyes of Pascoli's child: limpid but so easily troubled, full of the promise connected to the origins of life, perennially renewed, but destined not to come to fruition. His image appears clear and somewhat indifferent; there is something clandestine and hidden about one who seems so close and yet is never fully there or even reachable; full of life and pervaded with the pathos of death.

---

[131] A veritable science of analogies connecting nature, reality, unconscious and semi-conscious feelings is at the core of all symbolist poetry. The soul becomes, once again, that element at once separate and inseparable from the whole that was the essence of mystic philosophy. Binding the soul to all elements of body and mind, the poet can reach that center where all understanding is possible; in his view, the mysterious journey toward the truth may proceed only inwards: "The 'unconscious' is the subjective expression which identifies the very same thing we know, objectively, under the name of 'Nature,'" says Carus in *Nature et Idée*. He proceeds by identifying in the creations of madmen and poets *as well as in the fantasies of childhood*, the priceless vestiges of our original communion with all of life. In this sense, the voices of the soul, or of the unconscious, are the agents that remind us of our origins.

This child is, then, an intellectual construct; he cannot have a family, not even a mother; he does not have specific memories, nor does he recognize any rules of behavior or relationships. He stands for the desire to preserve, pure and intact, *after* the learning, *after* the experience, *after* all the books, the striking potential of the very young, knowing there is no other way to attempt to probe the mystery of existence and to be happy, at least while creating a new "naïve" poetry in technique and in spirit. The "naïve" poet never assumes he can change the phenomenic world nor the perception man has of it. He is happy just in confirming the reality of his place and of his situation: privileged, miserable, desperate, harmonious, at any rate not easily modifiable.

In his poetry, Pascoli frequently trespasses into the closed, anomalous territory that belongs to this Child and he offers us the quick impressions of his incursions with dignity and unrivaled grace. What he proposes in his treatise, by introducing the Child as a continual presence within, is the possibility of growing up young. Among the poet's suggestions, the most hopeful is certainly this invitation to view the child not as a means of escape or retreat, but as a grace of real life:

Is there, then, someone who has never felt any of all this? Maybe the Child is silent in you, professor, because you frown too much. And you, banker, do not hear him, amidst your assiduous and invisible counting. He sulks in you, farmer, as you dig and hoe and can never stop to look around a while; he sleeps, fists clenched, in you, laborer, who must stay closed up all day long in a noisy and sunless factory. But he is in everyone; I want to believe this.

(*L.C.,* III)

Neither a Paradise lost, nor a promised land to come, Pascoli's childhood is a human and modern dimension of our psyche lending eyes and ears to our adult blindness and deafness. The presence of the Child, "granted to all," goes beyond the interest of the scientist or the self-complacent mirage of the artist. It is a gift that every now and then comes back to the ones who are worthy of it. We must deserve the Child.

Selected Bibliography

Pascoli, Giovanni. *Tutte le opere: prose.* Milano: Mondadori, 1946.
_____. *Tutte le opere: Poesie.* Milano: Mondadori, 1948.

*** *** ***

Abrams, Meyer Howard. "Structure and Style in the Greater Romantic Lyric." H.
    Bloom, ed. *Romanticism and Consciousness.* New York: Norton, 1970.
Agamben, Giorgio. "Pascoli e il pensiero della voce." *Giovanni Pascoli: Il fanciullino.*
    Milano: Feltrinelli, 1982. 7-21.
Anceschi, Lucio. "Pascoli verso il novecento." Jolanda De Blase, ed. *Giovanni
    Pascoli.* Firenze: Sansoni, 1937. 15-34.
Ariès, Philippe. *L'Enfant et la vie familiale sous l'Ancien Régime.* Paris: Plon, 1960.
    Bachelard, Gaston. *La Terre et les rêveries du repos.* Paris: José Corti, 1948.
Bakhtin, M. M. *The Dialogic Imagination. Four Essays.* Ed. Michael Holquist. Trans.
    Caryl Emerson and Michael Holquist. Austin: U of Texas P, 1981.
Baldacci, Luigi. "Introduzione." Giovanni Pascoli. *Poesie.* Milano: Garzanti, 1974.
Bàrberi Squarotti, Giorgio. *Simboli e strutture della poesia del Pascoli.* Firenze: D'Anna,
    1966.
_____. *Gli inferi e il labirinto: da Pascoli a Montale.* Bologna: Cappelli, 1974.
_____. "Il fanciullino e la poetica pascoliana." *Giovanni Pascoli. Poesia e poetica* 19-
    56.
Battistini, Andrea and Ezio Raimondi. "Retoriche e poetiche dominanti." *Letteratura
    italiana.* Vol. 3. Ed. Alberto Asor Rosa. Torino: Einaudi, 1984.
Baudelaire, Charles. *Oeuvres complètes.* Paris: Laffont, 1980.
Bazzocchi, Marco Antonio. *Circe e il fanciullino: Interpretazioni pascoliane.* Firenze: La
    Nuova Italia, 1993.
    Beccaria, Gian Luigi. "Polivalenza e dissolvenza nel linguaggio poetico
pascoliano." *Giovanni Pascoli: poesia e poetica.* Rimini: Maggioli, 1984. 57-88.
Becker, Ernest. *Escape from Evil.* New York: The Free Press, 1975.
Béguin, Albert. *L'âme romantique et le rêve. Essai sur le romantisme allemand et la poésie
    française.* Marseille: Cahiers du Sud, 1937.
Benveniste, Emile. *Problems in General Linguistics.* Trans. Mary E. Meek. Miami: U of
    Miami P, 1971.
Bethlenfalvay, Marina. *Les Visages de l'enfant dans la littérature française du XIXe siècle.*

Genève: Droz, 1979.

Binni, Walter. *La poetica del decadentismo*. Firenze: Sansoni, 1936.

Boas, George. *The Cult of Childhood*. London: Warburg Institute, 1966.

Borgese, Giuseppe Antonio. *La vita e il libro*. Torino: Serie 3, 1913.

Burger, Ronna. *The Phaedo: A Platonic Labyrinth*. New Haven: Yale UP, 1984.

Caponigri, Robert. *Time and Idea: The Theory of History in Giambattista Vico*. London: Routledge & Kegan Paul, 1953.

Carson, Anne. *Eros the Bittersweet*. Princeton: Princeton UP, 1986.

Cecchetti, Giovanni. *La poesia del Pascoli*. Pisa: Libreria Goliardica, 1954.

Cerisola, Pier Luigi. *Giovanni Pascoli. Saggi di critica e di estetica*. Milano: Vita e pensiero, 1980.

Chimenz, Siro A. "Giovanni Pascoli e il fanciullino." *Nuova Antologia* (Nov.–Dec. 1933): 260-72.

Contini, Gianfranco. *Varianti e altra linguistica*. Torino: Einaudi, 1970.

Cospito, Antonio. *L'estetica dei poemi di Giovanni Pascoli*. Padova: CEDAM, 1953.

Coveney, Peter. *The Image of Childhood, the Individual and Society: A Study of the Theme in English Literature*. Baltimore: Penguin, 1967.

Croce, Benedetto. *Conversazioni critiche*. Bari: Laterza, 1918.

_____. *Giovanni Pascoli. Studio critico*. Bari: Laterza, 1906.

_____. *La letteratura della Nuova Italia*. Bari: Laterza, 1915.

_____. *Problemi di estetica*. Bari: Laterza, 1910.

Curtius, Ernst Robert. *European Literature and the Latin Middle Ages*. 1948. Trans. Willard R. Trask. Bollingen se. XXXVI. Princeton: Princeton UP, 1973.

Darnoi, Kenedy Dennis N. *The Unconscious and Eduard Von Hartmann*. The Hague: Martinus Nijhoff, 1967.

Debenedetti, Giacomo. *Pascoli: la "rivoluzione inconsapevole."* Milano: Garzanti, 1979.

Durand, Gilbert. *Les Structures anthropologiques de l'imaginaire*. Paris: Bordas, 1969.

Eliade, Mircea. *Images and Symbols*. Princeton: Princeton UP, 1991.

_____. *Myths, Dreams, and Mysteries*. New York: Harper Torchbooks, 1975.

_____. *The Myth of Eternal Return*. New York: Pantheon, 1954.

Felcini, Furio. "Il mito del 'ritorno' nella poesia pascoliana." *Quaderni pascoliani* 2 (1971): 96-125.

Ferratini, Paolo. *I fiori sulle rovine: Pascoli e l'arte del commento*. Bologna: Il Mulino, 1990.

Ferri, Teresa. *Pascoli: Il labirinto del segno. Per una semantica del linguaggio poetico delle Myricae*. Roma: Bulzoni, 1976.

Ferrucci, Franco. "The Dead Child: A Romantic Myth." *Modern Language Notes* (Jan. 1989): 117-33.

Feuerbach, Ludwig. *Thoughts on Death and Immortality*. Trans., introd. and notes James A. Mmassey. Berkeley: U of California P, 1980.

Flora, Francesco. "Il Decadentismo." *Questioni e correnti di storia letteraria*. Milano: Marzorati, 1949. 761-810.

_____. "La poetica pascoliana del 'fanciullino' e il 'fanciullo' di G. D'Annunzio." *Omaggio a Giovanni Pascoli nel centenario della nascita*. Milano: Mondadori,

1955. 200-07.

Foscolo, Ugo. *Le ultime lettere di Jacopo Ortis*. Torino: UTET, 1948.

Foucault, Michel. *Folie et déraison: Histoire de la folie à l'âge classique*. Paris: Plon, 1961.

Galletti, Alfredo. *La poesia e l'arte di Giovanni Pascoli*. Bologna: Zanichelli, 1918.

Garboli, Cesare. *Giovanni Pascoli. Poesie famigliari*. Milano: Mondadori, 1985.

Getto, Giovanni. "Pascoli critico." *Carducci e Pascoli*. Bologna: Zanichelli, 1957.

———. "Giovanni Pascoli poeta astrale." *Studi per il centenario della nascita di Giovanni Pascoli pubblicati nel cinquantenario dalla morte* Vol. 3. Bologna: Commissione per i testi di lingua, 1962

Giambattista Vico. *An International Symposium*. Ed. Giorgio Tagliacozzo. Baltimore: Johns Hopkins UP, 1960.

Giannangeli, Ottaviano. "Svolgimento della poetica e della poesia pascoliana." *Pascoli e lo spazio*. Bologna: Cappelli, 1975.

Gioanola, Elio. *La poesia del decadentismo: Pascoli e D'Annunzio*. Torino: Società Editrice Internazionale, 1972.

Giovanni Pascoli. Poesia e poetica. Atti del Convegno di Studi Pascoliani, San Mauro, 1-3 aprile 1982. Ed. Sanguineti et al. Rimini: Maggioli, 1984.

Goethe, Johann Wolfang. *Die Leiden des jungen Werther*. Zürich: Artemis-Verlag, 1962.

Goffis, Cesare Federico. *Pascoli antico e nuovo*. Brescia: Paideia, 1969.

Hillmann, James. *Senex and Puer: An Aspect of the Historical and Psychological Present*. Zürich: Rhein-Verlag, 1968.

———. *Loose Ends*. Dallas, Texas: Spring Publications, 1975.

Huizinga, Johan. *Homo Ludens: A Study of the Play Element in Culture*. New York: Harper, 1970.

Jesi, Furio. *Letteratura e mito*. Torino: Einaudi, 1968.

Jung, Carl Gustav and Karl Kérényi. *Essays on a Science of Mythology: The Myth of the Divine Child and the Mysteries of Eleusis*. New York: Pantheon Books, 1949.

Kuhn, Reinhard. *Corruption in Paradise: The Child in Western Literature*. Hanover: UP of New England, 1982.

Leonelli, Giuseppe. "Introduzione." Giovanni Pascoli, *Poemi conviviali*. Milano: Mondadori, 1980.

———. *Itinerari del Fanciullino: studi pascoliani*. Bologna: CLUEBB, 1989.

Leopardi, Giacomo. *Discorso di un italiano intorno alla poesia romantica*. Introd. F. Flora. Cappelli, 1970.

Lévinas, Emmanuel. *De l'existence à l'existant*. Paris: Fontaine, 1947.

Luzi, Mario. "Giovanni Pascoli." *Storia della letteratura italiana*. Milano: Garzanti, 1968. 8: 733-811.

Marcazzan, Mario. "Dal Romanticismo al Decadentismo." *Letteratura italiana. Le correnti*. Milano: Marzorati, 1956. 2:663-896.

Mariano, Emilio. "Gabriele D'Annunzio e Giovanni Pascoli ovvero l'Ellade e la Grecia." *Convegno internazionale di studi pascoliani*. Barga: Tip. Gasperetti, 1983. 2:9-85.

Marti, Mario. "Appunti sul Pascoli prosatore: temi e ritmi del 'fanciullino'". *Studi per il centenario della nascita di Giovanni Pascoli pubblicati nel cinquantenario della morte*. Bologna: Commissione per i testi di lingua, 1962. 2:79-88.

Mattalia, Daniele. "Croce e Pascoli." *Studi per il centenario della nascita di Giovanni Pascoli pubblicati nel cinquantenario dalla morte*. Bologna: Commissione per i testi di lingua, 1962. 1:131-47.

Mauron, Charles. *Des métaphores obsédantes au mythe personnel*. Paris: José Corti, 1963.

Mengaldo, Pier Vincenzo. *La tradizione del Novecento*. Milano: Feltrinelli, 1980.

Morabito, Francesca. *Il misticismo di Giovanni Pascoli*. Milano: Treves, 1920.

Nava, Giuseppe. "Introduzione" a Giovanni Pascoli. *Canti di Castelvecchio*. Milano: Biblioteca Universale Rizzoli, 1989.

_____. "Pascoli e Leopardi." *Convegno internazionale di studi pascoliani*. Barga: Gasperetti, 1983. 2:117-38.

_____. "Introduzione" a Giovanni Pascoli. *Myricae*. Firenze: Sansoni, 1974.

Pasolini, Pier Paolo. "Pascoli." *Passione e ideologia*. Milano: Garzanti, 1960.

Pazzaglia, Mario. "Poetiche di Myricae." *Atti del Convegno pascoliano di San Mauro*. Firenze: La Nuova Italia, 1991.

_____. "Il ritorno a San Mauro." *Testi ed esegesi pascoliana: Atti del Convegno di Studi pascoliani*. Bologna: CLUEBB, 1988. 187-211

Perugi, Maurizio. Introduzione a Giovanni Pascoli. *Canti di Castelvecchio*. Milano: Il Saggiatore, 1982.

_____. "Fra Dante e Sully: elementi di estetica pascoliana." *Giovanni Pascoli. Poesia e poetica* 383-410.

_____. "Morfologia di una lingua morta: i fondamenti linguistici dell'estetica pascoliana." *Convegno internazionale di studi pascoliani*. Barga: Gasperetti, 1983. 2:173-233.

Petrocchi, Giorgio. *La formazione letteraria di Giovanni Pascoli*. Firenze: Le Monnier, 1953.

Rogers, Robert. *The Double in Literature*. Detroit: Wayne State UP, 1970.

Romagnoli, Sergio. "Il Pascoli commentatore e la scuola carducciana." *Studi pascoliani*. Bologna: L'Archiginnasio. 2: 241-57.

Rossi, Paolo. *Immagini della scienza*. Roma: Editori Riuniti, 1977.

Russo, Luigi. "La poetica del Pascoli." *Belfagor* (1955): 121-37.

Salinari, Carlo. *Miti e coscienza del decadentismo italiano*. Milano: Feltrinelli, 1960.

Sanguineti, Edoardo. "Attraverso i poemetti pascoliani." *Ideologia e linguaggio*. Milano: Feltrinelli, 1965.

Sapegno, Natalino. "Nota sulla poesia del Pascoli." *Il Ponte* (1955): 1766-71.

Schiaffini, Alfredo. "Giovanni Pascoli disintegratore della forma poetica tradizionale." *Omaggio a Giovanni Pascoli*. Milano: Mondadori, 1955.

Schiller, Friederich., "Über naïve und sentimentalische Dichtung." *Theoretische Schriften*. Frankfurt am Main: Deutscher Klassiker Verlag, 1992.

Schinetti, Pio. "Pagine inedite di Giovanni Pascoli." *Il Secolo XX* (Maggio 1912.): 377-92.

Serra, Renato. *Scritti critici*. Firenze: Le Monnier, 1958.

Sully, James. *Studies of Childhood*. New York: D. Appleton, 1896.

Tilgher, Adriano. *L'estetica di Giovanni Pascoli: studi di poetica*. Roma: Libreria di Scienze e Lettere, 1934.

Traina, Alfonso. *Il latino del Pascoli: saggi sul bilinguismo poetico*. Firenze: Le Monnier, 1971.

Travi, Ernesto. "Miti della prosa pascoliana." *Studi in onore di Natalino Sapegno*. Roma, 1975. 3: 827-48.

Tropea, Mario. "Giovanni Pascoli." *Pascoli, Gozzano e i crepuscolari*. Bari: Laterza, 1976.

Valgimigli, Manara. "Pascoli e la poesia classica." *Giovanni Pascoli*. Ed. Jolanda De Blase. Firenze: Sansoni, 1937. 3-30.

_____. *Uomini e scrittori del mio tempo*. Firenze: Sansoni, 1965.

Vallone, Aldo. "'Vedere' 'udire-sentire' 'piangere-lagrima' nella poesia pascoliana." *Studi pascoliani* 2:89-120.

Vico, Giambattista. *The New Science of Giambattista Vico*. Trans. Thomas Goddard Bergin and Max Harold Fisch. Ithaca: Cornell UP, 1968.

INDEX